DENMARK

A MODERN HISTORY

W. GLYN JONES

CROOM HELM
London●Sydney●Dover, New Hampshire

© 1986 W. Glyn Jones
Croom Helm Ltd, Provident House, Burrell Row,
Beckenham, Kent BR3 1AT
Croom Helm Australia Pty Ltd, Suite 4, 6th Floor,
64–76 Kippax Street, Surry Hills, NSW 2010, Australia

British Library Cataloguing in Publication Data

Jones, W. Glyn
    Denmark: a modern history. — Rev ed
    1. Denmark — History
    I. Title
    948.9   DL148

    ISBN 0–7099–1468–7

Croom Helm, 51 Washington Street, Dover,
New Hampshire 03820, USA

Library of Congress Cataloging in Publication Data

Jones, W. Glyn.
    Denmark: a modern history.

    Bibliography: p.
    Includes index.
    1. Denmark—history—19th century. 2. Denmark—
History—1900–   I. Title.
DL156.7.J66   1986   948.9'05   86-6224
ISBN 0-7099-1468-7

Printed and bound in Great Britain

CONTENTS

PREFACE

In revising and updating my *Denmark* from 1970, I have continued to observe most of the principles then obtaining. This book remains the work of a literary historian intruding on the territory of the historian proper. Certain changes, however, have been made. In particular, the details of party gains and losses in elections to the Danish parliament in the present century have been almost totally omitted in the hope that the broader outline thus produced will be more effective than the mass of detail in the original version. For similar reasons the original detailed appendix on Danish social legislation has been removed, and relevant material has instead been incorporated into the main body of the text. The appendix on the Danish West Indies has likewise been taken out, making room for slightly longer appendices on the Faroe Islands and Greenland.

As a literary historian, I feel it natural now to include rather more cultural history than was the case in the original publication. In no way does this become a history of culture, far less a history of literature, but the sections on the arts have been expanded a little in the hope of reflecting in a modest way the interplay between political and social history on the one hand and the arts on the other.

As this is an updating rather than a new work, the importance of the Politiken and Schultz histories, to which I drew attention in the original preface, has again to be mentioned. However, as the bibliography will indicate, these have been complemented with more modern views of the most recent period.

WGJ
Newcastle upon Tyne

Map of Denmark showing the former Danish provinces in Sweden and the North German Duchies. The dotted line going south of Ribe across Jutland shows the 1864–1920 frontier. The line south of Tønder to Flensburg shows the present frontier. (Drawn by Dept. of Geography, University College London, 1970.)

NORWAY

0   km   200

BOHUSLEN

SWEDEN

Skagen   Gothenburg

Skagerrak   Varberg

Aalborg   Kattegat

HALLAND

Randers   Halmstad

Viborg

JUTLAND   BLEKINGE

Aarhus

Horsens   Helsingborg

SCANIA

Vejle   Copenhagen   Lund

Esbjerg   Roskilde   Malmø

ZEALAND

1864   Ribe   Odense   Sorø
-1920   Nyborg Korsør
1920   Haderslev
                Aabenraa FUNEN   Bornholm

Tønder   Rønne

                Sønderborg   Baltic
                                      Sea
                Flensburg
SCHLESWIG
Gottorp
                Schleswig   Rügen

                Kiel   WEST

HOLSTEIN   POMERANIA

                Lübeck
LAUENBURG

Hamburg   MECKLENBURG

1   c. 850–1814: EARLY HISTORY IN BRIEF

The story of Denmark is one of a territorially small country which, once it was organised as a single unit, came to play a dominant role in north European history. Placed at the crossroads of trade north and south and east and west, and always at least partly in control of the entrance to the Baltic, it is a country which has had an importance far in excess of its size. For a period it led the Kalmar Union, that union of the northern countries which was in fact the largest unified kingdom in Europe, taking in not merely Denmark, Norway, and Sweden, but Finland to the east and Iceland and Greenland to the west and north. Even when the Union was dissolved, Denmark retained the whole of Norway and the Swedish Sound provinces, the southernmost of which, Scania, remained loyal to Denmark for centuries. Denmark was long in at least partial control of what is now northern Germany as far south as Hamburg, and the north German coast has also known Danish rule. Yet her undoubted expansionist dreams in the early period brought their reactions, and Denmark had to relinquish her Baltic domains to Sweden and subsequently her southern duchies to Germany, becoming for a period at the end of the nineteenth century even smaller than she is today.

Socially the changes have also been enormous, from the Viking Age, when there was a certain equality among the people, to the rise of the nobility and aristocracy culminating in the seventeenth century. From being chieftains elected by common consent, the kings became absolute monarchs whose power was virtually unlimited and whose desire for glory rivalled that of Louis XIV himself. Subsequently the desire for equality reasserted itself, and the king's power diminished, until the advanced democratic system of today gradually evolved, a system in which there is still place for a monarch. The claim made by Rollo's Vikings on the Seine that they were all equal could perhaps be made again today, with about the same degree of accuracy.

The Viking Age and Early Denmark

In the twentieth century Denmark has little significance as a focal point of trade routes, though the widespread use of the free harbour in Copenhagen still helps to maintain something of its former importance. A thousand years ago, however, it was a different matter, and Denmark's importance as a trading centre was to have more than passing significance.

The Viking conquests were certainly partly occasioned by the need for trade and the discovery that wealth could perhaps be acquired by other means than peaceful trading. Conditions in both England and Normandy were such that the Viking marauders were able to plunder and subsequently to colonise or conquer.

In 878 the Danelaw was established, and by 1033 all England was under the Vikings. The year 911 saw Rollo in possession of Normandy as the first duke after his warriors had laid waste the land around the Seine. How many of these Vikings came from Denmark it is difficult to say, as the English tended to call them all Danes, whether they were from Denmark or Norway, while the French tended to call them Norsemen. There was little to distinguish them by, and even the languages were closely related. The Swedes went eastwards, trading and establishing colonies in Russia, of which Novgorod is the most famous. According to the Arab diplomat Ibn Fadlan, the Swedes were well established on the Volga in the early part of the tenth century, and it is largely thanks to his lengthy account that we have first-hand evidence of the customs and manners of the Vikings. Still farther afield the Vikings went to Byzantium, which they called Miklagard, and whence they brought fresh wealth.

With the increased wealth came an increasing population and this was doubtless partly responsible for the establishment of colonies in places of less immediate attraction, the islands of the north of Scotland, the Faroes, and Iceland, which were colonised largely by Norwegians and only came into Danish ownership with the Nordic Union under Margrethe the First.

Yet these Vikings, for all their warlikeness and strength, were strikingly receptive to foreign cultures wherever they established themselves. Celtic influence can be traced in early Norse literature and in the carvings and metalwork of the Viking Age. In England, where they found a people to whom they were distantly related, and with whom they could communicate in their own language, they were gradually assimilated into the population, and the same thing happened even in the Russian colonies. In Normandy assimilation also took place, and the military skills of the Vikings were duly responsible for the superiority of the Norman warriors who invaded England in 1066. In religious matters, too, the Vikings were tolerant of a different culture and receptive to it, and all the evidence points to an easy assimilation to a religion superior to their own — even if the ancient Norse religion left its mark on popular superstition for centuries after the conversion of the North.

While the Vikings were thus ravaging far and wide, the population at home was gradually fashioning Denmark in the shape she was to have for centuries. The southern frontier with Germany was still vague, but it stretched roughly to the Ejder — a fact which was to have repercussions in the nineteenth century — while the sea formed a natural boundary between Denmark and the other Nordic lands. The people were farmers, and by about 1250 they had settled the entire country and founded the villages which to this day are the basis of Danish rural society.

Independent farmers had either to pay taxes to the king or to provide him with military forces. While the small ones chose to pay tax, the wealthier and more powerful preferred to provide the military assistance. Consequently, a new class emerged who expected and received privileges from the king, and on whose support the king could rely to strengthen his own position in the country. This brought about a close relationship between the king and an incipient nobility at a time when the king was trying to centralise power. In time, however, as the nobles themselves sought to consolidate their rights, the resultant split between them and their monarchs was to have far-reaching consequences. It must be remembered in this connection that the kings of Denmark were elective monarchs, and although it was customary to choose the new king from among the sons of the previous one, it was by no means an unbreakable rule.

Another source of increasing power in the eleventh century was the Church. The first attempt at converting Denmark to Christianity was made by the Anglo-Saxon bishop Willibrordus around the year 700. He went to Denmark and was received by an early king, Angenthjor, whom, however, he failed to convert, finding him 'more cruel than any animal and harder than any stone'. Nevertheless, Angenthjor received Willibrordus well and allowed him to take thirty young Danes to Holland to be converted to Christianity. One suspects that it was Willibrordus' plan to send them back to Denmark as missionaries, but there are no records of this ever having been done. It was in fact another hundred years before a concerted effort was made to overcome paganism in Denmark. The first step was taken by the Emperor Louis the Pious who sent Ebo, the Archbishop of Reims, to Denmark with the aim of converting the people. Ebo knew King Harald, and in the year 823 he and a group of priests went to Denmark where they were allowed to preach and make converts. In 826 King Harald himself, together with a following of about 400, was baptised.

Although that year, with the baptism of Harald, is recognised as the year in which Denmark became Christian, it was not until the baptism of Harald Bluetooth in 960 that the Church can really be said to have established itself on Danish territory. The conquest of England in the following century strengthened its influence still further, for England had already long been Christian, and although politically dominated by Denmark was herself able to exert a cultural influence.

Even so, the Church was by no means an established church. It fell to King Knud II (St Knud) and his next successor but one, King Erik the Kind-hearted, *Erik Ejegod*, finally to establish it in all its power and independence. A new archbishopric was created in Lund, which at that time was in Danish territory, and in 1104 Asser was made Archbishop of Lund and therefore Primate of the North. As a further gesture of the close relationship between Church and Crown, the king now managed to introduce a system of tithes, which made the Church financially independent and enabled it to increase its influence. Another result of this new and regular influx of wealth to the Church was that it was now possible to build churches in stone instead of wood as hitherto, and so permanent buildings were erected, not least among which were the great cathedrals.

The Age of the Valdemars and Danish Expansion

King Erik had been a strong and determined monarch. He was succeeded by a weaker man, and for a generation the country was plunged into a series of civil wars, as kings fought against pretenders, and the throne became an object of dispute. It was not until 1157 that true stability was brought to the country with the acceptance as king of Valdemar I, and the period of growth and power known as the Age of the Valdemars was thus introduced. It lasted from the accession of Valdemar I, Valdemar the Great, to the death of Valdemar II, Valdemar the Victorious, in 1241, and alongside the kings the central figures in this age of glory were the three archbishops of Lund–Eskil, Absalon, and Anders Sunesøn.

When Valdemar I came to the throne, Denmark was weak, ravaged by the civil wars of the past decades, and overshadowed by Germany. Like his predecessors, Valdemar had to acknowledge the Holy Roman Emperor as his overlord, but he began to turn this dependence to his own advantage. During the period of weakness, the Wends, the Slav peoples of the Baltic, had taken the opportunity of ravaging the Danish coasts and plundering the villages, in much the same way as the Vikings had plundered others in earlier centuries. Valdemar set about putting an end to this. To do so he needed the help of the Saxons, who were also enemies of the Wends. His armies supported theirs and took a small share of the booty, until they were powerful enough to conquer the Wendic stronghold of Rügen on their own.

Denmark was gradually fortified and began to assert itself as a power to be reckoned with both in Scandinavia and in the Baltic as a whole. Yet Valdemar had other plans which were equally ambitious and equally important to the country's internal affairs. So far the monarchy had been elective, and the main voice in choosing the new king had been that of the people, expressing themselves in *things* — the ancient Nordic gatherings of the people where laws were formulated and recited, and lawsuits heard. Valdemar wanted to strengthen the monarchy and make it independent, and between 1165 and 1170 he succeeded in his aim. In this he had the full support of Archbishop Eskil. No longer was kingship to be the gift of the people; it was to be bestowed by the Church instead. Although in theory the *things* continued to influence the choice of king, in practice hereditary monarchy was instituted. It was still not absolute monarchy, and until the seventeenth century it became the practice for each elected king to sign a charter limiting his powers. But in effect the system was in full flower, the monarchy strong internally and externally.

It enjoyed, moreover, the powerful support of the Church. When as an old man Eskil was forced to resign his archbishopric, the obvious choice as his successor was Absalon, who had so far been Bishop of Roskilde and Valdemar's right-hand man. Absalon was not merely a zealous churchman, but a first-class organiser and military mind, a mixture not unknown elsewhere in the medieval Church. He was bent on centralising power in Denmark and breaking down the influence of the various regions. When Valdemar died in 1182 and was succeeded by his son Knud, Absalon was able to continue the policies of Valdemar for the next two decades. It is Absalon — often referred to as the founder of Copenhagen — who fuses the reigns of the two Valdemars into one glorious age.

His policy was one of expansion, and whereas Valdemar had been forced to acknowledge the emperor, Knud refused to do so. This refusal led to war, but Denmark was now strong, and gradually took possession of Mecklenburg and Pomerania as well as the territory as far south as the Elbe, including Lübeck. The most important trade centres in the north of Europe were thus now under Danish rule. Only one year after Absalon's death, Knud was succeeded in 1202 by Valdemar II. The expansionist policy continued, and by 1219 Denmark owned the whole Baltic coast as far as the eastern boundary of Estonia. But Valdemar II had gone too far. In 1223 he was taken prisoner by Count Henrik of Schwerin, and before he was released Denmark had to give up most of her Baltic possessions, while the southern boundary was drawn at the Ejder. Even here seeds of future trouble had been sown, as the population in the area was no longer purely Danish. It contained many Saxons who had moved in from Holstein when Denmark was in possession there, and their presence was to be felt again in the nineteenth century with the Schleswig-Holstein problem.

Instead of external expansion, Valdemar II now worked for internal growth, and his reign saw profound internal changes in the country's administration. The legislative power, which hitherto had been with the *things*, passed more and more into the king's hands, as was made plain by his giving the people the Jutish Law of 1241. It was a law of good government, and it codified what in fact had been traditional law before this time. The country was now unified both administratively and legally, and a change was taking place from a primitive society to one which was sophisticated for the Middle Ages. There was no longer general equality among the people, but neither were there any slaves (*thralls*), as there had been under earlier rule. Instead a community based on the three estates was emerging, and as a whole it was a community which could equal those of other European countries, with a literature, the ballads, and a culture of its own, a country with the ability to build and to fashion an architecture distinct from that of other countries.

After the Valdemars

The following sixty years, until about 1300, were a period of economic growth in Denmark. Scania became a great trade centre, with merchants from the East and West meeting there, exchanging goods or purchasing Danish products. One consequence of this activity was the rapid emergence of a Danish merchant, or *borger* class, while the trade centres developed into towns. The increased prosperity led to the development of new crafts, and the establishment of craft and trade guilds.

In the country districts, however, times were not so good, and the number of independent farmers fell from about 50 per cent of the total about 1250 to between 10 and 15 per cent around 1400. This was partly the result of political conditions which made life unsafe unless a farmer enjoyed protection (*vornedskab*) from some noble lord. And if it was enjoyed, it was at the price of giving up the ownership of land and adopting a system of leasehold. A different legal relationship developed when a farmer who was crippled by tax handed over his land to a noble or to the Church, both of whom were untaxed, and leased it back from them for less than his tax would have been. But he sacrificed his freedom by doing so. When times were bad, he had to pay his dues in labour instead of money, and thus developed the system of villeinage (*hoveri*) whereby a small farmer was forced to work for his landlord when required. By 1350 the system which was to last until the eighteenth century was beginning to take shape.

Politically these were troubled times. Valdemar II made his sons dukes in various parts of the country, and they quarrelled as to the succession and their rights under the new king, Erik Ploughpenny. Under these conditions Schleswig acquired a degree of independence not enjoyed by any other part of the country. Duke Abel of Schleswig, one of Erik Ploughpenny's brothers, fought for the independence of his duchy, and finally, with the support of the counts of Holstein — still completely independent of Denmark — murdered his brother and was made King of Denmark. Two years later he fell in battle, and although he left two sons, the Danes chose another of Valdemar's sons as Christoffer I. Abel's sons could do little in face of this, as they had no legal claim to the Danish throne, but they did manage to secure the semi-independence of Schleswig. Schleswig drifted closer to Holstein, and when in 1460 King Christian I of Denmark was elected Duke of Schleswig and of Holstein against a promise never to divide the duchies, the seeds of the nineteenth-century conflict were planted deep.

Meanwhile, the weakness of the kings after Valdemar the Victorious encouraged the Danish nobles to increase their power, and a struggle developed between them and the Crown. It was a contest in which the nobility won, but which brought untold trouble to the country as a whole. In order to maintain his power and in an attempt to put down a rebellion which had been set in motion in Jutland and Funen by Count Gerhard of Holstein in 1326, King Christoffer II had to pawn large parts of Denmark. Holstein was in virtual control of Jutland, having taken it as a pledge for a sum of money which Christoffer had no hope of raising. Another Holstein count, Johan, was in control of Zealand and Scania.For a time it even seemed possible that Denmark might cease to be a unified state, and for eight years after the death of Christoffer II, the country was without a king.

Yet his son, almost symbolically named Valdemar, was to succeed in reuniting the country. In 1340 Count Gerhard was murdered in Jutland. The nobility of Denmark, disunited as they were, were tired of strife, so was the Church, and so were the ordinary people. The only hope was seen in the re-establishment of the monarchy, and negotiations led to the election of the son of the former king. It was to be his duty to free the country from foreign domination by paying off the money which was being extorted from it.

No one was better suited to the task. Valdemar IV was strong of character and determined, and these qualities he combined with shrewdness and ruthlessness. Within twenty years he had reunited the country. He had had to sell Denmark's one remaining Baltic possession, Estonia, but otherwise had restored the kingdom to its former status. At the same time he strengthened the Crown by seizing much of the land which his predecessors had given up to the nobles. As had happened before, however, a king went too far. In 1361 Valdemar attacked the Swedish island of Gotland and won it, but this move was to lead to his virtual downfall. Sweden, Holstein, Schleswig, and, most important, the Hansa, whose fleet Valdemar defeated in 1362, joined forces against him. The Peace of Stralsund (1370) had its price: the Hansa was given a number of outposts in Scania and the right to trade there for fifteen years.

The Kalmar Union

In 1375 Valdemar died without leaving a male heir, and as the other line with claims to the throne had also died out, a king had to be chosen. The choice fell on Oluf, the five-year-old son of Valdemar's daughter, Margrethe, and King Haakon VI of Norway. King Haakon himself was the son of the King of Sweden. In 1380 Haakon died, and Oluf succeeded to the Norwegian throne, thus uniting the two kingdoms in a union which was to last until 1814.

During Oluf's infancy, his mother ruled in his place, and when Oluf died in 1387, she was chosen as queen in her own right. Yet Margrethe had other ambitions, and their fulfilment turned out to be easier than anticipated. Sweden was also torn by internal strife between the Crown and nobility, and the nobles invited Margrethe to become Queen of Sweden. In the civil war which followed, she and her supporters were victorious and by 1389 the whole of Scandinavia, including Finland, was united. To ensure the continuance of the union, Margrethe had her nephew, Erik of Pomerania, crowned King of the North in 1397, at which time she also executed a formal document of union, known as the Kalmar Union. The idea was that Scandinavia should be a form of federation, with each country enjoying its own internal legislation, but united under one monarch and with a single foreign policy. However, Margrethe, herself a Dane, caused resentment by giving her own countrymen high office in Norway and Sweden without extending similar privileges in Denmark to Norwegians and Swedes. Small as she was, Denmark was the most powerful and highly developed member of the Union, and the possibility of Danish domination was already obvious.

Margrethe succeeded in keeping the Union in being, but Erik of Pomerania was less successful, and finally lost his throne in 1439.

This was not, however, before he had carried out important and far-reaching economic reforms within Denmark. In order to increase the wealth of the towns, he insisted that much foreign trade should go through Danish merchants instead of direct from Hanseatic merchants to his subjects. He also required that certain trades should only be carried out in the towns. Another way in which he sought to strengthen his country's finances was by introducing a toll on ships passing Elsinore; thus 1429 saw the start of the Sound Dues which were to be such a bone of contention in later centuries.

The Union did not come to an end with the overthrow of Erik, and his successors tried, with varying success, to keep it in being. Christian II, however, was a more purposeful king than those who had gone immediately before him, and he intended to maintain his proper authority in Sweden by any means at his disposal. When a rebellion broke out under Sten Sture, he fought hard against what was a truly national uprising, and he won. But Christian had seen this sort of situation before, and determined that it should not be repeated. After his acknowledgement as King of Sweden, he arranged for his coronation to take place in Stockholm in 1520. To celebrate the occasion he had called together the flower of the Swedish nobility and the most powerful burghers and clerics. Some of them had been opposed to Christian in the uprising, but he had granted them an amnesty. Now, at the height of the celebrations, he closed the gates of the castle of Stockholm and arrested his guests. A show trial for heresy was engineered, and once the accused were found guilty of the charges, there was only one sentence possible: death. No fewer than 82 of the King's 'guests' were executed, by which action Christian hoped so to cow the Swedes that they would refrain from further revolt. To make his policy even more impressive, he carried out a series of bloody reprisals against those who had opposed him as he subsequently made his way back to Copenhagen.

Yet his actions had the opposite effect to what he had intended. In 1518, at the height of the rebellion, Christian had managed to secure six Swedish hostages, whom he had taken to Denmark. One of them, Gustav Eriksson, a member of the powerful Vasa family, was lodged with a relative in Jutland, but managed to escape, and by way of Lübeck made his way back to Sweden. He was chosen as leader in a revolt which drove Christian II out of Sweden and finally put an end to the Kalmar Union. All that now remained to Denmark of what is now Sweden, were her ancient provinces along the Sound. Christian's unpopularity was not confined to Sweden, for his policies had created enemies elsewhere, both at home and abroad. Lübeck was worried about his intentions, and so was Holstein. Holland's indignation with Denmark had been aroused by an increase in Sound Dues, and because Dutch skippers who refused to pay the extra charges had been arrested and their men in some cases conscripted. At the same time the Danish nobles were unhappy with Christian's brutal methods and felt themselves threatened.

The ordinary people were, however, less dissatisfied; many of the internal reforms which Christian introduced were in their favour. He continued the policy, started by Erik of Pomerania, of increasing the wealth of the towns, giving them wider trading rights; he sought to reform the currency; he introduced new laws which were to be valid for the whole country and replaced the old medieval regional laws; he sought to limit both the power and the wealth of the nobles and the Church.

Sensing that Christian's object was to make Copenhagen the centre of Baltic trade in place of Lübeck, that city decided to support the Swedes in their struggle against Denmark. At first the Lübeck authorities merely gave help to the Swedish rebels, but it became apparent that war was unavoidable. In August 1522 a Lübeck fleet sailed against Denmark, to be joined later by ships from Danzig and other Hanseatic cities. Together they wrought havoc around the coasts.

This action coincided with unrest in Jutland, where one of the King's sheriffs, who was probably typical of the rest, had been murdered for his brutality. The King repaid in kind, burning the city of Ålborg where the murder had taken place. By the end of the year a group of Jutlandic noblemen came together in a conspiracy aimed at bringing down Christian, and they made contact with Duke Frederik of Gottorp, who also distrusted him. In January 1523 they renounced their oaths of allegiance to the King, and the province of Jutland came out in open rebellion. After bloody battles the Jutlanders and Holsteiners won possession of Jutland and Funen, leaving Christian with just Zealand. There news came to him of an impending invasion; the plans were so well thought out and the opposing forces so overwhelming that Christian had to flee. On 13 April he sailed from Copenhagen for

Holland, whence he hoped to return with a new army. In his place Duke Frederik of Gottorp was proclaimed King Frederik I.

He was made king by the grace of Lübeck and the Danish nobility, and as such he was in many ways bound by what they wanted of him. In particular, he was forced to give the nobles greater privileges than they had had before. The chief sufferers were the ordinary people. It was not long before those who only a few years earlier had been rebelling against Christian II, were wishing for his return, a desire committed to writing in what is considered to be the last of the Danish ballads, the *Ballad of Christian the Second and the Nobles*. It is an allegory portraying Christian as the eagle who is forced to leave the forest by the hawk — the nobility. The ordinary people, portrayed as the smaller birds, complain bitterly of the oppressive hawk, and long for the return of the eagle: 'May God help the poor eagle flying over the wild heath; he knows neither shelter nor refuge where he dare build a nest. But the eagle is building in the mountains.' In Jutland the peasants showed signs of rising against the new oppression, while in Scania a large-scale rebellion got under way and had shown signs of succeeding before it was finally crushed.

The Reformation

There was more, however, to the discontent in the country than mere political oppression. Already in the final years of Christian II's reign, the first signs of the Reformation had appeared in Denmark. Christian himself had shown some sympathy for the Lutheran cause, and had engaged in discussions with the leading Catholic spokesman, Poul Helgesen, on the new teaching. Both were in basic agreement as to the need for introducing reforms within the Church, and at first both agreed that the reform should be from within, and not aimed at any break with Rome. In time, however, Christian changed his views on this.

There were two main causes of discontent in Denmark. First, there was the manner in which bishops and high-ranking prelates were chosen and rewarded. Although the Church in Denmark was under the authority of Rome, it was customary for the King to choose the Archbishop of Lund and all the bishops, and the choice confirmed by the Pope. This had given rise to abuses, not least because it was in the Crown's interest to choose its prelates from among its own supporters, irrespective of whether they were spiritually suited. The bishops were a political and military power in the country, and this side of their activities was of interest to the King. In addition, being entitled to a third part of the Church's income from tithes, the bishops were exceedingly wealthy men, and lived in a high style. At the other end of the clerical scale there were the mendicant friars, who in recent years had become a veritable plague in Denmark; and although they and their orders were pledged to poverty, the vows were not kept. The sale of indulgences was, of course, a thorn in the flesh in Denmark as elsewhere.

When Frederik came to the throne in 1523, he was determined to consolidate his kingdom, and thus he sought to avoid taking sides in the religious dispute which was growing in intensity. A Catholic himself, he made it his aim to be neutral and to allow the Lutherans a certain freedom. In practice, as the new faith gradually began to gain support from the lower classes, he began to lean more and more towards them. He gave protection to the leading Danish reformer, Hans Tavsen, when he was preaching in Viborg, and in time he allowed most of the Catholic churches there to be pulled down, despite protests. Tavsen was called to Copenhagen, where he was also allowed to preach, and there, too, he enjoyed royal protection, despite the fact that Frederik never became a Lutheran. Even had he wished to do so, he could scarcely have become a Protestant for fear of upsetting the German Emperor. On the other hand, he did not wish to make too great a stand against the Lutherans for fear of losing popular support.

And popular support was just what he needed. Christian II was trying to make a comeback. After an abortive attempt to make an early return, he had settled in the Netherlands for a time, when he had in practice become a Lutheran. Now the Emperor, Charles V, who was Christian's brother-in-law, offered to help him provided that he returned to the Catholic faith and promised to fight for its restoration in Denmark if he succeeded in re-establishing himself. The promise was made, though whether it would have gone the way of so many of Christian's other promises, it is not easy to say. At all events, he gathered an army and attacked Norway, where he dug himself in, though without achieving any notable victory. Under pressure from Lübeck, who wanted him out of the way, Christian was offered a safe conduct to Copenhagen to negotiate. He went and was enticed to Sønderborg Castle, where he was imprisoned many years before being removed to Kalundborg for the remainder of his life. He died in 1559.

Christian was taken prisoner in 1532. The following year Frederik I died, and the fate of the Reformation was seen to depend on the choice of his successor. He had two sons, and the elder, Christian, was more likely to succeed him. However, Christian made no secret of his Lutheran leanings, and thus his younger half-brother, Hans, who was only twelve years old and a Catholic, was favoured by most of the nobles and all the bishops. Yet when the choice was finally made, it was for Christian. And by 1536 the Reformation in Denmark was a fact.

A new church constitution was worked out with the help of Johan Bugenhagen. There was to be a state Church, with the King as its head, and its teaching was to be in accordance with that of Luther. There were to be no bishops and the main administrators were to be called intendants. (With the passage of time they have again taken the title of bishop, though the idea of hierarchy is no longer present in the Church of Denmark.) The intendants were installed by Bugenhagen at a ceremony in Copenhagen, whereby the Danish Church demonstratively lost its claim to Apostolic Succession — in contrast to the Swedish Church, which claims to have kept it. The new constitution provided the close link between the established Lutheran Church and the Crown, which was to be the basis of the absolute monarchy some hundred years later. And so eager were the leaders of the new Church to maintain this position that they made vigorous efforts to keep out any other doctrine. They were vigilant not only against Catholicism — though without the excesses which were found in Britain under similar circumstances — but also, and zealously, against any other form of Protestantism. The new Lutheran Church soon showed itself to be intolerant in the extreme.

Rivalry between Denmark and Sweden

During the following century, however, Denmark became preoccupied with more worldly matters. Trade prospered, and thanks to rising prices and plentiful supplies of money in southern Europe, Denmark succeeded in exporting more corn than ever before. Later, under Christian IV, there was to be a period of veritable mercantilism with the establishment of an East Indies Company based on a small colony which Denmark managed to found in Tranquebar.

As prices in northern Europe did not rise at the same rate as those in the south, trade flourished in the Baltic, and the number of ships, especially Dutch, making for the Baltic ports increased rapidly. During this period Denmark was the dominant power in this part of the world, and although she did not interfere with trade, she controlled the approaches through the Sound, still being in possession of both coasts. Sweden, on the other hand, was badly furnished with ports. The only part of the present west coast which she owned was a small enclave at the mouth of the Göta river (where Gothenburg now stands). To the east, Denmark owned the island of Gotland, and thus commanded the east coast of Sweden as well.

Sweden determined to try to free herself from this Danish domination; but Denmark had no intention of being reduced in stature; on the contrary, at one time she cherished the ambition of re-establishing the Kalmar Union. The result was a series of wars between the two countries, spread over the greater part of a century: first the Nordic Seven Years War (1563–70), the result of King Frederik II's attempts to re-establish the Union. In fact, little was achieved by this war, except considerable devastation, and at the end of it things were much as before.

Sweden next turned her attention to Russia, and managed gradually to acquire mastery of the entire eastern Baltic, as far as Estonia. In time this domination was extended right round the Baltic, until Sweden bordered on Denmark to the south as well as to the north. Such Swedish power was not to Denmark's taste, and Christian IV attempted to put an end to it by bringing Denmark into the Thirty Years War and securing the north coast of Germany. This episode, which lasted from 1625 until 1629, led to a resounding defeat and the occupation of Jutland by Wallenstein's forces, until the Danes made a promise not to take any further part in the war.

From the Swedish point of view, however, mastery of the Baltic was of paramount importance, and they now followed Wallenstein's example and occupied Jutland. By the resultant Treaty of Brømsebro in 1645, Sweden acquired some of the Danish provinces in the north of the Sound, and also ensured freedom from Sound Dues both for the Swedish mainland and for all Swedish possessions in the Baltic. The Dutch, for their part, were delighted to see the Danish monopoly of power broken, and they managed to have the Sound Dues reduced at the same time.

The next stage in the struggle between Denmark and Sweden came in 1657 when Sweden was fighting a nationalist uprising in Poland. Denmark, now under Frederik III, saw the chance of revenge and declared war on Sweden. Again the Swedes immediately occupied Jutland, while the Danes withdrew to Funen, where they appeared to be safe. Then the unforeseeable happened. In the extremely harsh winter of that year the water between Jutland and Funen, and between Funen and Zealand, froze over to enable the Swedish army to cross the ice on foot and thus make for Copenhagen. By the terms of the Treaty of Roskilde, Denmark now had to give up her possessions north of the Sound, and Sweden acquired the entire coastline south of the Norwegian border. Some parts of central Norway also went to Sweden. Peace seemed to be restored, and Denmark humiliated, but Sweden did not trust her southern neighbour to keep out of the war she was still waging in north Germany, and consequently broke the treaty within months by invading Zealand without warning, the object being to take over the whole of the country. This was too much for the Dutch. Little as they had liked the Danish mastery of the Sound, they did not relish the prospect of Swedish domination either, and they sent a fleet to the relief of Copenhagen, which had withstood a lengthy siege. There was also an uprising in the occupied parts of Denmark, and this, together with an attack by Polish and Brandenburg forces on Sweden, forced her to sue for peace. In 1660 the Treaty of Copenhagen acknowledged that Sweden had been defeated, but did not give back to Denmark all the provinces that Sweden had taken after the Treaty of Roskilde. It was in the interests of all parties to the treaty that neither Sweden nor Denmark should be in sole control of the Sound, and consequently Sweden was allowed to keep the Sound provinces — whereby that country took on something like its present shape. A position of some stability had now been reached, and the wars between Denmark and Sweden were over.

Internal Developments and the Establishment of the Absolute Monarchy

Despite the many wars and the expenditure connected with them, this period, and especially the years up to about 1600, was one of economic growth, symbolised perhaps by the architectural glories of the age of Christian IV. Yet the benefits were not evenly distributed. Exactly what advantage came to the farming community is not clear, but it is certain that as a whole this period saw a further loss of freedom to the farmer. He became less an independent farmer, whether an owner or a lessee, and more and more a man in the employment of the local landowner. The King was the first to set the trend towards increasing the size of his estates, which he did both by exchanging outlying farms which he owned for others closer to the royal domain, and also by refusing to renew land leases when the lessee died. The example was quickly followed by the nobility, and the sixteenth and seventeenth centuries thus saw the emergence of large estates in Denmark, together with the construction of impressive mansions. The farmers, meanwhile, could never be sure of continuing their leases, nor indeed be certain that they would not be forced to move from one farm to another. And at the same time they were compelled to put in more time working for their landlords. With the increasing size of the estates came a need for more help, and it was quite natural that the landlord should require it of those who had worked for him in the past, with the difference that what had once been a limited duty now became unlimited and dependent on the landowner's needs and whims. In another sense, too, the landowners benefited from change: it was customary for dues to be paid in kind rather than in money, and the amounts payable were fixed. Now, with rising prices, it was thus the landowner, not the lessee, who stood to gain.

The economic changes also favoured the towns, and the period was thus characterised by the emergence of a limited middle class. Denmark, freed from the domination of Lübeck merchants and not yet under the thumb of the Dutch merchants who finally took their place, started overseas trading on her own account. The trade was organised from the towns, and townspeople derived the main benefit from it. Furthermore, it became the policy of Christian IV to give some form of state support to trade, both by partially financing overseas companies such as the East Indies Company, and also by encouraging home-industry. For this latter purpose clothing and silk industries were started, but in the long run they lacked both the capital and the skill necessary to keep them going. These and other attempts, however, did benefit the emerging middle class, and the end of the sixteenth century saw the establishment of a Copenhagen bourgeoisie which was to play an important part in establishing the absolute monarchy when the final struggle between the Crown and the aristocracy got under way in the second half of the following century.

Since the rise of the aristocracy as a political power with the privilege of forcing a charter upon each king before allowing him to take the throne, and indeed with the theoretical right to depose a king if the occasion arose, there had been an obvious source of strain between the nobility and the king. In practice the nobles had not been as strong as the theory might suggest, but no king was happy at the thought of having his power thus limited. Nevertheless, each king had been to a great extent militarily dependent on the nobility. In times of war he looked to the nobles to provide his armed forces, and in return they were given widespread privileges, especially with regard to taxation. In the first half of the seventeenth century, however, things began to change. The wider use of firearms made the king less dependent on the foot-soldiers whom the nobles could provide, and at the same time the nobles were less wealthy than they had been. Indeed, many of the ancient noble families were impoverished by the seventeenth century, while others had died out. The king's power on the other hand, was obviously in the ascendant.

Frederik III's chance to break the power of the nobility once and for all came immediately after the siege of Copenhagen. In order to encourage the citizens to hold out, he had promised Copenhagen special privileges, including that of deciding how much tax they should pay. Accordingly, a meeting of the estates was called in September 1660 to decide the question, and the citizens and clergy insisted that all, including the nobility, should pay taxes. Despite attempts to avoid the issue, the nobles had to give in. Sensing their new influence and realising that they as well as the king would have advantages from seeing the power of the nobles reduced, the Copenhagen citizens then went on to suggest that the king should be declared a hereditary monarch, which would, of course, put an end to the system of charters. The king made at least a pretence of hesitating, but he made sure that the gates of the city were closed so that no noble could slip out and avoid the issue. Then he decided to accept the offer, and was acclaimed hereditary king amidst great ceremony, during which he made a show of friendship towards the leaders of the Copenhagen citizens, some of whom he then appointed to posts which would hitherto have been reserved for the nobility.

A new constitution of some sort to cope with the changed circumstances was clearly necessary, but here agreement proved difficult and looked like being impossible. The delegates preferred to leave this question to the king himself. The result was not quite what they had foreseen. In 1661 the king whom they had invited to become a hereditary monarch sent out a document for signature in which he called himself the *absolute* hereditary monarch, and on its progress round the country from one noble to another, no one dared to withhold his name. When in 1665 the constitution was finally published, it was seen that Frederik III had indeed taken absolute power. Whether this had been his intention in 1660, it is not possible to say with any certainty, and it may be well to remember that in 1661 Louis XIV of France was proclaimed absolute king. Once his absolutism had been recognised, however, Frederik III set about consolidating a system as arbitrary as could be found anywhere else in Europe.

The only limitations placed on him were that he should support the Lutheran Church and ensure that the kingdom remained united. Yet none of the Danish absolute monarchs made any attempt to act as a true despot. Although final decisions were left to the king, he was usually content to accept the recommendations of his closest advisers, who formed a Privy Council. The members of this Privy Council were themselves mainly drawn from the top ranks of the various departments of the administration, known as colleges. Basically the same as the modern concept of Ministries, these colleges were run not by one responsible Minister, but by committees drawn from the senior officials in them. Where the king did make greater use of his prerogative was in the choice of civil servants and advisers, and in the way he bestowed the favours which were eagerly sought.

Now that top posts were no longer reserved for the aristocracy, there was competition for them, and for resultant distinction and possible ennoblement. Christian V's leading minister and adviser, Peder Schumacher, reflected the possibilities and dangers to which the new system gave rise. He was a commoner, the son of a rich wine merchant, who worked his way to the very top by means of his own ability, but then, thanks to a rather over-subtle foreign policy, was brought down by the enemies and rivals he had created. The significant aspect of Peder Schumacher's career is not to be seen in his fall, but in his rise to power and influence — and ennoblement under the name of Griffenfeld. Under the old dis-

pensation a commoner would never have had such chances, and
the country would have lacked the benefits which his brilliant mind
brought to its problems.

The kings trusted such people as Schumacher because of their
total dependence on the goodwill of the Crown. On the other
hand, the old noble houses could scarcely be relied on, having
been ousted from their position of power; and so the absolute
kings began systematically to bring in new upstart aristocrats
either from outside Denmark or from the Danish Third Estate.
These new men took over much of the land which the impoverished Danish nobility had owned, and they began a period of
more intensive abuse of the peasantry than had been seen before.
Demanding as the old nobility had been, they had had something
of a patriarchal attitude towards the farmers, an attitude not
shared by the new aristocrats. These men merely wanted as large a
profit as possible, and they forced the farmers even more into
subservience, insisting on three or four days' labour from them
each week. The farmers' own land was consequently neglected and
a humiliated peasantry reached the nadir of its fortunes. Its legal
status was ill-defined, and even when the king in 1702 ended
vornedskab, its lot scarcely improved; for to prevent peasants from
fleeing and leaving the new aristocracy short of labour, a new rule
was introduced whereby no man between the ages of 14 and 36
could leave the estate on which he had been born. In effect, the
farmers were reduced to a form of serfdom.

The rather exaggerated love of grandeur which has often gone
with absolutism also had its effect on late seventeenth-century
Denmark. It persuaded the kings to build magnificent squares and
palaces — Kongens Nytorv in Copenhagen is one example — and
it gave rise to the baroque style in architecture and poetry. But the
one field in which glory could be won by the absolute kings would
be in the recovery of the Swedish provinces, the loss of which had
been an enormous blow to national pride. Denmark was allied to
Holland, but Sweden with France, and it was obviously impossible
for Denmark to wage war on Sweden while she had such an ally.
However, in 1675 the pretext and the opportunity came. France,
herself at war with Holland, persuaded Sweden to attack
Brandenburg, where a defeat was inflicted on the Swedes. Denmark could wait no longer, and after occupying Sweden's small
ally to the south, Gottorp, which included parts of Schleswig, the
Danes landed an army in Scania where it was well received by the

local population,. It was still a dangerous move, to which
Griffenfeld was opposed, and it was because he played a double
game with France in order to keep her from interfering that he was
finally brought down. France did, however, refrain from interfering, and Denmark won the Scanian War. Yet once more the
wishes of a major power, France, prevented the return of the old
Danish territories. Despite terrible losses, Denmark was allowed
to keep nothing of what she had conquered.

But Denmark was still not prepared to give up the attempt, and
a *rapprochement* with France took place just at the same time as
Sweden made a move to improve relations with England and
Holland, who had previously supported Denmark. This new con-
stellation was in existence at the beginning of the Great Nordic
War, which lasted from 1700 to 1720, the war in which the Swedish
king, Charles XII, fought against Russia only to be beaten by the
Russian winter when he marched on Moscow. The final outcome
of the war was that Sweden once and for all lost most of her Baltic
possessions, while Russia for the first time came to play a
dominant role in the Baltic. Denmark failed to regain the Swedish
provinces, however, and merely achieved an end to the Swedish
freedom from Sound Dues and the cessation of Swedish support
for Gottorp. As a result of this Frederik IV was able to strengthen
his own position in Schleswig, while allowing the Duke of Gottorp
to keep Holstein. It was hoped thereby to remove the frontier
problem to the south and north. Peace between Denmark and
Sweden seemed likely.

The Eighteenth Century: Pietism and Enlightenment

It has already been remarked that the Lutheranism which came to
Denmark with the Reformation in 1536 led quickly to a new
orthodoxy and intolerance. Nevertheless, the close connection
which existed between the Lutheran state Church and the Crown
meant that little could be done to overcome this or to allow new
ideas to penetrate into Denmark. It was not until the beginning of
the eighteenth century that any new development took place with
the arrival from Germany of the pietist movement. There was no
obvious desire to stray from the strictly Lutheran teaching, but
merely to intensify the spiritual life, and so it was difficult for the
state Church to prevent the spread of pietism. By 1720 Frederik IV

himself was sympathetic towards the new movement, and his successor Christian VI was himself a convinced pietist. All entertainments were now forbidden on Sundays, and pietist influence also brought about the closing of Copenhagen's Royal Theatre for a period, just when Ludvig Holberg, the greatest dramatist in the North, was at the height of his creative powers. On the other hand, the pietists laid great stress on charitable acts and help for those in need. Among these were children in want of education, and under the pietists an attempt was made to provide a minimum of schooling for all, an attempt which met with only limited success because of opposition from the landowners who had to finance it, and the farmers who would rather have their sons in the fields than in the classroom.

Under the pietists, too, Sunday church attendance became compulsory, and masters were responsible for seeing to it that their servants complied. Punishments were laid down for refusal to attend. Then in 1736, to celebrate the two hundredth anniversary of the Reformation, a new law was introduced, making Confirmation compulsory; only on being confirmed did a citizen acquire full civil rights.

Nevertheless, the pietists' interest in education can be seen not only as a special aspect of their creed, but as the forerunner of the Enlightenment which replaced pietism later in the eighteenth century and led to an increased interest in education generally. At the end of the century institutions such as the School for Civic Virtue were founded. This was a private, liberal, experimental school, inspired by German ideas, and aiming to give as wide an education as possible — as it turned out, far too wide. In effect it was a reaction against the established grammar schools, mainly medieval establishments often attached to the cathedrals. Here learning was by rote, entirely devoid of inspiration, and the interminable learning by heart was aided by the liberal application of corporal punishment. N. F. S. Grundtvig, the nineteenth-century pioneer of the Folk High School movement in Denmark, called them 'the black schools'. Establishments such as the School for Civic Virtue went to the other extreme, but they inculcated in the pupils a true and lasting love of their schools, and of learning in general.

Yet experimental as they were, they were symptomatic of an age which was realising the need for educational reform. Despite the fact that education was in theory compulsory, the law had never been enforced. In any case there were not enough teachers to go round and none were properly trained. In view of this grim situation, and as one effect of the reforming zeal which spread throughout the country with the Enlightenment, a school commission was set up in 1789. Its report formed the basis of the School Act of 1814 which really did introduce a new era into Danish education. It provided for free schooling for all, though parents who wished either to teach their children at home or send them to private schools were entitled to do so. For failing to comply with the law, parents were liable to heavy fines, and in cases of noncompliance the law was to be enforced. The new schools were henceforth to be paid for out of taxation, not by the landowner on whose land they had been situated, as had hitherto been the case. In addition, provision was made for the training of proper teachers by the establishment of training colleges, though decades elapsed before the supply was sufficient to satisfy all needs. The nineteenth century benefited from the new School Act, but it was essentially a result of the eighteenth century's philanthropy.

On a different level it was also an offshoot of the peasant reforms — which were one of the major achievements of the late-eighteenth century. Stemming from a happy combination of philanthropy, a period of increasing prosperity, an enlightened monarch, and perhaps a touch of Rousseauist idealism, the peasant reforms saw a reversal of the trend towards the oppression of the farming community which had been such an obvious characteristic of the past three or four centuries. Now, as liberal thought spread wider in ruling circles, a commission was set up in 1786 to consider peasant reforms.

Its first result was an Act setting out a farmer's legal rights. Hitherto, lessees had been entirely at the mercy of the landlord, and although many lords of the manor took a genuine, if condescending, interest in their tenants, others were less inhibited and looked only to their own gain. If a lessee died, it was easy for them to demand compensation from the widow for repairs to the farm, while on the other hand they never made any allowances for improvements. The new law stipulated that the question of increased or decreased values should be decided by a disinterested party. Nor was the landowner any longer able to inflict corporal punishment on a farmer, though he was still entitled to do so in the case of smallholders and labourers. The following year brought an end to *stavnsbaand*, the system under which farmers had been tied to the estate on which they lived, and which had been introduced in 1733 to ensure a plentiful supply of labour for the landowners. With this change the landowners lost their grip on their tenant farmers, and thus some need for a statutory limit to the work a farmer was forced to do for his landlord also became necessary. In fact *hoveri* was now normally the subject of some arrangement between a landlord and his tenant, and in many cases the arrangement was for an annual payment. Thereby the farmer was left in peace and the landowner was provided with funds to pay for a labourer. Under the new system it also became common for the farmer to buy back his farm instead of leasing it. The state encouraged this, and by 1814 some 60 per cent of Danish farmers were once more independent. They were not thereby made wealthy, and many had a hard time because of falling prices, but they acquired a self-esteem which they had not had for centuries. They were becoming a modern equivalent of the independent farmers of former ages, and it has been argued that the new self-respect of these farmers coupled with the obviously growing influence which was to be theirs, provided the basis for the modern democratic system.

Such progress was only made possible by another reform, introduced as early as 1781 by the otherwise conservative Prime Minister Hoegh-Guldberg. Until then the basis of Danish agriculture had been the strip system, which had made impossible any real improvements in agricultural methods. In 1781 an Act was passed to encourage the parcelling out of land and containing the provision that if this was demanded by one single landowner in a village, then it must be done. The problems of dividing the land out justly, taking into account both the amount and the quality of the land owned, were enormous, and it took many decades to implement the Act fully — but it established the basis for farmers to work in their own way instead of being limited by the common policy of the village, and led to far greater efficiency once a farmer was freed from his duties to his landowner. The scene was now set for the upsurge of agriculture which was evident by the end of the nineteenth century, because land which had previously been left untouched for common grazing, could now be brought under ever more intensive cultivation.

Prosperity, War, and Poverty

The agricultural reforms had coincided with a period of increased agricultural and national prosperity. Thanks to a growing population resulting from the Industrial Revolution, Britain was transformed from a corn-exporting country to a net importer. Denmark was among those countries which benefited from this turn of events, and such a turn, combined with the introduction of a corn monopoly in Norway, meant good news for farmers. The reforms were in no small part due to the new opportunities and need for better organisation which followed this good fortune.

Denmark's economy also profited initially from the wars between Britain and France at the end of the eighteenth century and from the American War of Independence, in all of which the country declared itself neutral and sought to trade with both sides. Denmark also earned great sums in the Far East, while Copenhagen achieved its old objective of becoming the centre of trade for the Baltic. By 1784 the government put an end to trade restrictions — which in their turn had led to smuggling — and Denmark was able to enter the nineteenth century in a period of affluence and free trade.

Danish trading policy and the earning of such large sums in foreign trade were not without their dangers. None of the belligerent powers was pleased to see Denmark trading with its enemies, and in particular Britain sought to stop and search Danish ships and confiscate cargoes whenever there was the slightest excuse. In 1780, therefore, Denmark joined with Russia, Prussia, and Sweden in an armed neutrality aimed at safeguarding trading rights in America, and was largely successful in doing so until the end of the War of Independence in 1783. However, when Britain was again embroiled in war with revolutionary France, Denmark was less successful, and the decision to organise a convoy system met with immediate British opposition. Denmark gave in, but went on to join the second Armed Neutrality with Sweden and Russia. After this apparent disrespect for an agreement just made, Britain in 1801 sent a fleet to Copenhagen. The Danes had to yield and accept the British demand that they should withdraw from the Armed Neutrality.

The difficulties in which Denmark found herself, caught between two major warring powers, were a sign of things to come. The position was aggravated when Napoleon announced the Con tinental Blockade in 1806, and even more so when Britain set in motion a counter-blockade. Denmark, dependent as always on the sea for communication, both between its own islands and between Denmark and Norway, was at the mercy of the British fleet. Nor is it surprising that the British government, after the events of 1801, was scarcely sure of Denmark's position. In fact with Napoleon to the south and the Royal Navy on the sea, Denmark was mainly interested in keeping out of trouble.

After the signing of the peace treaty between France and Russia at Tilsit in 1807, the position became even more complex. Russia joined in the Continental Blockade, and, although this was not known, the intention was to force Denmark and Sweden to join in too. Sensing this, Britain started pressing Denmark for an alliance, a provision of which was to be that Denmark should deliver her fleet to Britain as a pledge. The Danes were aware that if this happened, France would invade Jutland, and there was no knowing what might happen. On the other hand, if a decision was made for an alliance with France, the outlook for trade was bleak. In the event, they played for time, and tried to work on the fact that while the British were in Copenhagen making demands, the Crown Prince was in Kiel with his army. But they wavered too long, and the British lost patience. In order to force an alliance on the Danes they occupied Zealand and bombarded Copenhagen for three days, during which they laid parts of the city waste and killed hundreds of civilians. When at the end of it all the city gave in, the British confiscated the entire Danish fleet and sailed off with it.

Had they played their cards better and been less impatient, it may well be that they would have gained what they wanted, for on the whole the Danes sympathised with their cause. But by behaving in so high-handed a manner, and by cowing the city into surrender and then taking the fleet, they made themselves the object of hatred and resentment in Denmark for a long time to come. The bombardment of Copenhagen was felt deeply by the Danes as a national humiliation, and it gave rise to an upsurge of nationalism which, let it be admitted, had already been there in embryo since the domination of the court by German administrators in the middle of the eighteenth century.

In these circumstances an Anglo-Danish alliance was out of the question, and instead the Danes joined Napoleon. But it was too late, and it became obvious that they were on the losing side; a side, moreover, that the average Dane did not love. Attempts to break with France and to join the alliance against Napoleon were thwarted by Sweden. There the new king, Carl Johan, himself formerly one of Napoleon's generals had been promised Norway once the war was over, provided Denmark was on the losing side. Thus, in 1814, a year after a state bankruptcy had been declared, Denmark had to sign the Treaty of Kiel and found herself reduced from influence and relative affluence to insignificance and poverty.

2   1814–1864: LIBERALISM, NATIONALISM AND THE AFTERMATH

It is a truism to say that the explanation of the present century is to be found in the last, but the validity of this statement in the case of Denmark is perhaps more striking and of greater immediate significance than it is for some other countries. The nineteenth century saw the final transformation of Denmark from something approaching a major European power to a very small nation indeed, one so small that the possibility was mooted that she might be absorbed into the German Confederation.

This confederation, formed in 1815, was itself a result of the Napoleonic Wars. Not only did it include purely German states, but also, in view of the sovereignty of some of its member states, it impinged on non-German countries. The King of the Netherlands was concerned as Grand Duke of Luxembourg, and the King of Denmark as the Duke of Holstein and Lauenburg, both of which were members of the confederation. The confederation was a fairly loose association and its only military power was based on contingents from each state. There was no navy, though Prussia had plans for one. On the other hand, by the middle of the century the Danish navy bore some resemblance to its former strength, and the British representative at the diet of the confederation suggested in a letter to Palmerston in 1848 that Denmark should be persuaded to enter the confederation. This would head off Prussia's plans for naval strength and would also ensure that no Nordic union of any sort would be created, once more putting both coasts of the Sound under the control of one power.

Yet together with the rapid decline in Denmark's international prestige went, especially in the second half of the century, a determination to build up within her frontiers and to make good the wealth and power she had lost outside them. The two focal points in this process were to be found in 1814 with the loss of Norway, and in 1864 with the loss of Schleswig and Holstein. At the end of this period Denmark was smaller than she had been for centuries, and would in fact have been smaller still if the Swedish negotiators in 1814 had realised that historically Greenland, Iceland, and the Faroes had belonged to Norway. As it was, Denmark was allowed to keep them and in place of Norway was given Swedish Pomerania and the island of Rügen by way of compensation.

In practice, west Pomerania and Rügen were only held by Denmark for a short time, and were exchanged by Prussia for Lauenburg, a territory which suited Denmark better, since it bordered on Holstein. Subsequently, however, this was to prove more of an encumbrance than an advantage. Of more immediate benefit was the fact that Prussia paid Denmark a large sum of money as compensation for the difference in the size of these territories. Denmark was bankrupt, and the addition of between 2 and 3 million *rigsdaler* to her financial resources was only too welcome.

Discontent in the Duchies

Meanwhile, in a different field, the difficulties which were to face Denmark over Schleswig-Holstein and Lauenburg already began to make themselves felt. With the end of the Holy Roman Empire in 1806, Denmark had incorporated Holstein under the Danish Crown, carrying the ancient association between the duchy and the kingdom to its logical conclusion. Now, however, Frederik VI felt compelled to allow Holstein to join the newly established Confederation of German States, while himself remaining Duke of Holstein. Thus the ambivalence in Holstein's position *vis-à-vis* Denmark became more pronounced. There were now direct ties with Germany as well as with Denmark, and in Holstein it was hoped that the Consultative Assembly, to which Frederik VI had agreed, would become a sort of local diet with increasing powers. In fact the assembly was not established until 1831, when the King allowed the formation of similar bodies in Schleswig and in the kingdom proper.

These assemblies were the direct results of the July revolution in Paris, news of which reached Copenhagen in August and was received with enthusiasm by the greater part of the population, though not by the King, who saw that the course of events could lead to the end of his absolute rule. There were no real revolutionary tendencies in Denmark, where absolutism was felt to have a restraining rather than an oppressive effect. The King was well intentioned, and this was appreciated by the people as a whole. The pressure to introduce reforms originated outside Denmark, and was originally directed at Holstein. Metternich, the leading spokesman of the German Confederation, reminded Frederik that Denmark had agreed to give Holstein a constitution, and now Prussia, which had allowed a consultative assembly to be formed in 1823, added her voice and together with Hanover demanded the establishment of an assembly for Holstein.

In Holstein itself a movement began with the aim of forcing the Danes to grant a constitution. The leader of the movement, Uwe Lornsen, had been a member of the Danish administration and had been attached to the central administration in Copenhagen. In September 1830 he applied for, and was appointed to, a relatively minor post in the island of Sild, where he was sufficiently close to events in Holstein to take a direct hand in them. It was his intention to separate Holstein from the central administration and to establish an administration within the duchy itself, probably in Kiel. At first he met with little popular response, but the movement grew and by the end of the year Lornsen was able to publish suggestions for a constitution for Schleswig-Holstein, providing for elections and the establishment of a legislative assembly. The king, however, should have the power of veto if he objected to any proposed legislation.

Although Lornsen's pamphlet was eagerly read by liberals in Kiel, it ran into opposition from both the moderates and the upper classes, who might well want an independent or semi-independent Holstein, but wished to run it themselves, not to see it in the hands of liberals and revolutionaries. In Denmark it was quickly appreciated that the whole idea ran counter to Danish policy. While the Danes saw both duchies as distinct entities with different historical relationships to Denmark but none the less as part of the country, Lornsen's view was that Schleswig and Holstein formed an indivisible unity. He was arrested for activities prejudicial to the state, and subsequently sentenced to a year in prison. By treating him in this way, Denmark made him a martyr to his cause, which flourished more vigorously than it might otherwise have done. The idea spread that Schleswig and Holstein should be fused into a single independent state, and there was nothing Copenhagen could do to alter this. It spread despite the fact that the King, acting in fearful anticipation of events in the duchies as well as under pressure from Germany, proclaimed his willingness to establish consultative assemblies in both duchies as well as provincial assembles in Denmark itself.

Provincial Assemblies and Reforms

In February 1831 he ordered legislation to establish four such assemblies, to the delight of politically mature Danes, but less to the liking of the Holsteiners, who saw this policy as running counter to their desire for a union between Holstein and Schleswig. Nevertheless, by the end of May preparations were completed and a royal proclamation issued establishing four assemblies, one each for Holstein and Schleswig, one for Jutland, and one for the islands. They were to be elected on a limited franchise, and they were to include representatives of the university and the clergy. Their functions were to be advisory and their spheres of influence limited. However, they were to have the right to petition the king for legislative proposals of their own. The aim was to make the four assemblies as alike as possible, though those in the duchies were finally given more extensive rights to advise on local government.

Despite opposition it was decided not to place the budget before the assemblies, but in fact a statement of national finance was published the day before the first meeting of an assembly — and it gave ample scope for discussion. These four advisory assemblies were the first step in the process of moving from autocracy to democratic government. Even though it was only a modest step, it did mark the first occasion on which the Danish people had been able to have any say at all in the government of the country since the introduction of absolute rule in 1665.

Although the main lines for the assemblies were laid down in 1831, it took time to work out detailed proposals, and to arrange for elections. It was not until May 1834 that the final arrangements were made as to rules and eligibility for election. Only then was it announced that the assemblies would meet in Roskilde (70 deputies), Viborg (55), Schleswig (43), and Itzehoe (47), none of them major centres of population, and all of them removed from possible sources of trouble. The position of Iceland and the Faroes was solved by allowing them representatives in the Roskilde assembly, which was the first to start functioning, in October 1835.

There were no political parties, but delegates, who were more representative of the country than might have been expected from the limited franchise rules. They soon divided into two broad camps of conservatives and liberals, with the liberals pre-dominating. Under the leadership of Tage Algreen-Ussing the liberal faction demanded public knowledge of the workings of the state, especially of state finances, and they also worked for improved standards of education in schools other than grammar schools and for the abolition of press censorship. The farming community found champions in this group, but its views were not radical enough for some of the intellectuals and students under the leadership of Orla Lehmann. However, the division between the two liberal groups was not so big as to prevent co-operation between Algreen-Ussing and Lehmann.

Despite the agricultural reforms at the end of the eighteenth century, the farming community had not achieved anything like complete freedom, and moves got under way in the assemblies to improve the status of the farmers. On the whole the farmers were loyal to the King, remembering that it was the Crown which had granted their reforms. Now, however, they wanted more: greater opportunity to own their own land and complete freedom from *hoveri*. They also wanted to see conscription, which was still limited to the agricultural community, widened to include others. A petition to this effect was delivered to the King, but Frederik rejected it out of hand, thereby losing much of the support he had hitherto enjoyed. The farmers' sense of loyalty waned, and they turned to the liberal members of the assemblies for support, for-ming together with them the *Bondevennernes Selskab*, the Society of Friends of the Farmers, in May 1846.

In fact a limited reform programme was quickly carried out under pressure from this group. Although the main object — the enforced sale of land to those farming it — was not achieved until 1919, agricultural reforms were started in 1848. The condition of smallholders was improved, and conscription was extended beyond the farming community. In spring 1849 a commission was set up to look into further proposals for reform, the most important of which was perhaps the establishment of *Kreditforeninger* (Credit Societies), which attracted small savers and helped finance those farmers who by one means or another managed to buy the land they were working. These societies were one of the first expressions of the co-operative spirit which later in the century, and right up to the present day, was to be one of the main forces behind Danish agriculture. A similar venture to the Credit Societies was the establishment of the Zealand Farmers' Savings Bank in 1856, again intended to be run by the farming community for its own benefit, and partly with the object of freeing it from pressures from outside.

This increasing liberalisation in agriculture was accompanied by a liberalisation of trade and trading conditions in Denmark. In the 1840s the liberal trade principles of Adam Smith won increasing support in Copenhagen, where internal trade was still based largely on medieval principles, with the guilds and their antiquated rules still predominating. The first politicians to put free internal trade in their programme were the Friends of the Farmers, who adopted it in 1846; but it was not finally put into effect until 1857. The new proposals were radical in scope and did away completely with the guild system and also with the old monopoly of trade in the market towns. Now anyone was free to pursue any trade anywhere, and the field was cleared for much-needed improvements.

Almost symbolically, the old-fashioned street-lighting by oil lamps was done away with that same year, and gas-lighting was introduced into Copenhagen, while the old Sound Dues were finally abolished, thus making the use of Copenhagen more attractive for shipping than had previously been the case. The capital had rapidly been losing ground to Hamburg as a trading centre. Private banks were now being formed for the first time in Denmark, making a further contribution to the growth of trade under the initial leadership of C. F. Tietgen, who had first-hand experience of British methods and hoped to introduce them into Denmark.

Further help to trade within Denmark came from the opening of the railways, the first line, ironically enough, being that between Altona and Kiel in Holstein. This came into use in 1844, nineteen years after the first English railway and nine years after the first in Germany. By 1870 the railway system of today had in essence been laid out. Thus, it is true to say that by the 1860s both agriculture and trade, as well as industry, had been provided with the foundation for a period of expansion, so necessary for Denmark's survival after the loss of Schleswig and Holstein.

King Christian VIII, who succeeded Frederik VI in 1839, fulfilled much of his promise as a reformer. In addition to agriculture and trade reforms, his reign saw the overhauling of local government, a new charter for the government of Copenhagen, and a new law on the administration of rural communities. Yet although the reign of Christian was one of progress in these important, though limited, fields, it was one of *struggle* for reform in the wider constitutional field. Denmark possessed no real constitution, apart from the Royal Constitution (*Kongeloven*), which had established absolute rule in the seventeenth century. As Crown Prince and regent of Norway earlier in the century, Christian had granted that country the most liberal constitution in Europe. Danish liberals had looked forward to his accession to the throne of Denmark in the hope and firm expectation that he would do the same there. But Christian became more conservative with age, and aimed instead at maintaining the benevolent despotism which had developed over the past 150 years. Consequently, although willing to introduce specific and limited reforms, he was not prepared to alter the traditional basis of government.

Towards a Constitution for All

However, the wish to rule autocratically was not the sole reason for Christian VIII's refusal of a constitution. By this refusal he was not merely seeking to perpetuate the internal *status quo* in Denmark, but also to avoid the complications over Schleswig and Holstein which would inevitably arise in any attempt to write a specific constitution spelling out the relationship between the duchies and Denmark proper. The King sought to maintain the existing relationship between them, to follow what was known as the 'unified state' policy, according to which the Kingdom of Denmark and the duchies of Schleswig, Holstein, and now Lauenburg, should be unified under the one head of state. This policy was opposed within Denmark itself by the *Ejder Policy*, the adherents of which wanted to incorporate Schleswig into the kingdom proper and make a break with Holstein and Lauenburg. Finding a reasonable compromise was made more difficult because neither of the Danish solutions suited Schleswig-Holsteiners now the movement for national independence had begun. Although many of the inhabitants of Schleswig were Danish-speaking, while the remainder of the population of the duchies spoke German, there was a sense of unity between them, and they refused to be separated from each other. The two duchies must at all costs remain united, if necessary independently of Denmark. This solution, of course, found no favour in Denmark itself, and so any possible move was likely to cause intense dissatisfaction in one camp or the other. Yet the existing situation could not be maintained, partly because of the growing national feeling in the duchies and partly because of the demand of the liberal-minded Danes for a constitution. Consequently the constitutional struggle in Denmark became inextricably bound up with the Schleswig-Holstein question and, as no one would give way, an open conflict was seen as inevitable, especially later in the century when Bismarck began to develop his own aspirations in that quarter.

The question was further complicated at this stage by the dynastic problem. It was already fairly clear that Christian VIII's son, later Frederik VII, would be the last of the Oldenburg dynasty. In Denmark itself a female succession was possible, but the Holsteiners would not accept this and the attitude in Schleswig was doubtful. The Schleswig-Holstein Assembly, in an attempt to avoid the danger that the Danish succession laws might be extended to Schleswig-Holstein, adopted a resolution demanding independence and indivisibility under the house of Augustenburg, to which the King replied by publishing an open letter maintaining the Danish succession laws in Denmark proper, Schleswig, and Lauenburg, but admitting some doubt as to Holstein. Again the seeds of discontent were not merely being sown, but were being given ample opportunity to germinate.

Partly under the influence of this pressure from the south, the Danes began to look to the other Scandinavian countries for support, and indeed Lehmann even went to the extent of suggesting a Nordic federation. The supporters of the 'pan-Scandinavian' movement could think of no reason why such a union as had once existed should not be revived, especially as the desire this time came from the people, whereas the original union had been purely political. There was great enthusiasm among certain elements throughout Scandinavia, especially students and intellectuals, not merely because of pressure from Germany, but also because of a certain distrust of Russian motives, and there was a feeling that a united Scandinavia would be a power to be reckoned with. The first climax to the movement came at a meeting of students in Copenhagen in 1845, when there was almost ecstatic support for the idea, too ecstatic to be long-lived, as was plainly shown by subsequent events.

In the course of the 1840s, certain changes occurred in the attitudes of the politicians who dominated the assemblies. Until 1848, when the liberals organised themselves into a group, there were no real parties as such. Some of those individuals who had previously been radical in their approach had become more conservative, and in general the liberal group had become more nationalistic in their outlook and had earned the name of National Liberals. The Friends of the Farmers were still the radicals among the politicians. Outwardly the National Liberals were *national*, and inwardly *liberal*, and after making gains throughout the forties they prevailed upon the King to grant a constitution. He ordered a draft to be made, and it was his intention to discuss the recommendations on 6 January 1848. Before he could do so, however, he was taken ill and died on 20 January. Despite hesitations, his successor, Frederik VII, was persuaded to pursue the constitutional proposals, and signed a declaration on 28 January 1848 to this effect. The final result was a constitution — of strikingly liberal bent — which took effect on 5 June 1849, guaranteeing religious freedom, freedom of speech, and the general liberty of the individual. The legislative power was to go to a *Rigsdag* elected by popular vote, and this *Rigsdag* should consist of two chambers, a lower house called the *Folketing*, and an upper house, the *Landsting*, the latter being elected on a more restricted franchise in order to give it a more conservative character. The King was no longer an absolute monarch, but he was given real political power, as his signature was necessary before any bill could become law, while he was entirely at liberty to choose his own Ministers, irrespective of the composition of the *Rigsdag*. The unity of the kingdom and the duchies was maintained, each being given equal status. The duchies, however, were far from being convinced that this equality would exist anywhere but on paper.

The Duchies' Reaction and the 1848 War

This distrust combined with the upsurge of national feeling that swept through Germany after the 1848 revolution in France, and a movement emerged to establish a provincial government in Schleswig-Holstein and to include the whole area in the German Confederation. It was finally decided to send a delegation to Copenhagen to seek a common constitution for Schleswig and Holstein and to ask permission for Schleswig to join the German Confederation, which meant in effect that Denmark would be giving up control of Schleswig. The immediate Danish reaction was to maintain the old unified state policy, but this led to a ministerial crisis, brought about by the National Liberals, which was only resolved by the appointment of a new ministry consisting of a coalition of conservatives and National Liberals intent on forcing through the Ejder policy. More significant than the change of policy was perhaps the fact that King Frederik VII on this occasion, 22 March 1848, declared that he would henceforth consider himself to be a constitutional monarch. Absolutism was finally at an end in Denmark.

The new ministry now made a final offer to the Schleswig-Holstein delegation. Holstein and Lauenburg would be granted a free constitution and be free to join the German Confederation. Schleswig, meanwhile, would be united to Denmark, but would be allowed its own diet and freedom in its internal administration. This proposal was not acceptable to the Schleswig-Holsteiners, who, in an attempt to break away, hastily formed their own provisional government in Kiel. War was clearly imminent, and Denmark mobilised.

Left to themselves the Schleswig-Holsteiners had no hope. By weight of arms the Danes gained the upper hand, and Frederik VII entered Flensburg. At this point, however, Prussia, spurred on by the desire for German unification, sent an army of 12,000 men to the north, and this, together with forces from the other German states, faced the Danish army with an enemy 30,000 strong. There was nothing for it but to withdraw to Funen, and a Prussian army entered Jutland.

Although Britain and France had guaranteed the status of Schleswig in 1720, and Russia had done the same in 1773, Denmark sought support only from Britain. It was refused, and an offer of mediation made instead. Meanwhile Russia persuaded Prussia to withdraw and after a sudden attack on the remaining German troops, made with the help of a contingent of Swedish soldiers sent as a symbol of pan-Scandinavian sentiments, Denmark accepted a cease-fire, together with Britain's offer of mediation.

Britain, together with most of the other major powers, saw a partition of Schleswig along the language border as a reasonable solution, but this the Danes would not countenance, and they even went so far as to draw up a new constitution including Schleswig as an integral part of Denmark. It was still their intention to unite the two realms, and on 26 February 1849 Denmark announced an end to the truce. At the beginning of April hostilities recommenced. By now, thanks to universal conscription, the Danish army had been increased to 41,000 men, who had to face a German/ Schleswig-Holstein force of some 65,000. After an initial defeat the Danes withdrew to Fredericia, but on 6 July they broke out and inflicted a resounding defeat on the enemy.

The battle of Fredericia has gone down in history as a glorious Danish victory. In one of his novels M. A. Goldschmidt refers to it as 'that glorious battle, one of the few known to history which almost seemed to be the work of a poet: an epic single combat of vast dimensions with a personal enmity between the 16,000 on the one side and the 16,000 on the other . . .' And Goldschmidt sees the victory as 'a dawn which after the passage of centuries once more sees the Nordic character rugged and indomitable, warriors who "without tactics" tramp, crawl, strike and bite their way to victory'.

Four days later a new truce was signed, and a commission consisting of one Prussian, one Dane, and one Englishman was set up to govern Schleswig, the southern part of which was occupied by Prussian troops, the northern part by Norwegians and Swedes. Provisional agreement was reached to give Schleswig its own con- stitution and not to tie it more closely either to Denmark or to Holstein. This was unacceptable to the Schleswig-Holsteiners, and when an unconditional peace was signed between Denmark and Prussia in 1850, they decided to fight on alone, despite the London Protocol of 4 July acknowledging the indivisibility of the Danish Kingdom, and signed by Russia, Britain, France, Sweden– Norway, and subsequently Austria, a declaration which in theory re-established the unified state policy. Without the active support of Prussia, Schleswig-Holstein could not hope to win against Den- mark, and its army was defeated in the bloody battle of Isted and subsequently again when it tried to make a stand at Dannevirke, the ancient fortification west of the town of Schleswig. Under pressure from Russia, Prussia agreed not only to refrain from fighting, but in fact to oppose Schleswig-Holstein nationalism, and accordingly the provisional government was dissolved early in 1851.

A Dual Constitution — and its Results

Thus Denmark, on the face of it, had won a great victory, although this final outcome was to a considerable extent the result of Russia's fear of nationalist movements and the pressure it exerted on Prussia. Moreover, Prussia herself, considering both Schleswig and Holstein to be German territory and knowing Holstein to be already a member of the German Confederation and thus susceptible to German influence, preferred to see them both under partial Danish control rather than have Holstein outside and Schleswig completely within Danish jurisdiction. In any case Prussia was not sympathetic towards the radical nationalism in Schleswig-Holstein itself. Thus there was in effect a return to the original position, to the old unified state policy, which for so long had been hateful to the Schleswig-Holsteiners, and which after the bitterness caused by the fighting was to prove even less palatable to them. The settlement was enshrined in the agreements of 1851 and 1852 which laid down that Denmark should henceforth consist of three parts: the kingdom, Schleswig, and Holstein with Lauenburg. Nothing should be done to tie Schleswig closer to either Denmark or Holstein; Holstein and Lauenburg should be free to continue membership of the German Confederation; the Danish constitution should not be valid in the duchies, which should each have assemblies with legislative powers. The following year the Treaty of London decided on the inheritance of the Danish throne: if Frederik VII should die without a male heir, Prince Christian of Glücksborg was placed next in line for the succession, which was to continue in his male line.

The agreements of 1851 and 1852 were not expressed in a new constitution until 1855. It was obvious that the liberal constitution of 1849 would have to be limited in some way, as it could no longer, according to the agreement, be valid for Schleswig and Holstein as well as for Denmark. The duchies were promised regional assemblies to settle their internal affairs, and then, after lengthy negotiations and to the consternation of the liberals in the *Rigsdag*, the 1849 constitution was limited to internal matters in Denmark proper, while arrangements were made for a new common constitution for the duchies and Denmark — in other words, a constitution covering foreign policy and general finance and defence. The legislative body for this common constitution was to be called the *Rigsraad* (State Council), to consist of 80 members, of whom 18 were to be elected by the *Rigsdag*, 12 by the Schleswig and Holstein diets, 30 by popular vote, and the remainder appointed by the King. Thus Denmark was for a time in the peculiar position of having two national assemblies, the *Rigsdag* for internal affairs and a more conservative *Rigsraad* for foreign affairs and for matters common to the kingdom and the duchies. The hope was that this constitution would unite the entire realm. It did not, and national differences emerged clearly at the outset when the new *Rigsraad* met and was immediately found to include Holstein members who spoke no Danish. To make matters worse, the Holstein Assembly refused to recognise the constitution.

Outside Denmark, the new constitution was accepted by Prussia and Austria, but opposition grew throughout the other German states. In 1856 Prussia and Austria complained that the 1851–52 agreements were being broken, and that the new version of the unified state policy was linking Holstein too closely to Denmark. A change of prime minister in Denmark in 1857 was intended to symbolise a more accommodating attitude and a move away from the unified state, but the Holsteiners were still not satisfied. The matter was brought up at the diet of the German Confederation, and in 1858 the deputies issued a declaration to the effect that the common constitution was not valid for Holstein and Lauenburg. In May an ultimatum was served on Denmark and the common constitution was annulled for the two duchies — an action which quietened the Germans for the time being. This was in effect a move back to the Ejder policy, which found support among both the National Liberals and the Farmers' Party, and was the obvious solution to the adherents of the pan-Scandinavian movement.

Meanwhile, proposals and counter-proposals on the status of Holstein were made and rejected, and in 1860 Schleswig complained of Danish pressures. Again Prussia insisted that Denmark was not keeping the 1851–52 agreements, and threatened to intervene in the dispute. In 1861 an ultimatum was served on Denmark, giving her six weeks to arrange affairs to the satisfaction of Prussia. The great powers also exerted pressure on Denmark to reach a settlement. Denmark refused, but did agree to direct negotiations with Prussia. This concession, however, was marred by the fact that by bowing to the nationalism of public opinion the Danish Prime Minister, C. C. Hall, implicitly made the Ejder policy official. He was not impressed with Bismarck when he met him, though even then Bismarck knew what he wanted, and consequently gave no ground. At the same time Britain, whose assistance Palmerston had promised in July 1863, announced her support for the German demands, thanks to the pro-German policy of Queen Victoria.

Relying now on support from Norway and Sweden, Denmark rejected all complaints, prepared for war, and in March 1863 incorporated Schleswig into Denmark proper and separated Holstein and Lauenburg from the kingdom. The hope was that Prussia would be too occupied with the Polish rebellion against Russia to intervene. The German reaction, however, was to threaten to occupy Holstein and Lauenburg if the constitution were not restored. But the Danes had now gone too far to retreat. Consequently, a new common constitution for Denmark and Schleswig was passed in the November of 1863, though by only three votes more than the required two-thirds majority and in the face of grave warnings. Even then it almost lost the royal assent, as Frederik VII died two days later, to be succeeded by Prince Christian of Glücksborg as Christian IX. The new king was not sympathetic to the new constitution, but finally signed it, though he was perfectly aware of the probable consequences.

Bismarck again demanded a return to the 1851–52 agreements, and as Denmark received no support from other sources, not even from Sweden — where the government was less eager than the king to embark on military adventures — Saxon and Hanoverian troops entered Holstein on 24 December 1863. Denmark was not prepared to fight there and withdrew to Schleswig. The Danish Prime Minister, D. G. Monrad, played for time, but Prussia refused to wait, and invaded Schleswig without warning. The Danes were outnumbered and their equipment was inferior. They retreated to, and then beyond, the Dannevirke fortifications, much to the dismay of the general populace, who had been convinced that Denmark would win as she had done before.

Danish intransigence was partly responsible for the failure of a peace conference called in London, and in June 1864 Prussia invaded Denmark proper. Denmark had little support from outside, and even pan-Scandinavian enthusiasm led to nothing but limited support from Swedish–Norwegian volunteers. Hopes for official support from Sweden remained unfulfilled.

Monrad was blamed for the Danish failure and dismissed. The new government under C. A. Bluhme sued for peace and accepted humiliating conditions from Prussia. Denmark had to renounce all rights to the three duchies, which meant that about a third of her territory was lost, together with a third of the population. Denmark had shrunk to her smallest-ever size since the formation of the kingdom many centuries before. The process of humiliation which had begun with the Napoleonic Wars was now complete and all dreams of glory were dashed.

The Economic Situation

Although by 1864 Denmark was politically at a lower ebb than at almost any time in her history, economically she was considerably better off than at the beginning of the century. After some years of prosperity at the end of the eighteenth century, the period of the Napoleonic Wars had been accompanied by raging inflation, so much so that by 1812 the currency had dropped to one-fourteenth of its face value. Money was now supplied by the expedient of printing more, and although some effort was made to stem the inflation by increased taxation, this was not entirely effective. Because of the prospect of the imminent collapse of the currency, speculation in foreign currencies increased, and attempts to stop it were scarcely successful. Indeed, the King himself indulged in it.

As a consequence, on 5 January 1813, Frederik VI proclaimed the bankruptcy of the Kingdom of Denmark. The nation's bank, the *Kurantbank*, established during the period of mercantilism in the eighteenth century, was closed and replaced by the *Rigsbank*, and all paper money was called in to be exchanged. For six *kurantdaler* one *rigsdaler* was issued, and even then the value was fixed at only five-eighths of par. In other words, the real reduction in money was to be to about one-tenth of its former face value, in addition to which property-owners had to pay a proportion of their property values to the state, if necessary by taking out state mortgages on hard terms. In 1818 the *Rigsbank* was again replaced, this time by the *Nationalbank*, an autonomous institution outside the immediate direction of the state. Despite further falls in value — at one time to only six per cent of par, corresponding to only one per cent of the old currency values — the new *Nationalbank* succeeded by means of a strict control of the amount of paper money in circulation in bringing the *daler* back up to par by 1838.

Meanwhile the country had suffered. In particular agriculture had at an early stage encountered serious difficulties, and a full-scale agricultural crisis developed around 1818 and lasted for a full ten years. This was a direct consequence of war, and reflected the increasing agricultural production throughout Europe as troops returned to more estimable work than shooting each other. With increasing output came falling prices, and in their wake came in 1815 the British Corn Laws, which hit Danish exports badly. The farmers' position was further complicated because many of them were in debt, having taken advantage of the eighteenth-century reforms and bought their own land. They were faced with enormous problems in paying off their debts, and many went bankrupt, while some few returned to a leasehold arrangement. Ironically, leaseholders came out of the agricultural crisis better than freeholders, as many of the dues were still paid in kind.

The repercussions of the agricultural crisis spread quickly throughout the community, hitting first shopkeepers and merchants in small towns, and then spreading to the larger towns. There they merged with crises which had reigned in Copenhagen business circles since 1816, and a series of bankruptcies rocked the business world.

The state did its best to help. Taxes on agriculture were reduced and farmers were allowed to pay some of them in kind. Next the price of corn paid in tax was raised above market levels, and finally paper money was accepted instead of silver for taxes paid in currency. The state also arranged for loans to farmers, but even then some went bankrupt, the state taking over their farms, only to have to sell them at a loss. Help for industry came in a relaxation of duty on many raw materials, with the object of enabling industry to start moving and to be self-supporting. But it all took a desperately long time. Nevertheless, the agricultural crisis was eventually overcome, and the economic situation was eased. The first sign of a change came with the liberalisation of the British Corn Laws in 1827 and 1828, which once more gave Denmark access to an important foreign market. At the same time the price of corn and other commodities in Europe began to rise with increasing demand based on the rise in population which occurred after the Napoleonic Wars. In the wake of the rising prices came a new optimism, which resulted in the gradual increase of land prices in Denmark. Between 1830 and 1845 prices rose by about 160 per cent in the richer agricultural districts. By 1863 they had doubled again.

There was also a change in attitude on the part of the farmers, the younger members of the community having been the first generation to benefit from the school reforms introduced in 1814. However imperfect the working of the system had been, owing to the economic difficulties, it had met with limited, yet increasing, success, and its effects were now being felt. The farmers were more receptive to new ideas and were willing to adopt new methods of cultivation and accept modern implements. They had also realised the necessity of improving the quality of their products if they were, in the long run, to maintain the rise in exports. It should also be remembered that this new and more enlightened generation of farmers was expressing itself through the Friends of the Farmers in the provincial assemblies. They were the transitional generation, marking the change from the eighteenth-century peasant to the highly skilled farmer of the end of the nineteenth century.

Agriculture still accounted for more than half of the working population in Denmark, and as its increasing difficulties twenty years before had affected the remainder of the community, so better conditions now brought about an improvement in trade and general living standards. Industry benefited too, but it must be noted that there was relatively little organised industry as such in Denmark. It has been said, and with some reason, that Denmark was comparable more to central European countries at this time than to western Europe. There was no real industrial revolution there, and while the country lagged behind the major industrialised countries, it was free from the social problems brought about by the Industrial Revolution in England, Germany, France and Belgium. When the change did come, relatively late, those responsible for dealing with the problems had gained in worldly wisdom and could learn from other countries' experience. The consequence was a very advanced means of dealing with the problems of industry, from which Denmark emerged in the forefront of industrialised countries. This late and sophisticated adaptation to the industrial age has doubtless had far-reaching effects on Denmark in the twentieth century.

Little wonder then that the years from 1813 to about 1840 were a period when Denmark was without a foreign policy. There was no energy and no resources to do anything except improve the country's financial status. The national outlook was limited by this, and it was a period of *petit-bourgeois* conformism, during

which Frederik VI became as restricted as his people, an absolute
monarch with narrow ideals, who was dutifully applauded by his
loyal subjects when he was rowed around the canals of
Frederiksberg Park in Copenhagen on a Sunday afternoon. This
was indeed symbolical of his position and outlook, and of those of
his subjects. For despite misfortunes, he remained by and large a
popular king who seemed to reflect his age. As well as being an
absolute monarch, he was a citizen king who was close to his
people and loved by them. 'Only one feeling really united high and
low alike, both sexes and all ages: respect for the king', wrote the
dramatist Thomas Overskou in his autobiography.

The Position of the King

Just how close he was to them is also reflected in Hans Christian
Andersen's autobiography, *The Fairy Tale of My Life*, when he
tells how in his early days in Copenhagen he had tried to find, and
succeeded in finding, patrons who would help him on his way. One
of them, Jonas Collin, seeing in Andersen not a writer of future
international fame but a boy who, given a decent education, would
be able to make a contribution to the life of his country and
become a useful citizen, went to the King for financial support for
Andersen — and got it. This was the action of the absolute king,
and the populace at large preferred to view him in this light rather
than dwell on his political ineptness. Bishop Mynster, the Primate
of Denmark, was probably giving voice to the general feeling on
the King's death in 1839 when he wrote:

> None of us was left alone on earth as long as we had him. What
> comforted me was the fact that difficult times were ahead,
> which, weakened by old age, he would have been less able to
> meet: and it would have given me great pain to see my old king
> as a mere shadow of what he had been, guiding the state with an
> uncertain hand in face of the breaking storms.

The bishop's doubt as to whether the King would have been able
to rule successfully in the coming years is obvious, but what is
equally significant is the feeling that 'none of us', none of the
Danes, was friendless as long as Frederik was alive. He took a
direct and personal interest in his people's life and conditions, read

criticisms of his administration in the newspapers, and if, on starting investigations, he found the criticism justified, he took action. He was his own ombudsman. When he discovered corruption in the civil service in these difficult years, he stepped in and personally saw to it that it was dealt with. He was the absolute monarch, and he felt his people's wellbeing to be his personal responsibility. As the Swedish poet Geijer said of him, 'In his person Danish absolutism is almost certainly the most paternal on earth'. Yet Geijer linked this with the narrowness and lack of vision which certainly distinguished everyday life in Denmark at that period, and which were reflected in many aspects of Copenhagen life.

Life in Copenhagen

Copenhagen was in many ways a city of paradoxes. It was the capital city, but with a population of under 120,000, scarcely bigger than a provincial town in countries larger than Denmark, and, having lost its monopoly of overseas trade because of post-war reorganisation, was giving way in importance to the Danish provincial towns themselves. As far as size was concerned, however, there was a considerable margin: Odense was next with just 8,700 inhabitants, while of the other towns only Elsinore, Ålborg, Århus, and Randers exceeded 5,000. Nevertheless, their influence was growing because of their significance as trading centres, not least with Copenhagen's main rival, Hamburg, where credit was easier to come by. Yet in Copenhagen, the centre of Danish absolutism, the home of the civil and military authorities, the seat of the only university in the country, the ideas of liberty and equality which swept through Europe after the French Revolution were gradually making themselves felt. So far they were less obvious in the political field than in the realms of literature and religion.

The concept of individualism was asserting itself: the individual's right to his own ideas and beliefs, the literary swing away from the universality of Classicism to the Romantic cult of genius and individuality. There was the attempt to find a different metaphysical explanation to the problem of existence from that implicit in orthodox Lutheranism: Hans Christian Ørsted, the discoverer of electro-magnetism, tried to find a scientific-metaphysical explanation, while N. F. S. Grundtvig sought to combine patriotism with a personalised religion. Sectarian movements were also in evidence. Within the field of orthodoxy itself, Bishop Mynster sought to introduce a new spirituality after the barrenness of eighteenth-century rationalism. The transition to individualism is to be seen no less in the architecture of Copenhagen itself: after the fire of 1795 and the British bombardment of 1807, the ruined areas were gradually rebuilt. Whether through lack of funds after the state bankruptcy of 1813 or a predilection for the strict, unadorned lines of neo-Classicism — or a happy coincidence of both — the original task was assigned to C. F. Hansen, who planned the entire centre of Copenhagen on a neo-Classical pattern. The old City Hall (now the Law Courts), the adjacent prison, the Cathedral, and the Metropolitan School behind it, were the outstanding achievements in this genre, though there were many town houses of less impressive dimensions as well. Hansen was, however, unable to finish his work, and his successor Peder Malling, one of his pupils, introduced a more individualistic style of neo-Gothic, and juxtaposed it to Hansen's buildings in his design for Copenhagen University. In architecture the transition from the controlled lines of Classicism to the bolder inventiveness of individualism came later than in other spheres, but its evolution followed the general pattern, and the outstanding buildings of the 1840s are varied and individualised, like St Ansgar's Church and the Synagogue in Krystalgade.

Nevertheless, it was not until the middle of the century that the transition from the old city to the modern capital really began to gather impetus. Until 1870 Copenhagen was still a city within its ramparts, as it had been for centuries. Permanent buildings were not allowed outside the gates within the immediate vicinity of the ramparts, and thus housing for the denser population had to be packed into the area which Copenhagen had occupied for the past 200 years. The result was a bewildering number of flats and houses packed together in a labyrinth of passages and courtyards, and overcrowding was appalling. In many cases two families are said to have had to live together in a single room.

The four gates to the city were shut at night until 1821, when Nørreport was left open to pedestrians — against payment of a toll. Carriage and coach could neither enter nor leave, and all wheeled traffic was forbidden in the city at night.

Even during the day few people drove to their destinations, as distances were short, although there were cabs for those who wanted them and, in a time of poverty, could afford them. Relatively few people went out at night to seek entertainment, and when they did so they found the streets, already filthy and without drainage of any sort, ill lit by oil lamps. Even these were not lit on moonlight nights. Watchmen, in dress which corresponded to the antiquity of their task, patrolled the streets and called out the hours, as they had done since the seventeenth century:

Three O'clock

Now hastes black night away,
And morning fast approaches.
God, keep from us alway
All evils and reproaches.
　The clock has now struck three.
　Oh, Saviour bless'd
　Give grace and rest.
Let us keep faith with thee.

Klokken tre

Nu skrider Natten sorte,
Og Dagen stunder til,
Gud, lad dem blive borte,
Som os bedrøve vil:
Vor Klokk' er slagen tre.
　O Fader from:
　Vend Du os om
Din Naade os bete.

Entertainment

Entertainment was largely limited to private visits. People were fond of company, even though the entertainment they could offer was modest in proportion. At the same time some sort of café life was beginning to emerge, and though somewhat sordid at first, it began to brighten up and offer a more attractive and reputable form of diversion by the middle of the century. Restaurant life had been unknown in Denmark in the eighteenth century, but in the last decades what were known as *Schweizerkonditorier* — cafés serving cakes, liqueurs, punch, and chocolate — had begun to appear, and their numbers increased in the first decade of the nineteenth century. They were given impressive names, such as Gianelli, Pedrin, Pleisch but, according to the politician Orla Lehmann, the names were their only charm as late as the 1830s:

> You entered an unpleasant murky room. On a series of small tables there were tallow candles in brass candle sticks, each accompanied by a small pair of iron scissors. They were not lit until a customer sat at the table, and then they were put out again as soon as he left. The customers sat with a glass of punch — and regular guests would have a long-pipe which the waiter kept for them on the premises. They sat with a news-paper in their hands, or carried on halting conversations in a half whisper. It is impossible to imagine a less elevating sight than this sleepy finish to a sleepy day's work.

In the 1840s, however, with the opening of Kehlet's Café, things improved, and cafés gradually became a recognised part of Copenhagen life.

There was little else in the way of public entertainment for the average Copenhagener, and when the weather was good he found his pleasure in walking about the capital — in the park on the eastern side of the city, in Kongens Have, the colonnades of Christianborg, or on the ramparts themselves until they were demolished in 1870 — all well away from the stench of the over-crowded districts. In 1822 the Royal Art Gallery was opened, and in the winter this, together with the various museums, attracted a considerable number of visitors.

In good summer weather many citizens would walk outside the city boundaries, probably to Vesterbro, which became a popular place of amusement, and where a theatre for light entertainment was opened in 1801 by an Englishman named Price, who was later joined in the venture by his two brothers. One of the attractions of this theatre was Italian pantomime under Giuseppe Casorti, but when, in 1833, the Price brothers tried to introduce the more lavish English pantomime, it was a failure. A walk beyond Vesterbro brought one to Frederiksberg Park, where a café was opened in 1813; but few went further than this unless they were going on what was a traditional annual outing in the forests around Copenhagen. Even then most people walked, and the route they followed was the inland road. The coastal road was little used in those days, and in parts it was covered by thick sand and virtually impassable. There are accounts of groups of trippers hiring a farm waggon to go that way, and all having to climb out and push the waggon along. It was not until relatively late in the century that this road was improved and made into the main road to the north of Zealand. There was little demand for improved communication along it, as pleasure-seekers by and large preferred the inland route. The sea did not have the romantic attraction in the nineteenth century which it has since acquired; it was considered cold and insensitive, and the Danes preferred the more idyllic surroundings inland. The cult of the idyll, perhaps thanks to Rousseau and the eighteenth century, held a great attraction for them, and those who had the opportunity spent the summer 'in the country', renting houses or rooms, depending on what they could afford, in the most idyllic spots available. A few wealthier families owned summer residences.

The pleasures of nature were, however, reserved for the summer. In the winter the people of Copehagen were left to their own devices, to entertainment in the home, song and dance, and occasionally for the more well-to-do, a private chamber concert. Interest in music was widespread, and these chamber concerts played a part in the lives of many cultured families, and gave Romantic composers such as Gade, Hartmann, and Rung a welcome outlet for their talents both as composers and performers. It was Hartmann who in 1850 founded the Copenhagen Music Society and thereby gave the Copenhageners their first opportunity of hearing classical orchestral music. Previous to this there had been sporadic performances of opera by an Italian group from 1842, which had proved popular, and in 1843 Jenny Lind had made her first appearance and carried the city by storm.

There was meanwhile one well-established source of public entertainment which enjoyed enormous popularity: the Royal Theatre. Then, as now, it put on a mixed programme, and it was the centre of Copenhagen cultural life. It enjoyed a social function also, attracting everyone who made any pretence of belonging to the cultured classes, and there was considerable competition to obtain tickets. As Hans Christian Andersen points out in *The Fairy Tale of My Life*:

At a time when politics played no part at all in Denmark, the theatre was the 'public interest', the most important theme of conversation for the day and the evening: the Royal Danish Theatre was probably also to be considered as one of the foremost in Europe: it certainly was in possession of considerable talent.

And he goes on:

Meanwhile, if I may be allowed to say so, the theatre was my club-room each evening: I still went there regularly. Just that year I had been given a seat in what was known as the 'Court Stalls', which were only separated from the rest of the stalls by an iron bar: it was the custom that every author who produced one play for the theatre was given a free seat in the pit: two plays gave him a seat in the pit stalls, and three gave him admittance to the 'Court Stalls' . . . the part of the stalls where the king gave seats to his courtiers, diplomats and leading officials . . . I, too, gained this honour. Thorvaldsen, Oehlenschläger, Weyse, and several others were there as well at the time.

Through Andersen's complacent-cum-childlike delight at being admitted to the Court Stalls, the reader perceives something of the esteem in which Copenhagen's major artistic talents were held. Perhaps this was the final expression of the patronage of an absolute monarch, but the populace as a whole derived a genuine and personal pride from the artistic achievements of the age, and in a city as small as Copenhagen the artists and literary figures themselves were as well known as television has made their modern counterparts in a more diffuse and impersonal society. It is a fact that when writing his pseudonymous works Søren Kierkegaard used deliberately to take regular short strolls through the streets of Copenhagen to give people the impression that he was wasting his time and to convince them that he could not possibly be writing. As for national pride in the achievements of one man, the return of Thorvaldsen from Italy was a national occasion on which the entire population of Copenhagen went to greet him.

The Royal Theatre, a meeting-place for Copenhagen society, had nurtured the leading talents of the Danish literary scene.

Adam Oehlenschläger, the first and in many ways the greatest of the Danish Romantics, had had his heroic dramas of the Ancient North performed there. Carsten Hauch, Oehlenschläger's contemporary, had seen his plays acted on the same stage. In the second generation of Romantics, Johan Ludvig Heiberg had been one of the leading attractions, and Hans Christian Andersen himself had both light plays and operas, for which he had written the libretti, produced there. To have a play performed in such surroundings was the token of success, of acceptance as a writer of talent, and — as Andersen also points out — it was the writer's best source of income.

The Cultural Scene

The catastrophic economic conditions and the difficult political situation in the first half of the nineteenth century, when its new and impotent role forced the country to turn its gaze inwards, nevertheless formed the background to an unprecedented burgeoning of Danish literature. The period from 1803 to about 1830 is known as the Golden Age — an era of grandiose achievement, high Romantic tragedy, rolling verse, historical novels, and deeply felt and inspired hymns. If any period can belie the theory that literature cannot flourish in a period of national collapse, it is this epoch of Danish history.

The apparent paradox hinged, however, on the coincidence of a number of factors. First was the arrival of the Romantic philosophy of Schelling, brought to Denmark from Germany by Henrik Steffens. This in itself had an immediate liberating influence after the constrictions of the end of the Enlightenment. It created the philosophical foundation for a new attitude to literature and enabled writers to indulge in new literary forms and to renew the literary language. It taught, among other things, the idea of the unity of nature and the spirit, of past and present, the unity indeed of all things; and as examples of this unity, writers treated Nordic themes in literary forms which belonged to the South, while historical themes suddenly took on a new significance for the present time. Accordingly dramas and epic poems appeared dealing with the heroic age of Scandinavia, written by Oehlenschläger, Grundtvig, and Hauch, while Ingemann wrote his historical novels in the manner of Walter Scott. This movement also produced what is known as the Aladdin motif, after the idea which Oehlenschläger expressed in his play *Aladdin*. This deals with the theory that certain people are chosen by nature, or God, or the gods, to achieve greatness, and that nothing can stop them, however weak and ill-suited they may otherwise seem. Thus Aladdin is shown not to deserve the greatness which is thrust upon him, but all the machinations of Noureddin, the sorcerer, in fact the representative of eighteenth-century rationalism, cannot prevent him from winning the princess.

The twin themes of former national greatness and of the possibility of being chosen to be great, despite all appearances, assumed a special significance for Denmark after 1814. Romantic-patriotic drama dealing with the heroic past appealed to a population looking for an escape from the sordid present, and served as a source of inspiration for many years. At the same time the Aladdin concept also took on new proportions: it was not only of use as a literary theme, but it could be applied to individuals — Oehlenschläger felt that he himself exemplified it, as did Hans Christian Andersen — and it was also possible to apply it to a country. Denmark began to see herself as an Aladdin, especially after 1848 when Prussia was forced to climb down. The fact that this was largely due to the pressure of more powerful nations was ignored, and some romantic and patriotic Danes saw themselves in the role of an Aladdin, chosen to be great, and not to be prevented even by such a powerful nation as Prussia. There is little doubt that this upsurge of national self-assurance and implicit faith in what nowadays might be referred to as a country's destiny was largely responsible for the climate of public opinion which forced events towards the catastrophe of 1864. The final defeat then, coming after a period of growing self-confidence, gave a staggering blow to national self-assurance and had an effect which can only be described as traumatic.

Meanwhile, although the Aladdin theme had certainly survived as long as this, the other, escapist, aspect of the Romantic age had gradually been replaced in the 1830s by what is known as poetical realism. The new generation of writers concentrated more on a mixture of fantasy and realism based on contemporary Denmark, and especially on life in Copenhagen. This process coincided again with the emergence from the financial doldrums and the approach to parity of the currency, reached in 1838. With this increasing affluence, and the retreat in time of the Napoleonic Wars, nationalism and escapism, typical of the Golden Age, became less attractive and less relevant, while the present gradually ceased to be something to escape from.

Thus Poul Martin Møller could write his character poems *Scenes from Rosenborg Have* and his unfinished novel *The Adventures of a Danish Student*, both of which are distinctly and firmly based on contemporary Copenhagen, and written with a deftness of touch and a humour long absent from Danish literature. The first generation of Romantics, filled with an awed sense of their divine calling, had taken themselves very seriously, but the second generation felt themselves less as chosen tools of the gods and could thus use a lighter style. Even J. L. Heiberg, the chief exponent of Hegelian philosophy in Denmark, and a man who took his philosophical work very seriously indeed, allowed himself in his light and elegant plays to be inspired by recognisable elements of everyday life in Copenhagen. Although he transcends this school, Hans Christian Andersen really belonged to it — witness the Copenhagen of *Ole Lukøie* and parts of *The Tinder Box*, and the quite specific and recognisable mansions at the beginning and end of *The Ugly Duckling*. Søren Kierkegaard also betrays close affinities with the school in the novels which form part of his work, notably *The Diary of a Seducer*, of which the Copenhagen scene is an integral part.

In the visual arts, too, this is referred to as the Golden Age. The sculptor Bertel Thorvaldsen rose to international fame greater than that of any other Danish artist of his day. His work was commissioned on the one hand by Napoleon and on the other by the Vatican, while in Poland he wrought statues to Poniatowski and Potocki. In his native land his works were legion. His statues are noted for their sense of form and their harmony; in the eyes of his critics Thorvaldsen is too cold — though it has also been suggested that he was forced to restrain himself because of Danish taste in his day. There *are* statues of greater sensuous beauty, and that of Maria Barnatinskaja (1818) shows the restrained sense of the human body which was part and parcel of Thorvaldsen's art.

The bourgeois restraint which seems to have implanted itself on Thorvaldsen's art likewise makes itself felt in the paintings of the period. In their way, these are in keeping with the literature of the age, linked to the life of the Copenhagen bourgeoisie, whether in the portraits of C. W. Eckersberg, C. A. Jensen and Constantin Hansen, or the idyllic but lively Copenhagen scenes of Christen

Købke and Wilhelm Marstrand. As time went on, Copenhagen, though still the focus of Golden Age art, was extended to include other urban and rural scenes. Many of the painters, not least Constantin Hansen, formed a Scandinavian artists' colony in Rome, which also served as a constant fount of inspiration.

Although it did not achieve the international standing which was even at that time recognised in Thorvaldsen, and which has more recently become recognised in the paintings of the period, Danish music, too, thrived. J. A. P. Schultz, the German-born musician who settled in Denmark. began with his *Lieder im Volkston* (1782–90) the song tradition which continued throughout the nineteenth century up to Carl Nielsen and beyond; a gentle *Lied*, less complex than those of the great German Lieder-writers, but charming and immediate in their simplicity. The genre was now taken up and developed by C. E. F. Weyse, the composer of six symphonies and the music for many plays, but still most famous for his songs. Based largely on texts by his contemporary Romantics, and like them reflecting the idyllic escapism of his time, he is also associated with the growing interest in folk song.

N. F. S. Grundtvig and the High Schools

Outstanding among all the writers of his time in his significance for contemporary and later Danish cultural life was Nicolai Frederik Severin Grundtvig. Internationally less known than Kierkegaard and Andersen, though with growing recognition, Grundtvig was a baffling mixture of poet, theologian, educationist and prophet. Theologically speaking, he was something of a sectarian, but he was never excluded from the state Church and was able to found one of the two main wings of the Danish Church as it exists today; though in another country he might well have suffered the fate of a Wesley. Certainly, Grundtvig was at one time placed under state censorship for his criticism of the rationalist teachings of some leading theologians, and attempts were made to limit his freedom. In his Romantic mixture of patriotism and Christianity he also expressed that trend towards individualism which was an essential aspect of Romanticism in Denmark as elsewhere, and which in Danish minds was linked to the idea of genius. The search for the individual and the desire to give to the individual the opportunity to express himself was also one of the motive forces behind

Grundtvig's idea of the folk high school, a product of Danish Romanticism which has played such a formative role in the life of the ordinary people. Having suffered from the old grammar school tradition of education, Grundtvig was determined to work for a school of a different type. During a stay in England in 1829, he was fired by the dynamism he found there, and which he saw as springing from the English ideal of freedom, which he could only contrast with the passiveness of the benevolent autocracy in his native land. One feature which particularly impressed him was the growth of liberal studies and learning in the newly-founded London University (now University College London), itself an expression of the achievement of freedom from tradition. This, combined with the community spirit which he found in the Cambridge colleges, was instrumental in inspiring Grundtvig with his vision of a 'high school in Sorø'.

There was no thought of establishing a new Danish university on the lines of either Cambridge or London. Grundtvig, for all his learning, had too much patriotic and missionary zeal to be interested in establishing an exclusive academic institution. His idea was to start something which could be a seat of general learning divorced from the examination-ridden grammar schools, the 'black schools' as he called them. The original intention of founding such an institution at Sorø was shelved and finally abandoned. Instead, the first high school was opened at Rødding in 1844, as part of the effort to support Danish culture in the areas close to the German border. This was a move reflecting the true function of the high schools, namely to foster Danish patriotic sentiments and combine them with a liberal Christian outlook: 'Man first — then Christian', as Grundtvig himself put it. In addition the schools were intended to attract students from the rural areas and give them some feeling for cultural values.

Under the leadership of Christen Kold rather than Grundtvig himself, the schools were a great success and attracted large numbers of young adults from country districts. Although originally a Grundtvigian concept, the idea was later taken up by the more evangelical wing of the Danish Church, Inner Mission, and a number of political institutions were subsequently added to the list. The high school is now a flourishing institution, with a much wider horizon than in the nineteenth century. Although the new educational opportunities offered by mass media, university extension courses and evening classes at one time caused numbers to diminish, the unemployment rate of recent years together with a modernisation of the programmes on offer has brought about a noteworthy revival as the schools have once more been able to play an important role in modern Denmark.

It is difficult to estimate the influence of the high school movement on Danish life as a whole, however easy it is to produce statistics and figures. Nevertheless, it is reasonable to suggest that it is partly responsible for the genuine interest in culture and art, so strikingly widespread in modern Denmark, and ultimately for the proportionately large number of books read by Danes. The high schools have also fostered amateur art and crafts, and it would not be unreasonable to suggest that they have played an important part in fashioning the sense of taste and design which are so striking a part of the present Danish make-up.

Ecclesiastical Strains

Theologically speaking, Grundtvig was an individualist in a rather different sense, in that he was one of many at that time who rebelled against the conformity of the previous age and sought to find a new and more living expression for the Christian faith. During the eighteenth century, rationalism had succeeded in removing all truly metaphysical aspects of Christianity and reducing it to little more than a moral code. The move away from this came with Romanticism at the beginning of the nineteenth century, and while Bishop Mynster sought to preserve the unity of the Danish Church at the same time as he introduced a more spiritual element into it, Grundtvig and others like him sought to introduce completely foreign elements. The ordinary people had found the Lutheran Church unsympathetic and drifted towards these new teachers and others whose teaching was further removed from the Lutheran orthodoxy — Baptists and Methodists were perhaps chief amongst these, but there were also Moravians and numerous other small sects, some of which, being run by laymen, were put down with a hard hand, as laymen were by law not allowed to lead religious movements. Søren Kierkegaard was representative of this tendency to rebel against the state Church, except that he was not disposed to try to create a sectarian community. His significance was rather that of religious individualism taken to its logical conclusion, and precisely because of this he can be firmly placed in the Romantic individualist tradition.

By 1864, then, Denmark had progressed to the point at which she could begin to be transformed into the Denmark we know today. Her frontiers were much shorter than they had been half a century before, and her population had shrunk to little more than half of what it had been. Yet, counter to the catastrophes in the field of foreign policy had gone the preparations for a period of expansion at home. Most of the remains of the former systems had been removed within a noticeably short period of time. The age of absolutism was past, the limitations on trade had been removed, and the means were beginning to be put at the disposal of industry to enable it to establish itseif in the forefront of the Danish economy. Although Denmark was basically an underdeveloped country in the period around 1820, by 1864 things were looking very different. In agriculture, too, new methods of cultivation had been introduced, drainage had improved, and, perhaps fundamentally of more importance, the financial means needed to expand were available. And so was the will to improve matters. The farmers had experienced an age of liberation. The smallholders had not, but their turn was to come later in the century with the emergence of the working classes as a power to be reckoned with.

3 1864–1901: TOWARDS A TRANSFORMATION

Denmark's internal political affairs during the period up to 1864 had been concerned largely with the ending of the absolute monarchy and the related problem of instituting a suitable constitution. There had been an almost monotonous series of constitutional crises. Politically speaking, the period which ends in 1901 with what is known as the change of system, is concerned with the continuation of that struggle and of the related phenomenon — the emergence of political parties. The battle now was not against the absolute rule of the King, but against rule by cabinet, the cabinet being appointed by the King. In the face of an increasing liberal majority in the lower house of the *Rigsdag*, the upper house had a built-in conservative majority and was backed by the cabinet. It was only in 1901, after a period of bitter conflict which at one time led to violence, that the parliamentary system was finally established with the understanding that the government must be drawn from the majority in the lower house.

Reactions after Defeat

Whether they deserved it or not, the National Liberals were given the blame for the defeat of 1864, and there could no longer be any question of their forming a cabinet. The King looked for new men to lead the country, and found them in a class which had been largely out of politics for many years, the great landowners. They had been eclipsed by the farmers and their representatives because they had been unwilling to enter into public debate with them and had accordingly not fought elections in great numbers. It was their view that Denmark should no longer be governed by the academics who formed the discredited and by now reactionary National Liberals, but that they should be replaced by landowners and the upper-middle classes. They wished to replace the November constitution (forced upon Denmark by events in Schleswig-Holstein and already removing some of the freedom granted in 1848) by one far less liberal in content. In this they were opposed by the farming classes, expressing themselves through the Friends of the Farmers, who wanted to leave the 1849 constitution untouched. A return to this constitution in its entirety was throughout the whole of this period one of the main objectives of the farmers and the party that emerged around them. However, the election of 1866 gave a narrow majority of members of the *Rigsdag* in favour of revising the constitution, and after protracted negotiations between the parties most directly concerned, it was decided to leave the *Folketing* untouched, but to introduce new arrangements for electing the *Landsting*. The franchise for this was to be severely limited, and based on land and money, in addition to which the King was himself to appoint 12 of the proposed 64 members. Despite attempts to dissuade him, Christian IX signed the new constitution which came into force on 5 June 1866 and remained in force until 1915. He then chose to appoint his Ministers, as was his prerogative, from the *Landsting*, completely ignoring the wishes of the *Folketing*, although it was a body considerably more representative of the wishes of the people.

The first Prime Minister under this new constitution was the largest landowner in the country, Count C. E. Frijs, the owner even then of over 500 farms, an enlightened patriarch who accepted appointment from a sense of duty rather than from political ambition. As his Foreign Minister he chose J. B. S. Estrup, a consummate and determined politician who was subsequently to become a symbol of aristocratic rule. The only gesture to the National Liberals was the appointment of a professional civil servant as Minister of Justice. Nevertheless, the landowners were prepared within limits to work with the National Liberals, partly with the object of withholding influence from the farmers' representatives, whom neither considered to be sufficiently well educated to have a say in government. Thus even at this early stage there were signs of co-operation between the landowners and the intellectuals in what was the beginning of a political structure based on class.

What followed was a period of relative political stagnation. However, a number of much needed social reforms were carried out and a catastrophe in foreign affairs was avoided by the unwillingness of the government to accede to the emotional demands of the people, the way thus being cleared for a period of expansion after the advent of democratic government in 1901. It was at the same time a period of internal conflict, as improved educational standards and a changing social pattern made people unwilling to accept a form of aristocratic, semi-authoritarian government from a group which came to represent an ever-smaller section of the *Rigsdag*. There was also considerable resentment at the system of representation. The electoral law allowed for single constituency members to be elected. This gave a built-in majority to the wealthier rural interests at first, as about three-quarters of the population still lived in the country districts, while many of the wealthier townspeople also owned land in the country and could thus be counted as belonging to that class. The working classes, on the other hand, were almost entirely disenfranchised.

Yet is was precisely this upper-class government which contrived to keep Denmark out of the Franco-Prussian War of 1871. The temptation again to intervene in international politics had already emerged in 1866, when Denmark had considered taking sides in the conflict between Prussia and Austria in the hope of regaining Schleswig and Holstein. The French government had then advised Denmark to remain neutral, and were able to include in the final treaty between the two powers a clause allowing the northen part of Schleswig to return to Denmark when the local population showed its desire to do so by means of a free vote. This clause was, of course, couched in such vague terms that Bismarck was able to ignore it completely, and he proceeded after the Peace of Prague to incorporate the duchies completely into Prussia.

It was hardly surprising, therefore, that the Danes were inclined to join forces with France when events started to lead up to the Franco-Prussian War. The Danish army had been modernised, and the romantically tinged, rather unrealistic patriotic spirit which had been decisive in 1848 and 1864, and which had since been fostered by the folk high schools, again began to make itself felt. However, the government was now less inclined to be swayed by popular sentiment and stood firm. France wanted an alliance, and sent the Duc de Cadore to Copenhagen to negotiate. The Danish government, however, was sufficiently hard-headed to demand that France should show some sign of success before Denmark would commit herself to entering the war, and when news of a French defeat arrived in Copenhagen, Denmark decided to remain neutral and to maintain indefinitely the provisional declaration of neutrality which had been issued when the war began. Some Danish politicians hoped that because of this Bismarck would return at least part of Schleswig, but they were soon disappointed. Bismarck had no such intention. He merely received no excuse to annex yet more of Denmark. 'Le Danemark est si peu de chose', the Duc de Cadore is said to have remarked in an unguarded moment — and Bismarck's behaviour indicated that he thought likewise. The duchies were to remain in German hands for a further fifty years. Prussia set about tying them closer to the German states, and a Prussian style of administration was introduced, as was conscription into the Prussian army. Even in the face of significant emigration to Denmark, this policy was carried through.

Although annexed by Prussia, and thus for a time outside the direct control of Denmark, the duchies continued to exercise the Danish mind. Yet the effect of losing the duchies was a blow to Danish national pride rather than the economic disaster that the loss of Norway had been only fifty years before. Denmark was not ruined by the wars with Prussia, and was quickly able to recover from the financial strain which had inevitably accompanied them. Indeed, in a country reduced in size it was easier to concentrate on the task of reforming and modernising, and on the constitutional and political internal problems with which she was faced. In one sense there was a direct economic gain from the loss of Holstein: Hamburg, the old trade rival of Copenhagen, was less accessible and the balance of trade altered significantly.

Conflict in the *Rigsdag* and the Emergence of Political Parties

During its first years the new 1866 constitution worked relatively smoothly, despite the unabated opposition of the farmers' representatives. This was in great part due to the able government of Count Frijs, who managed to mediate between the different points of view and especially between the two chambers of the *Rigsdag*. He avoided issues that might have led to a direct confrontation between them. In 1870, however, he resigned, and his successor, Count Holstein, was not a man to continue the policy. Indeed this very choice was sufficient to bring about a consolidation of the opposition forces, who with some reason felt they were the spokesmen of the people. The resultant increased tension caused the loose political groupings which had so far dominated the *Rigsdag* to change into embryonic political parties.

Broadly speaking, there were four more or less distinct groups in the *Rigsdag* in the early 1870s:

(i) The landowners and their supporters, who dominated the indirectly elected *Landsting* and represented the views of the upper classes.

(ii) The old National Liberals, the second main group in the *Landsting*, consisting largely of intellectuals and academics.

(iii) The so-called Centre Party, which was akin to the National Liberals but opposed to their increasingly conservative outlook. It drew its support from a less limited class than the National Liberals, and was considerably more liberal in its social and economic outlook.

(iv) The farmers' representatives who, while putting forward a show of unity in their opposition to the present government, in fact contained a number of disparate elements ranging from radicals to Grundtvigians, whose national aspirations were akin to those of the National Liberals.

It was this fourth group who first formed a true political party under the name of the *United Left*, the name itself indicative of the reforming aims with which the party began. And indeed it soon produced Denmark's first political manifesto. It aimed first and foremost at government by the people, with a return to the 1849 constitution. It also put forward a series of demands for political and social reforms: a more equitable taxation policy; universal suffrage in local elections; freedom for the farmer from the remains of the leasehold system; and greater independence for the state Church. In two other fields the party's spokesmen were less radical and more national. In Schleswig they wanted to see a border drawn up based on the wishes of the people living there, a solution similar to that subsequently agreed upon in 1920. They also called for a strengthening of ties between the Scandinavian countries, though this part of their programme was left vague because of a division of opinion within the party. It was a demand close to the hearts of the Grundtvigians but it failed to fire the imagination of the rest of the party. In general, the Grundtvigians among the party's supporters — nationalistic and financially well placed — were rather more conservative in their attitude, keenly aware of disagreements on fundamentals with other factions within the party — factions whose far-reaching demands for social equality were based, they felt, on hatred rather than on Christian charity. The seeds of dissent existed within the Left from its very inception, and the disparity of its various groups was in time to lead to new splits within the party, the formation of new groups, and finally to a split into two distinct and separate parties. Meanwhile 49 members of the *Folketing* (with a total of 102) belonged to the United Left. The demand for parliamentary democracy was not entirely unselfish, for the deputies of the Left saw a *Folketing* majority within their grasp. And they achieved it in 1872.

This parliamentary opposition was in essence the voice of the farmers. It was not the voice of the smallholders and farmworkers, nor was it that of the increasing urban working population. Indeed, although the demands for equality made by some factions within the Left would have favoured the workers, they were not really interested in them. The Social Democrats did not so far exist as a political party within the *Rigsdag*, though socialist ideas had begun to gain ground in Denmark in 1871. Pamphlets had been distributed opposing the rather patronising ideas that the workers should be educated. Significantly enough a parliamentary commission set up in 1874 had the task of examining 'how and to what extent the state can help to raise the workers' spiritual and material conditions and, more especially, protect them against undeserved poverty, particularly in their old age'. When the commission published its report in 1878, one of its suggestions was connected with the gulf which the commission saw between employer and worker:

> If the gap is to be closed, and if dissatisfaction and conflict, which by the nature of free competition must be created between capital and labour, are to be avoided, then it must, in the view of the undersigned members of the commission, be through a new pattern of conciliation in the arrangement of the industrialised society. The conflicting forces must be reconciled: the worker can be related to the concern for which he works in such a way that he wishes for its success: his courage, his loyalty, and his hope must be strengthened by the prospect that by means of orderliness and thrift he can progress from his position as a wheel in the machinery, to one where he can be in control of it.

These were far-sighted words for a commission in 1878. However, in 1871, this was not the way along which the thoughts of the socialists were directed. Instead, they were arguing that their aim should be to unite the workers and to achieve political power. It was their belief that they could win two-thirds of the seats in the *Folketing*. The pamphlets gradually achieved a circulation of some 3,000. The editor was anonymous, but was in fact a certain Louis Pio, who on seeing the success of the venture, started to organise a Danish Internationale. He won 700 members in Copenhagen, was in touch with Marx for a time, and proceeded to organise a series of strikes. In April 1872 he brought about a strike of 1,200 bricklayers, and his daily newspaper, *The Socialist*, which developed from the original pamphlets, called a mass meeting for 5 May. The government, aware of Pio's violent statements and foreseeing trouble, banned the meeting, and when Pio made it clear that he would ignore the warning, he was arrested. The meeting was cancelled, but it was too late: workers assembled as planned, and were dispersed by force, though without any loss of life.

The government now banned the Danish Internationale, and Pio and his colleagues were imprisoned, in Pio's case for five years, though he did not serve the whole sentence. Meanwhile the workers reorganised themselves in workers' associations and trade unions. By the time Pio was released in 1875 there were some 30 trade unions in Copenhagen, and between 70 and 80 in the rest of the country. Pio again took an active part in the movement, but was scarcely suited temperamentally to the changed conditions, and in 1877 he emigrated.

As yet neither the Left nor the Social Democrats appealed to the radical intellectuals. The previous generation's intellectuals had gone to the National Liberals, and some still did so, but those who wanted to see new ideas introduced into a backward Denmark had nowhere to go. They found their solution in a movement which originated in 1871, but which to begin with did not have connections with a political party. However, the Modern Breakthrough, as it came to be known, had direct political implications from the start, and as time went on developed such a close connection with the radical wing of the United Left that it cannot be omitted from any review of the emergence of political parties in Denmark. In the autumn of 1871 a young academic, Georg Brandes, began a lengthy series of lectures at the University of Copenhagen entitled 'Main Currents in European Literature in the Nineteenth Century'. He contrasted what he saw as the dynamic literature of other countries with the uninspiring products of contemporary Denmark. He sought now to infuse literature and intellectual life in general with a new desire to examine, to debate, to query. The ideas were not all new; they had been current elsewhere for years, but they all fell at one time upon a Denmark which had been cut off from such ideas in the rest of Europe, and they made an enormous impression on the young people who were looking for some new channel for their idealism.

In literature, in philosophy, in private discussion and public debate, the new ideas were expressed vehemently. Honoured institutions were attacked as irrelevant to modern society: marriage, chastity, piety, were condemned, and efforts were made to introduce a new morality based on the materialist conception of man. More conservative members of society saw the very foundations of Danish culture threatened, and they fought hard to stem the rising tide of radicalism.

It was not surprising that these conservative forces, sensing the political implications of the various opposition movements within and without the *Rigsdag*, should also seek to organise themselves. In 1875 J. B. S. Estrup was appointed Prime Minister. In 1876 he and the landowners, the National Liberals, the Centre Party, and a small number of independent conservative members came together in the *United Right*. The party sought to defend its conception of Danish culture, by military means in face of threats from abroad, and by opposing radicalism in all its forms at home. It was prepared to supervise a gradual organic development and to work for an improvement of the condition and moral standing of the working class — an aim quite different from that of the Left. Its position was essentially defensive from the start, and as part of its system of defence it aimed at a co-ordinated organisation at local level. The Right became the first of the parties to develop a close-knit organisation, though in this it was closely rivalled by the Social Democrats.

J. B. S. Estrup and Autocratic Government

In appointing J. B. S. Estrup as Prime Minister, the King was aware that he was giving the task to a man who only had the following of a minority in the *Folketing*. His majority in the *Landsting* did not promise to make life easier for him, as there was no provision in the constitution for what should happen in the event of a serious clash between the two chambers. However, Estrup was thought to have the strength necessary to carry through a conservative policy in face of a Left opposition. He was a man of culture who from the start had been critical of the liberal provisions of the 1849 constitution, and when elected to the *Landsting* in 1864 he had played a leading role in working out the less liberal 1866 constitution. He saw it as his duty to defend Danish society as it had evolved so far, and to prevent any radical incursions into the *status quo*. Basing himself on the idea that the ownership of land gave rise to independence of mind and love of country, he argued that the ownership of land should be accompanied by political privilege, and so his political aim became and remained that of maintaining the supremacy of the upper classes. A further argument in favour of political privilege for landowners derived from the fact that taxation was based on land, and the more land a man owned, the greater was the weight of taxation he had to bear. Thus, the argument went, he should get something for his money. The Left answered by maintaining that the tax system should be altered.

With the changes then taking place in the country's economic structure and the emergence of a new, wealthy urban middle class, so far untaxed, it is not surprising that taxation was to become a major factor in the coming parliamentary struggle. On the one hand, the more or less unprivileged farmers represented by the Left, wished to see taxation extended to include the urban middle classes by the introduction of income tax. On the other hand, the landowners were unwilling to remove one of the arguments in favour of their own privileges, while the urban middle classes for purposes of their own had no interest in seeing income tax introduced. Both the latter groups were represented by the Right.

While taxation was thus one bone of contention between the two major parliamentary factions, the issue was complicated and given greater significance by antagonism of a completely different nature. Estrup was of the opinion that Denmark must be able to defend herself in any eventuality, and with this in mind he proposed to fortify Copenhagen. The Left opposed him, not so much because they were pacifists — the colourful and radical Viggo Hørup and his group being the exceptions — but because they saw the opportunity of using the defence question as a means of bargaining their way to parliamentary democracy.

The immediate confrontation between the two parties came

over the budget. According to the constitution, no bills could become law until passed in identical form by the two chambers. The Left saw this as a possibility of stopping any bill of which they did not approve. For their part the Right pointed to another clause in the constitution empowering the government to legislate by decree in an emergency if the *Rigsdag* were not in session. In strict legality, therefore, it could legally dismiss a recalcitrant *Rigsdag* and enact temporary legislation by extra-parliamentary means. The Left, on the other hand, maintained that such an act was illegal, and fought for years for the re-establishment of 'legality'.

Trouble started in the 1876 session, when the government presented a defence plan costing 71 million *kroner*. (The currency had changed from *rigsdaler* to *kroner* in 1875.) The Left suggested an alternative plan costing 30 million, to be coupled with the introduction of income tax. The government refused, and it proved impossible to reach a compromise. Estrup therefore dissolved the *Folketing*, and new elections were held in April 1876. The result was typical of many thereafter: the Left increased its representation, this time to 74 of the 102 seats, but there was no change in the parliamentary situation. The government was, and remained, the Right.

The Left now consistently refused to assist the passage of government legislation, and when 1 April 1877 was seen to be approaching without any signs of a compromise agreement on the budget, trouble was obviously brewing. On 4 April the *Folketing* session was closed. On 12 April there followed a provisional budget by decree, though it did not include points on which no agreement had been reached with the opposition during budget negotiations.

Dissention in the Opposition

Disillusion set in when the *Folketing* reassembled and the majority of Left members showed themselves to be in favour of co-operation with the Right. Indeed, feelings ran so high that a dissident group under the leadership of Berg and Hørup broke away from the main party and formed the Radical Left group.

Faced with the Left in disarray, Estrup saw an opportunity to strengthen his position, and dissolved the *Folketing* once more. His judgement proved correct, and the Right won 9 extra seats in the election, giving them 35, while the two Left factions were left about equal in strength. Estrup, using his considerable political skill, manipulated the two Left groups, and by so doing succeeded in pushing through more reform bills than had been passed for many years. Smallholders' credit societies were formed to give financial aid to smallholders; an act was passed establishing savings banks; and another by which the state bought up the Zealand railways. In order to do this Estrup had leaned heavily upon the support of the Radical dissidents, but he then unexpectedly reached a compromise agreement with the Moderates on a new army act, according to which the army was increased in strength, but the period of service reduced. However, the passing of the act brought to an end the co-operation between the Berg–Hørup radicals (strongly anti-militarist in outlook) and the ruling Right Party. It was the Moderates who now seemed in favour of compromise.

The year 1880 saw the election to the *Folketing* of Edvard Brandes, brother of the radical literary spokesman Georg Brandes, and one of his most ardent supporters. Edvard Brandes thus forged the link between the radical literary movement outside the *Folketing* and the radical political movement within it. An outspoken atheist, he was an admirer of radical movements throughout Europe, and tried to introduce their ideas into Denmark — as did his brother Georg in a different field. It was natural that he should join the Berg –Hørup group. They became the vehicle for the new ideas and in time attracted a new class of intellectuals into the party. The difference which existed between them and the moderates was such that it was obviously only a matter of time before a fundamental split developed, sufficient to start off an independent radical party.

An Impotent Left and Dictatorial Rule

When trouble arose over the budget again in May 1881, Estrup repeated his former tactics and dissolved the *Folketing*. This time he did himself no good, and the Right was reduced to 32 seats. With progress still impossible, yet another election was called, after which the Right was reduced still further to 26 members. A completely new factor in the 1884 election was the appearance of two Social Democrat members representing Copenhagen, a city which had so far been dominated by the Right.

With a result such as this it was doubtful whether Estrup could carry on: a minority government of now 19 against 83 was scarcely likely to be effective. Moreover, it was felt that the likelihood of a Left government was increased by the fact that one now existed in Norway without immediate chaos being apparent. Yet the Danish Left was as disunited as ever, and although some co-operation was possible between the various groupings, it was of a nervous kind, in which cultural as well as tactical and political differences were becoming increasingly apparent.

Under these conditions there was virtually a stalemate in the *Folketing*, with the result that it was dismissed and a provisional budget proclaimed in April 1885. Under the terms of the proclamation, the government was enabled to collect taxes, though not in excess of the original estimates on which negotiations had been carried out. However, there was a great difference between this and the previous provisional budget in 1877: this was not limited to such clauses as had already been agreed between the parties.

The Left reacted furiously, and there was open talk of revolution by many of its members. Their leaders, however, were not in favour of such extreme action and merely advised farmers not to pay their taxes. Some did refuse for a time, but to little avail. Others joined together to form 'rifle clubs' in order 'to combat enemies at home and abroad'; and the formation of co-operative ventures and stores, already proceeding apace, was speeded up as a political gesture towards the Right.

No government could ignore such widespread agitation, and a fresh provisional law was proclaimed forbidding the importation and distribution of weapons for the rifle clubs. Teachers were forbidden to take part in political agitation, and folk high schools agitating for the Left lost their state subsidy. A close watch was kept on public gatherings, and when Berg, immediately before delivering a speech, had the chief constable of Holstebro removed from the platform, he was gaoled for six months.

Yet nothing happened. The Left threatened to boycott the 1885–86 *Rigsdag* session, but in the event they attended as usual. When the Right suggested taking the entire question of the provisional laws to the Supreme Court, the Left refused on the assumption that the judges would almost inevitably take the side of the Right. There was deadlock again over the budget, and when an unsuccessful attempt was made on Estrup's life, the entire *Rigsdag* was dismissed and a series of new provisional laws issued by decree. These established an armed militia to maintain order, extended the powers of the police, limited the freedom of the press, and laid down penalties for spreading false rumours or encouraging violence. The most violent protest against the regime came in 1887, when there was a minor riot at Brønderslev. It was put down without bloodshed, though many of the rioters were thrown into goal.

Yet still nothing was achieved, and the campaign by the Left began to lose momentum. Had its leaders been men of sterner calibre, there might have been a different outcome, but for all their fury, none of the leaders, not even the fiery Viggo Hørup, was prepared to accept the responsibility of leading a revolution. Seen in retrospect, at least from one point of view, their protests against the dictatorial regime were pathetic, a fact with which the author Henrik Pontoppidan makes play in some of his short stories. Yet there is another side to the picture. Come what might, the Left leaders decided to keep within the constitution — how could they do anything else when their perpetual cry had been that the Right was acting in conflict with the constitution? They knew they had legality on their side and they were determined not to undermine that position.

Nevertheless, since the policies of obstruction and protest had failed, a change in tactics was called for. Accordingly it was decided to embark on a policy of negotiation, to force the government to keep the *Rigsdag* in session in order to discuss a whole series of suggestions for reform. But the Right countered by dissolving the *Folketing* and holding elections. There was a record turnout, and the Right increased its representation to 27 seats against a combined opposition of 75. The Left was now even more willing to negotiate than before, but still no agreement was possible. So resort was again had to a provisional budget by decree.

In 1889 the Left published a comprehensive programme for reform, demanding reductions in customs duties and in military expenditure; the proclamation of neutrality; old age pensions; financial aid in sickness and for disablement; a limit to the hours of work; the right of the workers to form unions; the provision of state aid to smallholders to enable them to buy land; votes for women; a reform of the legal system; and greater freedom for the churches in Denmark — an ambitious programme, which provided the basis for legislation for years ahead.

Whether or not under the influence of this programme, the

election of 1890 led to a new reduction in the strength of the Right to 24 members, while Left members tended to be radical at the expense of the Moderates. Two Social Democrats were also elected to the *Landsting*, again a landmark in Danish politics.

The Social Democrats were now becoming more and more of a power in Danish political life. They were well organised and were making demands for reform which went beyond those of the Left. Moreover, they were at last beginning to make progress among the farmworkers in the rural areas, a preserve which had hitherto belonged to the Left, who were worried by this new development and moved more towards a policy of negotiated reform. In fact during the years to come both the Right and the Left were interested in pushing through a reform programme, not so much out of reforming zeal, but from a desire to maintain their positions.

The Left Achieves its Object

Berg died in 1891, and with him went one of the main obstacles to negotiation between the Moderate Left and the Right, who together passed a law on Sickness Benefit Societies in 1892 and also co-operated to prevent the payment of a state pension of 2,000 *kroner* a year to Georg Brandes, as was suggested by the Radicals. Collaboration between the two factions went as far as an electoral pact in the *Folketing* elections of 1892, when the Right maintained its position with 32 seats, against the Moderates' 38.

The policy of mutual concession continued, with the immediate result of further reform legislation and subsequently an attempt at a true political reconciliation. A compromise was reached on the fortification question and it was agreed that the remaining provisional laws should be repealed. Briefly, the terms of the reconciliation agreement were that while some defence plans were to be continued, the aim of all defence measures was to be the establishment of Danish neutrality, for which the government was to try to obtain the recognition of the great powers. It was duly accepted by 54 votes to 44. Edvard Brandes resigned his seat at this, and Hørup refused to consider further nomination. Estrup, who had symbolised the struggle between the parties, carried out his threat to resign as Prime Minister in August 1894, though he remained a member of the *Landsting*.

This was not, however, the end of rule by the Right, though the new government under Tage Reetz-Thott, consisted chiefly of men who had worked for reconciliation and were eager to co-operate with the Moderates. The country as a whole, however, was not happy with this arrangement, and in the *Folketing* election of 1895, which took account of twelve new constituencies, both the Right and the Moderates, acting in concert, lost seats.

The Right had had its day. By 1898 they were reduced to only 16 seats in the *Folketing*, and that same year they lost a further three seats in the *Landsting*. Estrup resigned, and many members even of the Right were now in favour of a Left government.

Although the Smallholdings Act was passed, together with a new Primary Education Act, in 1899, there remained the great stumbling-block of taxation. The Right was itself disunited on this and the government had to resign because of pressure from the rebels within its ranks. The new government could not rely on their support, and it only succeeded in getting the bill through the *Folketing* by leaving out all controversial clauses. The *Landsting* split on the taxation issue, and in 1900 a group of rebels left the party and joined together as the Free Conservatives.

The *Folketing* election of April 1901 was held under entirely new conditions as, to discourage political pressure-groups, a law had been passed introducing the secret ballot. The result was a resounding victory for the Left Reform Party and an almost total eclipse of the Right, now reduced to eight seats, the smallest group in the *Folketing*.

In July the King, as expected, asked the government to resign, and called for the formation of a Left cabinet under the leadership, not of a parliamentary politician, but of a university professor of law, J. H. Deuntzer. The demands of the Left had been met at last, and 1901 thus finally saw the establishment of parliamentary democracy. The event has become known as the Change of System.

The Industrial Scene

Politics were not the only sphere of Danish life to undergo a development of some significance in this period. It was a time of rapid change outside the *Rigsdag*, in almost every sphere of activity, and some of the most important took place in the field of industry and industrial relations.

The industrial change which took Denmark once and for all away from the ancient pattern of industry and production came late. When it did come, it was partly the result of changing industrial patterns and methods elsewhere, but also the direct consequence of the liberalisation of internal trade in 1862. Before that, the guild system had been in full operation and the way in which trade had been carried on had been strictly limited. Now, with liberalisation, people were free to carry out any trade as and where they pleased. The guilds no longer had any significance, at least not beyond running such activities as sickness benefit societies. There had been some apprehension about the effect of this radical change of system, but the worst fears were not realised, although increased competition did have adverse effects on some workers.

Although a thousand or so industrial firms had been founded before 1864, these were small concerns and there had so far been little that one could call major industrial enterprises. By 1872 the number had risen to 1,400, but of these 800 still employed under ten men each, while only 54 were big enough to employ a hundred men or more. The increase was significant, however, and the new freedom to pursue any trade, together with rising prices in the 1870s, led to a further rapid increase. A few concerns in Denmark were now so big as to be beyond the resources of individuals, and the formation of limited companies began. Burmeister and Wain, the shipbuilders and the largest establishment in Denmark, went public in 1872 and was followed by many others: 17 in 1872, 69 more by 1875. Many of the companies thus formed are still in existence today.

At the same time, commercial activity increased. There was a move to expand international trade and the free harbour was built in Copenhagen. Communications improved internally with the expansion of the railway system and both internally and externally with the changeover from sail to steam. Easier transport meant that industry could develop in the provinces as well as in Copenhagen, and the period saw an increase in the populations of the provincial towns as well as Copenhagen, though the capital grew more rapidly.

This increase was due not merely to a marked growth in population, but also to a drift from the villages and the countryside. The intensification of mechanised farming as well as the industrial breakthrough were behind this, and the growing proletariat had to be controlled and organised.

The workers had their representatives, or would-be representatives, in two fields. The Social Democrat Party sought to gain, and gradually achieved, political influence. On a different level the trade union movement emerged and grew parallel with industrialisation. Although in Pio's day there had been a close connection between trade unions and politics, it was now decided that the unions should not engage in political activity or be directly connected with the Social Democrat Party.

They set about improving working conditions and wages, and encouraged a wave of strikes, mainly in Copenhagen but also elsewhere in the country. By 1898 the various unions agreed, for the sake of the movement as a whole, and also in order to avoid hurting each other as a result of their activities, to join together in the Association of Trade Unions (*Det Samvirkende Fagforbund*) with the object of co-ordinating their efforts.

They were presumably also spurred to this move by the fact that in 1896 the employers had organised themselves into the Employers' Association (*Arbejdsgiverforeningen*). This new association was obviously created to protect the employers' interests in the face of growing union strength, and the possibility existed of a conflict between the two major organisations. It came in 1899. Before this, individual employers had reacted to strikes by introducing lock-outs, and one major example had taken place in 1885, involving the locking-out of 1,300 workers from 24 factories. Now, in 1899, one strike led to the locking-out of 40,000 men for a total of 19 weeks, an event of such seriousness that many experts were concerned for the long-term effects on the economy. In the end the dispute was settled largely because of near-exhaustion on both sides, but the basis of the settlement has had great significance for industrial relations since that time. The workers gained recognition of their right to organise themselves, a right that some, but not all, employers had sought to deny them. Meanwhile the other clauses of the compromise settlement were just as important to subsequent peace, as they drew up terms for relations between the two sides of industry. No strike was to be called without a vote in favour by three-quarters of the executive of the union involved. A week's notice must be given. No strike or lock-out was to be supported by the unions or employers' organisations if called contrary to the rules. Agreements between unions and employers should be binding, and three months' notice must be given of intent to terminate agreements. It was also decided that efforts should be made to establish a compulsory arbitration tribunal, and this was in fact achieved in 1910. Thus the arrangement after the great lock-out at the turn of the century laid foundations for the civilised standard of relations which has existed in Danish industry ever since. It has been suggested that this one agreement outside the *Rigsdag* has been of more significance than any signed within it during the period at present under review.

Living Conditions

The transition from old-fashioned industry to the beginnings of modern capitalism, the change from a small society where each trader made and sold his goods, to one in which those with capital financed trade, while the others worked for them, brought a change not only in the pattern of trade and industry, but also in the pattern of society. The move from the countryside to the towns, occasioned by industrialisation, led to the building of potential slum areas. The new workers had to live in large blocks of flats, and the stress seems to have been more on cheapness than on quality. Many workers and their families lived in one-room flats with no toilet facilities; the luckier ones had two rooms, of which one was kitchen-cum-living-room, the other the bedroom. The blocks in which these flats were built were large, and behind the block facing the street came yet another block with possibly an even less attractive exterior and no view of any sort — the so-called *baggårde*, backyards. This system of building persisted for many years and was only done away with when local authorities began to take a greater interest in building standards and town planning after the turn of the century, and either refused to sanction these large complexes or insisted on better and wider roads, which automatically put a stop to this kind of development. The structures themselves were flimsy in the extreme, which pre-cluded any pretence of private life as everything could be heard from one flat to another. Although social histories tell of these flats, the best description is probably to be found in the social literature of the day, first and foremost in Martin Andersen Nexø's *Pelle the Conqueror*:

> Up through the narrow courtyards the entrance porches hung drooping and decaying towards each other, leaving a narrow

opening where clothes lines glided backwards and forwards with children's clothes and floorcloths. The dark wooden stairs ran in zigzags against the walls, popped into the entrance porches and went right up to the attic. From the porches and balconies, doors gave access to the flats or to long corridors which led into the interior of the massive block. But on *Pipmandens* side there were neither entrances nor railings from the second floor upwards. Time had devoured them, so that the stairs hung alone on their moorings: the ends of the beams still stuck out from the walls like rotten teeth stumps. A rope was hanging from above which could be used for support: it was shiny and black from many hands.

Nevertheless, buildings of this sort were not all that Copenhagen or the other major cities possessed, for together with the growing proletariat went an up-and-coming middle class — those who in one way or another had managed to keep up their independence or who had a sufficient income to maintain appearances. They, too, lived in apartments, though of larger dimensions, usually with a kitchen, though probably still not with toilet facilities. Mains drainage was still unknown.

Despite the lack of hygiene which marked the lower classes and many of those not so low, the standard of health in Denmark was improving at this time, owing partly to new medical knowledge and techniques of treatment and partly to the greater provision of health insurance associations, especially after the legislation in the 1890s. Many of the trade guilds, which had died out after the introduction of the Free Trading Act in 1862, had themselves organised a form of sickness insurance, and although the guilds themselves disappeared, this particular service was continued in the form of health insurance societies connected with individual trades or branches of commerce. Membership was of course voluntary, and in many cases limited to members of the particular trade; consequently a large section of the population was not covered at all. In cases of sickness, these people were either forced to accept poor-aid, with all its legal consequences, or to find a doctor willing to treat them without a fee. This was by no means as uncommon as might be supposed, and it was an accepted fact that many doctors varied their fees according to the means of their patients. This was also true when, as often happened, the doctor was paid a regular retaining fee covering any necessary services for a family and its servants throughout a year. The 1892 law on health insurance societies, while maintaining the voluntary principle, made provision for membership for all citizens whose income was below a fixed level, and consequently there was a rapid increase in membership, with, in the course of time, an improvement in standards of health.

Treatment also improved and new hospitals were founded. Finsen pioneered his light treatment for certain diseases and founded his institute, and at the very end of the period, in March 1900, Vejlefjord Sanatorium was opened in a first bid to end turberculosis. Along with the founding of hospitals went the need for suitable nursing staff, and in the 1880s the question was raised as to whether it was fitting for a young lady to undertake the work of nursing others, especially men, to health. Yet nursing became a profession open to young ladies of good family who for some reason or other had to fend for themselves. On the other hand, the fact that such young ladies had their difficulties emerges from Herman Bang's novel *Ludvigsbakke*, where the 'heroine', Ida Brandt, although left a considerable fortune after the death of her parents, is unwilling to live a life of leisure, and instead seeks to make a contribution to society by becoming a nurse. Her position is scarcely appreciated, for while the snobs of her day consider it beneath her dignity to have a profession, many of her fellows, learning of her small fortune, grumble that she has taken a post which could well have been filled by someone in more need of the money.

Drunkenness posed a particular problem. It was said at the turn of the century that one man in seven died of drink, and although this is probably an exaggeration there is no doubt that alcohol was the cause of many deaths. In Copenhagen alone there were approximately 300 cases of *delirium tremens* a year. By 1910 this had risen to about 700. The cause of this alcohol problem was not beer but *snaps*, which was then extremely cheap, known even as the poor-man's drink. Just how much was drunk it is difficult to say with any accuracy, but there are many examples in Danish literature from the period which indicate that workers, especially those engaged on outdoor work, were provided with a bottle of *snaps* each day to keep them warm. The annual consumption of *snaps* around 1880 is said to have averaged 17.5 litres per head of population, or 67 litres for every man over the age of 20. It is not surprising, therefore, that a movement aimed at total abstinence got under way and attracted widespread support. It is estimated that at one time almost seven per cent of the population belonged to it.

The obvious step which the government could have taken to reduce the consumption of *snaps*, that of taxing it, was not taken because of the political struggle in the *Folketing*. A compromise was reached by taxing beer, though it was pointed out even at the time that this was in fact taxing the lesser of two evils.

Rural Conditions

Chaotic as was the situation in the towns during this period of transformation, it was no better in the country districts. The change from the old patriarchal system to a class society was accompanied by inevitable strains and stresses. Despite the superficial unity between the farmers and the smallholding-labouring class, a widening gap had existed between them since the end of *stavnsbaand* almost a century before. While the farmers had developed from a community which rented its land into one which normally owned it, the smallholders had been left behind. A profound change in the relationship between these two groups had become apparent. Whereas previously the farmer had benevolently allowed his workers to dine in the same room as he did, now, with the increase in prosperity which enabled him to improve his house, he had a special room built for his workers instead. A class system sprang up, and if by any chance a farmer and his employees did eat together, they sat at table in strict order: the farmer and his family; the resident workers; and lastly the day labourers and the smallholders who were doing chance work on the farm. These latter were always given the worst treatment, just as the most difficult work was left to them. This was the normal state of affairs by the 1880s, though things had not gone so far in some of the more backward parts of the country, where the patriarchal system was still maintained.

Not only is it quite certain that the farmers began to treat their labourers as an inferior class, but it is also quite evident that they sometimes looked on them as little more than slaves. The labourers were housed in filthy rooms to which access was gained through the stable or cowshed. Several men might have to share a single room, some having to share their beds with each other or with the children who, from the age of about eight, acted as gooseherds or cowherds. Hygiene was almost non-existent and sickness was rife. The farmer had the right to beat the children who worked for him, and there is ample evidence that many took advantage of this if the child failed in his duty. There is some difficulty in discovering just how widespread this ill-treatment was, probably because, as is to be expected, the cases where it did not apply were not given prominence. The composer Carl Nielsen, for example, talks of his days as a gooseherd as a very happy time, though others who had lived the life talked of the frightening responsibility of looking after a herd of cattle all day long and the utter loneliness of life out in the fields.

Just as some farmers tended to exploit their workers, so local councils adopted an unsympathetic attitude towards families in need of financial help and treated paupers in the most humiliating manner. Whereas the poor had hitherto been helped by individual initiative, in the 1860s and 1870s a number of poor-law institutions were built, probably not so much out of a desire to be humane, as a wish to dissuade people from resorting to the parish. Many of the workhouses had the appearance and atmosphere of prisons, and it was said that many people commited suicide rather than be sent to them. There were obviously, says the novelist Skjoldborg in his memoirs, some good wardens as well as cruel ones, but he considered the whole system to be wrong and maintained that such institutions had awakened his feelings of social injustice.

After a good deal of discussion, the Ministry of the Interior decided in 1889 to revise the Poor Law, but not to change its basis completely. Comments were invited from all manner of qualified people throughout the country, and it emerged from their reports that there were two widely conflicting views. Officials and laymen with high humanitarian ideals looked objectively at the existing situation, while the local authorities consisted largely of well-to-do farmers who did not nourish tender feelings towards the less fortunate members of society whom they saw as potential financial burdens. This state of affairs explains, too, some of the abuses which had been current and were now stopped: the 'auctioning' of paupers, particularly children, to those who would take them into their homes for the lowest payment; and the system of the 'round' (*omgang*), by which paupers were forced to go from one farm to another, staying in each for a couple of days and working there for a meagre living. Then there was the practice of 'maintenance marriages' (*forsørgelsesægteskaber*), which was also prevented by the new Poor Law of 1891 — and which had in fact never been favoured by the authorities. When people had been living in a parish for a number of years they were entitled to receive poor-aid there. Women were entitled to it in the parish to which their husbands belonged, and so it was by no means uncommon for one parish to pay a man from another parish to marry some women (often with a large illegitimate family) who was a burden on it. The Poor Law of 1891 stated that illegitimate children remained the responsibility of the parish to which the mother had belonged before marriage, thus denying the local authorities the chief advantage to be derived from marrying off their pauper women to men from elsewhere.

The other main provisions of the new Poor Law were to clarify the question of where people were entitled to receive aid, to limit the power local authorities had over them, and to define just when a man could have cancelled his debt for any poor-aid received, and thus receive back the civil rights he had lost by accepting it. Five years were to be the norm: after five years' residence in one parish without poor-aid from another, people were entitled to assistance there; after five years without receiving poor-aid a man could be counted free from debt; and only after five years without poor-aid was a man free to marry without permission.

While, in retrospect, the Poor Law remained harsh, some provision was certainly also made for more humane treatment of paupers, and another bill was passed the same year providing assistance for old people who fulfilled certain conditions, the chief of which was that they had not received poor-aid for the ten years prior to their sixtieth birthday. It was left to the local authorities to decide what form the old-age assistance should take and they were able to put applicants into special homes if they wished — though not in poor-law institutions. There was some resistance from those most directly concerned, but the increasing number of beneficiaries can be deduced from the fact that payments made under the act rose from just under 3 million *kroner* in 1893 to almost 5 million in 1899. The payments were very modest at first, on average only 69 *kroner* per head in 1894, rising to 168 *kroner* by 1914.

Parallel with these early attempts to help the needy went a series of efforts to put smallholders on a new footing. These culminated in the first Smallholdings Act of 1899 which introduced the principle of state loans to smallholders to enable them to buy a certain amount of land for themselves. The aim was typical enough of the attitude of the better-off members of rural society, as the size of the plots which the smallholders could buy was not to be sufficient for them to live off them exclusively. Yet they were to be too big for the owner to take a full-time job in addition to running his smallholding. Thus those in need of labour were still assured of a plentiful supply.

With all its deficiencies, this Act was used to provide some 1,900 plots between 1899 and 1904. Its renewal in 1904 brought no major changes, but when it again came up for renewal in 1909, provision was made for the purchase of bigger plots, and thus the smallholder was enabled to take another step along the road to complete independence from his more wealthy colleagues.

The provision of 'state smallholdings' had from the start a far-reaching influence on the morale of the smallholders. They were now for the first time enabled to buy land for themselves, and the very fact that this represented for them a financial responsibility encouraged them to give of their best. It was sometimes said that the best models for agricultural methods were to be found in the smallholdings, not in the farms, such were the eagerness and determination with which they undertook their new tasks. As time went on provision was made for 'smallholders' tours', in which competent smallholders were taken to see the best results of their colleagues, so that they could learn from their methods. Evil tongues argued, perhaps with some justification, that smallholders going on these tours were often too old to benefit from what they learned, but there is no evidence to suggest that this was the normal run of affairs. With enhanced abilities and economic independence came a growing social pride, which led to the formation in 1910 of the Federation of Danish Smallholders' Societies, an organisation that was the living expression of a new class. Thus the period had seen the emergence and establishment of two distinct classes in rural Denmark: the modern farmer, progressive in outlook and well able to look after himself; and the smallholder, freed from the final traces of serfdom which had still been apparent even towards the end of the nineteenth century.

The farmers themselves had undergone a transformation which in its way was just as radical as that experienced by the smallholders. It all began in the mid-1870s with the appearance of cheap corn in the United States. Denmark had so far been a corn-exporting country, but could no longer compete. At the same time, thanks to the Industrial Revolution, Britain started importing large quantities of meat. The Danes saw their opportunity in this market, and within the twenty years from 1875 to 1895 they had more than doubled their exports of animal products. At the same time Denmark went over from being a corn-exporting to a corn-importing country, thanks to the increased quantities needed to feed the growing numbers of livestock. This happened despite the energetic efforts of the Danish Heath Society to cultivate the Jutlandic heath and grow corn on it. Between 1871 and 1914 the number of cattle in Denmark went up from 1.2 million to 2.5 million, pigs from 400,000 to 2.5 million, and poultry from 4.6 million (in 1888) to 15.2 million. Only sheep production dropped, owing to the increased competition from Australia resulting from the introduction of refrigerated ships.

Increases such as these were bound to bring about problems of distribution, while another problem was the quality of some of the products, notably butter. Danish butter at that time varied much in quality and had a poor reputation in Britain. Farm butter was said to be inferior to that made on the larger estates, and so in trying to improve and standardise the quality of farm butter there was at the same time the political motive of competing with the landowners. In 1874 an Århus merchant called Hans Broge suggested the formation of co-operative dairies in each village. In 1880 the first common dairies were established, in which the owners bought milk off the local farmers, but not on a co-operative basis. The first co-operative dairy proper was opened in 1882 in Hjedding, Jutland. The principle was that each farmer using the dairy should have a share in it, though the amount of capital required of each was minimal. Each farmer, whatever the size of his farm, was to have *one* vote in running the dairy and profits were to be shared according to the amount of milk delivered. The skimmed milk left after butter production was to be returned in proportion to each farm and used for pig rearing. This system was so democratic as to enable smallholders to take part even on the basis of their limited production, and also to have an active share in the running of the dairy.

The co-operative dairies were a success, and the following years saw a rapid increase in numbers: by 1885 there were 84 dairies; by 1890, 684; and 1895, 832. In an effort to stabilise quality, the state provided consultants who travelled round the country advising on the best methods and adopting a strict line with the inevitable few low-grade dairies. After 1888 a consultant was sent to Britain to keep a watch on what happened to Danish butter after import and to try to prevent adulteration — a not uncommon practice. In 1906 the Lur mark, the reproduction of the Viking horns (*lur*), was introduced as a trademark on the British market and in 1911 legislation was introduced laying down the quality of butter required before the Lur mark could be used — guarantee of quality at a very early date.

The same trademark was used on bacon, the export of which had increased along with that of butter from the early 1880s. Prior to this Denmark had exported live pigs to Germany, but in 1879 one Magnus Kjær had decided to produce bacon for the British market. He imported Yorkshire pigs and crossed them with pigs from his own district, and succeeded in producing a bacon attractive to the British consumer. This new trade was given a boost in 1887 when the Germans prohibited the import of live pigs or pig meat because of an outbreak of swine fever, and was further helped when they placed an import duty on live pigs in 1889.

The co-operative principle was adopted here, too, and the first co-operative bacon factory was opened in Horsens in 1887. More capital was needed to start a bacon factory than a dairy, and this problem was solved by serving a wider area, thereby attracting a larger number of farmers. By 1890 there were 10 such bacon factories; by 1895, 17; and by 1900, 26. In addition there was a small number in private ownership.

The dairies and bacon factories established the co-operative principle in Denmark, and this method of distribution was extended to cover fodder, seed, cement and machinery. A different aspect of the same principle was also to be found in the co-operative stores which began to open all over the country. They were inspired by the first English co-operative store in Rochdale, founded with the aim of securing commodities for the working people. Thisted Workers' Association, founded in 1866, had the same object, aiming at improving the workers' conditions by buying more cheaply and sharing the profit with those who took part in the venture. However, one great difference arose between the English and Danish stores; in England co-operative stores were essentially features of urban life while in Denmark they became established mainly in the country districts. This was because while the country people saw the advantages of the system, the workers from the towns were dissuaded from forming or joining co-operatives by the Social Democrats who feared that lower prices would ultimately lead to lower wages. Thus, until 1900, the co-operative movement in Denmark remained almost entirely rural, and did not acquire the working class image that became part of the parallel movement in England.

The growth of these stores was helped by an anomaly in the trading laws dating from earlier in the century. These had defined areas around the market towns where shops might not be built. But as the co-operatives were societies, not shops, the law could not prevent them from opening, and in these belts they thrived. There was also a certain political motivation, in that the co-operatives often aimed at opposing the established grocers, who were nearly always supporters of the Right Party, while the farmers nearly always supported the Left.

The main difficulty encountered by the co-operative stores was the lack of expertise. They were in fact run by amateurs and consequently some of them went bankrupt. A move to counter this came in 1884 when the co-operatives in Zealand amalgamated, while those in Jutland followed their example in 1888. An amalgamation of all the co-operatives in the country took place in 1896 when the Danish Co-operative Wholesale Society, which has been described as a co-operative within a co-operative, was formed.

The Arrival of 'Modern' Literature

At a time which saw so many changes in so many fields, it is not surprising that Georg Brandes should have made an impression with his assertion that literature only shows signs of life when it debates problems. These words, uttered in 1871, came at a particularly favourable time — a time when society was ready for a change after a period of stagnation, and when new techniques and new ideas at all levels were capable of ensuring an end to that stagnation. Brandes made his original impact not only because of what he said, but also because of when he said it. The result was a close affinity between the literary radicalism of Georg Brandes, and the political radicalism of his brother Edvard and Viggo Hørup. Little wonder that while the political radicals became known as the Radical Left, the literary and cultural movement for change was dubbed the 'Literary Left'.

Romanticism, or its echoes, had persisted until after the 1864 war. Some of its great figures, notably Hans Christian Andersen and N. F. S. Grundtvig, lived on until the 1870s, even if they could no longer be said to be figures of literary influence. Literary eyes were in fact almost all turned inwards, and in a society which itself was more or less indifferent to what was going on outside, it was natural that few new ideas should be introduced. Then, after 1864, came the transformation of Danish society and a gradual realisation that the culture hitherto obtaining was not valid for all time, that other countries had progressed both materially and intellectually. Thus, when Brandes started introducing new ideas from all over Europe, the time was ripe for progress. With him came the modern English and French philosophical ideas of John Stuart Mill and Auguste Comte; with him, too, came an upsurge of Darwinism. In the field of theology, the liberal, radical ideas of Strauss and Feuerbach were introduced. Marx was also brought into the picture, though his importance for Danish literature was at that time limited. All these ideas were in conflict with the established outlook and they led people to question all accepted conventions — marriage, religion, political institutions, family life, the position of women in society: nothing was left untouched. It was clear that in introducing the discussion of contemporary society into literature, Brandes was consciously forming a link between political and literary radicalism. In this he was ably helped by Edvard, who was politically more active at the same time as he was acknowledged to be almost as redoubtable as a critic — 'the best hated man in public life', Georg Brandes admiringly called his brother in 1883.

The fact that the time was ripe for Brandes' attempts to reintroduce a new, European, radical dynamism into Danish literature did not, however, mean that he had all his own way. He was opposed by the entire establishment, whether on political, religious, or moral grounds, and when the chair of literature became vacant at Copenhagen University in 1872 and Brandes was nominated for it by the retiring professor as being the only man qualified, he was not appointed. Feelings ran extremely high throughout the 'cultural debate', and book after book dealing with this period, be it fiction or biography, indicates the intensity of the struggle. In his autobiography, Johannes Jørgensen, later in life an opponent of this 'Modern Breakthrough', tells how as a child he was excluded from conversations concerning modern literature:

They spoke of 'this Ibsen', 'this Brandes', 'this Drachmann', and sometimes of 'this Zola'. . . . Most of what they wrote was supposed to be of little value: admittedly, Ibsen had previously written valuable works, such as *The Pretenders*, and to some extent *Brand*, but his latest play — about Nora or whatever her name is, who deserts her husband — is there supposed to be anything beautiful or elevating in that?

The same is to be sensed in the work of Henrik Pontoppidan, a loyal admirer of Brandes, who depicts him in his novel *Lucky Peter* as a certain Dr Nathan. There 'Dr Nathan' is referred to as 'this much fêted and much attacked man who more energetically and determinedly than anyone else had cleared the ground for a Denmark of the future and started a stir in the country, the likes of which had not been seen in any intellectual or spiritual movement since the "Reformation"'. Dr Nathan had attracted followers and created opponents, and the split between them was deep.

As it was, the Modern Breakthrough provided Denmark with an upsurge of new literature aimed at carrying out Brandes' demand for contemporary interest, and philosophically based on Darwinism and a new pagan humanism. 'There is no God, and Man is his prophet', remarks one of the characters in Jens Peter Jacobsen's novel *Niels Lyhne*, the story of a man who throughout his life fights with himself and with others for his atheist faith, and who finally, mortally wounded in the war of 1864, refuses the ministrations of a priest and 'dies the death, the difficult death'.

J. P. Jacobsen, the first and internationally the most influential of the writers of the Modern Breakthrough, points to something of a paradox in the movement. While many of the most thorough-going Brandesians are now relegated to the histories of literature, those writers who have achieved a lasting place in the Danish literary consciousness are all in varying degrees exceptions who only within certain limitations can be said to be representative of the movement. The medium of this kind of movement must obviously be prose. Yet Jacobsen started his career as a lyric poet, one of startling originality even, and during this time provided the cycle of poems which in their German translations Schönberg took as the text of his *Gurrelieder*. Even here, however, with the thwarted Valdemar cursing God and being condemned to hunt the forests of Zealand until the end of time, there is discernible the anti-Christian tendency of the Naturalist movement, the Modern Breakthrough.

After Brandes entered the arena Jacobsen abandoned poetry in favour of prose, and his work is among the most finely chiselled ever produced in Denmark, written in a language which at its best is rhythmic and almost poetry, but which at its worst is artificial to the extent of being mannered. In his attempt at finding the *mot juste*, Jacobsen reminds one very much of Gustave Flaubert, and in fact his first major novel, *Marie Grubbe*, is almost a Danish version of *Madame Bovary*. The theme had attracted other writers before Jacobsen, but the interest here is the psychological motivation, based on Jacobsen's Darwinist conception of human nature. Jacobsen's other novel, *Niels Lyhne*, is an attempt at examining one 'problem' of the day in its treatment of the theme of atheism.

Because he was not concerned with the immediate problems of Danish society, Jacobsen was able to give his work a more universal quality than was the case with any of the other writers of this period. However firmly his work was placed against a Danish background, it was in each case a historical one, and this in itself is sufficient evidence that Jacobsen was not primarily interested in society in the sense of social conditions. His 'problems' are of an ethical-religious nature, and as such could still be appreciated outside the borders of his homeland. Whatever he has done with the text, it is perhaps symptomatic that Frederick Delius should have chosen *Niels Lyhne* as the basis for one of his operas, *Fennimore and Gerda*. It is the universality of Jacobsen that distinguishes him from his contemporaries.

At the other end of the scale is Henrik Pontoppidan, who started life as an out-and-out social critic in a series of short stories dealing with the material conditions of the poor, and went on to produce a number of long novels in which material conditions play a smaller part, but, where Danish society is concerned, none the less are always of fundamental importance. As already indicated, *Lucky Peter* is concerned with Copenhagen at the time of Brandes, a city torn between the old and the new. This is a novel which might possibly be acceptable to an English-speaking public without any particular knowledge of Danish affairs, but the earlier trilogy *The Promised Land*, concerned with sectarian conflicts in rural Denmark, is scarcely destined to be read outside its homeland. Perhaps this is reflected in the fact that the first two volumes were once translated into English, while the third never appeared. Again, the third of Pontoppidan's great novels, *The Realm of the*

Dead, is closely tied up with the political situation, and it will only be fully appreciated by a reader who knows at least a modicum of Danish history. At the same time the author is concerned to chart the social developments of the age, showing how the new upstart families who had gained wealth from the new industrialisation were trying to assert themselves alongside the families whose culture was established, but whose wealth was diminishing. For all his radicalism, Pontoppidan obviously deplores the ensuing decline in cultural standards, as does Herman Bang in a parallel situation in his *Ludvigsbakke*. In his concern with social and political problems, and also in his discussion of ethical questions, Pontoppidan is well within the definition of the Modern Breakthrough. Where he differs to some extent is, however, in the ascetic solutions he seems to find to some of them.

Two other figures of the Modern Breakthrough are also to some extent exceptions to the rule. In a time of prose, Holger Drachmann was a lyric poet who at first tried to use his lyrical gifts in support of the new movement, but gradually drifted into a more expressly Romantic view of life. And Herman Bang, the Impressionist, is far more concerned with individuals than with society as a whole, although the social picture is important to some of his work. He is mainly interested in depicting those whom life has passed by: the nurse who sacrifices herself to the man she loves but who is rejected for someone with a larger fortune, or the gentle wife of a boorish stationmaster watching life slipping away and not being willing to make a break when another man appears on the scene.

These four men are the outstanding representatives of the Modern Breakthrough, even though literature with a social flavour has continued to be written even to the present day. One thinks in this connection of authors such as Aakjær, whose novels from the end of the nineteenth century and the beginning of the twentieth were fervent attacks on social injustice, or even of Jakob Knudsen who defended the *status quo* and discussed social and ethical problems from a conservative standpoint. Yet, within twenty years of its beginning, the Modern Breakthrough was spent and had to give way to a new form of literature, more lyrical and more abstract in character. In the late 1880s a new generation of authors appeared who, though at first Brandesian in outlook, soon began to tire of the grey prose which was the typical product of the time. And when they came across the French Symbolist poets, they found a literary form which appealed to their own deepest instincts. Social problems, and indeed society itself, were pushed into the background, and the new writers sought instead to establish something beyond materialism.

Thus the 1890s emerge as a decade of introspection and soul-searching, though this is only a partially true picture. The major writers of the breakthrough were still productive, while the second generation of realists — Aakjær and company — were also active. The lyric element, however, was the work of the most significant group among the younger generation, and the introspection of much of their poetry was echoed in their prose and in that of some of the younger writers emerging at the end of the 1890s. The two major writers in question, Johannes V. Jensen and Martin Andersen Nexø, have both achieved an international reputation for their later, more extrovert, work, but they both started off as typical products of the 1890s, exponents of the *fin de siècle* atmosphere which had developed.

There was no sudden change in the style of painting which had established itself earlier in the century, though P. C. Skovgaard began to take greater liberties with perspective and showed less concern with the photographic accuracy which his older contemporaries, all like himself pupils of Eckersberg, had sought. There was perhaps a greater concentration, too, on atmosphere than there had been only a few years before.

Meanwhile, a new element made its presence felt in the work of the two leading sculptors of the day, H. V. Bissen and J. A. Jerichau. Bissen was a natural successor to Thorvaldsen, though the calm of Thorvaldsen's classical lines was now broken, and there is a greater sense of life and individuality about his figures. The dress, too, is less stylised. For his part, Jerichau went much further, totally rejecting the ideals of neo-classicism and concentrating instead on strength and physical realism. His statue of Hercules and Hebe is in stark contrast to the work of his predecessors, with emphasis on the muscular male figure alongside the slight female figure of Hebe. The statue of the Panther Hunter, depicting the moment at which the hunter is about to plunge his spear into the panther is one of frozen dynamism, a snapshot of a violent action.

The change in Danish painting came with Niels Larsen Stevns on the one hand, with his simplified representation of figures and landscapes, and on the other with the group of painters who settled at Skagen at the end of the nineteenth century and established a colony of artists there. Foremost among them were P. S. Krøyer and Michael and Anna Ancher. They were at first akin to the neo-Romantic movement in literature, represented by Holger Drachmann (who himself spent much of his time in Skagen). Even here, however, there is a striking element of realism in their paintings — the elderly workman carving a piece of wood, or the famous painting of the girl in a kitchen. Both transcend the uncontroversial realism of an earlier age, both representing ordinary, working people in place of the middle and upper classes which had hitherto dominated Danish art. In her later art Anna Ancher shows the influence of the French Impressionists, both in her portraits — for instance that of her own mother — and in street scenes such as that from Østerby.

Krøyer went further than Anna Ancher in his realism. A pupil of Léon Bonnat, he experimented with the use of colour which he learned in Paris, combining it with a social conscience. This led him to a social realism of a totally different kind — the ordinary, weatherbeaten fisherfolk in a Danish fishing village, or the famous painting of Italian hatters working under appalling conditions and lined with the suffering brought on by social oppression. As a work of art it is notable for its use of light streaming through the window, illuminating the bodies and features of those working in otherwise almost total darkness.

Danish music was generally conservative, clearly reflecting the influence of the nineteenth-century German Romantic composers. The song tradition started by Weyse was continued by Niels W. Gade, for many years internationally the most famous of Danish composers, the protégé of Mendelssohn, to whose music his own bears some resemblance. His first symphony, 'On the Fair Plains of Sjølund' reflects the national character of much of nineteenth-century Danish culture, being largely inspired by Danish folk melodies.

P. A. Heise continued the Romantic tradition: his 200 songs were originally much in the mould of Weyse and Gade, though his later efforts were more experimental. The great change came, of course, with Carl Nielsen, who belongs principally to the next period, but whose first symphony, written between 1891 and 1892, heralds something new and dynamic, a turning point in Danish music. Indeed, it is now recognised as a new departure in music in general, being probably the first symphony anywhere to employ progressive tonality, and thus predating Mahler.

Society, politics and the arts had gone hand in hand in this final period of the nineteenth century, as indeed they had done before. These final decades had brought about an awakening of the social and political conscience which had transplanted itself to the arts, and for which literature and painting had become willing vehicles. It had been a period of immense drive during which Denmark, partly through reaction against the lingering romantic complacence of years up to 1864 and partly through the introduction of new ideas from other and more progressive countries, had undergone a profound but relatively peaceful transformation. By the turn of the century Denmark was on the road to becoming the country we know today, a country with a social conscience, with an economic urge and, by 1901, a democratic system. She had been transformed from an inward-looking and backward country to an outward-looking nation rapidly catching up with her neighbours.

The First Democratic Government

The King was scarcely enthusiastic in deciding to give in to popular pressure and introduce the principle of parliamentary democracy. He was loath to relinguish rule by the Right, and his basic dislike of the Left was apparent in his decision to use his prerogative and choose as his Prime Minister not the leader of the Left, J. C. Christensen, but an academic who had so far played little or no part in political life. Deuntzer may well have had Left views, but at least he was not a farmer. On the other hand, he was quite aware that it would be impossible to form a viable government without bringing in professional politicians as his chief Ministers, and this he set about doing. J. C. Christensen was naturally included, and so, after some hesitation, was the mercurial Viggo Hørup, although he was not a member of the *Folketing*. The new government was very different in character from anything that had gone before: instead of the academics and aristocrats of former times, it included schoolteachers, farmers, and, in charge of military and naval matters, men from the services with first-hand knowledge of the situation rather than professional politicians. There was a genuine effort to bring into the government politicians and non-politicians alike whose views could be classed as Left, and who were willing to devote themselves to spheres of activity in which they were specialists. Deuntzer also made a show of balancing in his government the conflicting views which were held by the various factions of which the Left was composed, factions with such strongly held principles that they were finally to lead to the breaking-up of the Left as a single party. The views of the Radicals and the Moderates were too incompatible for them to belong to the same party once that party had achieved power and had been given the opportunity of ruling and carrying out a policy. The bond that had held them together — the desire to defeat the Right and the knowledge that concerted action could best be expected to achieve this — was liable to dissolve at any moment. Then, as time went on, the smallholders, on whose support the

Left had also depended, discovered that in power the farmers were less inclined to look to the interests of the rural working classes than had been expected. As the government became more obviously a farmers' government, they withdrew their support from the party and moved instead to the Social Democrats. Parliamentary democracy had certainly been achieved, but new divisions and new struggles lay ahead.

In the *Folketing* the new government, within the limits laid down by its own divergent opinions, could command a majority, but this was not the case in the *Landsting*, where the Right still held sway. As legislation could only be carried through if a bill was passed in identical form in both houses, it appeared at first that Deuntzer's colleagues might still have difficulty in carrying out any serious programme of reform. However, they were helped by disunity within the ranks of the Right Party itself. The nine members of the *Landsting* who had broken with the Right in 1900 now officially launched an independent conservative party which they called the Free Conservatives. With this help the Left managed to push through many of the reforms it had so long desired. The first of these was to be tax reform.

The new taxation laws meant a reduction of land taxes in the countryside and an increase in property taxes in the towns. These were coupled with the introduction of direct income tax according to a sliding scale, though to a modern eye the forms it took were haphazard. It was not compulsory to fill in returns, and only about 60 per cent of those liable did in fact do so. The remainder were content to accept the assessment of the taxation authorities, a sign of how intimate Danish society as a whole was — the tax authorities obviously knew sufficient of their immediate neighbours' means to be able to tax them reasonably accurately. Symptomatically, a greater percentage of townsfolk preferred to fill in their assessment forms.

Change came in another field, too, where it was long overdue. Tithes were still the rule in Denmark, though instead of going to the Church as had been the case before the Reformation, they often went in effect to the local pastors. Henrik Pontoppidan, in his early satirical story *The Polar Bear*, gives a clear impression of how deeply rooted the custom was in the rural population by telling how Thorkild Müller, an unconventional pastor, sees the poverty of many of his parishioners, and decides with true Christian charity to forego his tithes. However, instead of being hailed as a man of vision, he actually loses prestige as his flock think he must be mad. The entire system was done away with in this 1903 tax reform, though provisions were made for compensation to be paid to those affected.

The other significant reforms introduced by the new government concerned education, and 1903 saw a new Education Act which remained the basis of education in Denmark until 1958. Until now schools by and large had been of two types: primary and grammar; and a grammar-school education had been reserved for those who could afford it. The grammar school led to the final Student's Examination, which gave access to the university. The new act made provision for free schooling not only in the primary stage, but also beyond it in what was called the middle school, with entry at the age of twelve. Entrance to a grammar school now came after the middle-school examination, with entry at about fourteen. The result of this new Act was to make education available to classes who had previously been barred from it, and to make for greater uniformity in the educational pattern. It is generally considered that this reform was a major step to breaking down the class distinctions which had existed until that time, but which are so significantly absent today. The local authorities were keen to adopt the new line laid down by the Act, and a great improvement in educational facilities was made. This was less marked, however, in the country districts than in the towns.

Nevertheless, the government did not in the main live up to its promises, and various sections of the community, especially the smallholders who did not benefit from the tax reform, felt that they had been let down. Moreover, there was the perennial question of defence. Hørup, as ever against spending on defence, had in practice little influence on the government. He was already a sick man when appointed Traffic Minister, and in 1902 he died. He was not replaced by a man of similar views, and thus opinion within the government swung towards accepting expenditure on defence. The more radical members of the *Folketing* began to react against the increasingly conservative attitude of the government — though this was to some extent due to the need for co-operation with the Free Conservatives in the *Landsting* — and as a countermeasure they formed the Radical Club, which aimed at the same drastic programme of reform that had formerly been that of the Left. In 1903 the Social Democrats increased their representation in the *Folketing* and sought to cause a split within the government on the defence issue. They succeeded, as the Army Minister had gone beyond his mandate and built defences without authorisation — and the first Left government fell in January 1905.

Compromise and Conflict

It was followed by a new government under J. C. Christensen who had exercised a dominant influence even when Deuntzer was Prime Minister. He was a negotiator *par excellence* who understood the need for compromise in order to achieve any reforms at all. His programme was ambivalent on the question of defence, but tended to be conservative. So high did feelings run that a group of eight anti-defence members threatened to break with the party and were finally excluded from it. This coincided with agitation for a more radical party which would carry out the reforms previously expected of the Left. In 1905 a convention in Odense launched a completely new political party which called itself the Radical Left (Radicals), obviously indicative of its sympathy with the radical programme of many members of the Left Party. The eight Left rebels immediately joined the new party and a radical reform programme was published.

The new party aimed first and foremost at proclaiming Denmark a neutral state and reducing all armed forces to the status of border- and coast-guards. Other reforms demanded were more help to smallholders (who had been disillusioned by the neglect accorded to them by the Left and the realisation that the tax reforms had benefited them less than the wealthier farmers); taxation based on land values according to the ideas of the noted American economist and social reformer Henry George; greater social equality, including women's right to vote; and far-reaching social reforms. These were in many ways a restatement of the old Left principles which were being forgotten and shelved as the party was moving towards a more conservative attitude. It was, of course, not the first time an effort had been made to maintain the radicalism of the programme originally formulated by the Left, but while the earlier breakaway groups had been shortlived, this new party had come to stay, and has subsequently played an important part in later Danish politics. Although springing from the Left, and thus having affinities with it, it has incorporated many ideas which are akin to those of the Social Democrats, and has thus on many occasions been able to form a coalition with both the other parties. Always a small party, it has often held a balance of power.

The defence question loomed large in public debate in the coming months, but no action was taken, as the government was awaiting the report of a defence commission set up some years previously. One complication was that it was not clear against whom Denmark was trying to defend herself. If the enemy were Germany, things would have to be organised differently than they would against Britain or France. The rest of Europe was dividing into the German or Anglo-French camps, and it seemed that a decision must be taken. Germany was herself seeking to gain Danish support, a desire reflected not only in general contacts, but also in the more liberal attitude adopted towards Danish sympathisers in the former duchies of Schleswig and Holstein. The government was inclined to seek a *modus vivendi* — though not an alliance — with Germany, while popular sentiment was pro-British. J. C. Christensen's attitude, which was also that of King Frederick VIII upon his accession in 1906, was to provide sufficient defence forces in Denmark to act as a deterrent to anyone who might wish to carry out a bloodless invasion.

When the defence commission finally produced its report members were seen to be in as much disagreement as the politicians. The decision about what measures to take seemed to be left to J. C. Christensen, but then, unexpectedly, any action he was contemplating was stopped by what was probably the biggest Danish government scandal of all time.

For a good while rumours had been circulating about the affairs of P. A. Alberti, the Minister of Justice. Questions had been asked in the *Folketing*, but had always apparently elicited satisfactory answers. Nevertheless the campaign against Alberti continued and in July 1908 Christensen was finally forced to ask for his resignation. In May that year Alberti, who was director of the Zealand Farmers' Savings Bank, had asked Christensen for a loan from state funds to save the bank from going into liquidation. At a particularly difficult financial period the request was granted and the state was given mortgage deeds as security. The deal was, however, kept secret. New rumours developed about Alberti, news of the transaction leaked out, and finally Alberti himself, no longer a Minister, admitted embezzlement of a sum totalling 9 million *kroner*. In the resultant examination of his affairs, this was in fact shown to be a conservative estimate and the true total turned out to be 15 million. Alberti was disgraced and in 1910 sentenced to eight years imprisonment, and thus disappeared from the political scene. But Christensen was left to cope with the crisis which Alberti had occasioned. He was himself entirely blameless — though perhaps he should have seen through what was going on — but in mid-September 1908 he was forced to resign together with his government, with the defence question still unresolved.

Nor was it resolved until 1909, when a compromise agreement was reached, allowing for some fortifications to be maintained, while plans for others were to be scrapped.

The government which brought about this compromise was itself shortlived. It only lasted for six weeks and was in its turn brought down by the new Radical Left members. It was thus only natural that the problems of forming a government should fall to that party, though even with the support of the Social Democrats it was to be a weak minority government incapable of taking effective measures. Consequently, yet another election was held in May 1910.

Both the Radicals and the Social Democrats maintained their strength, but the position of the other parties altered decisively. The various factions of the Left had again combined and fought as one party under the simple name of Left, and by so doing had won 57 seats, while the Right had been reduced to 13. This new amalgamation of the various factions within the Left meant that the major parties which have dominated Danish politics in recent years had been formed: the Right, the Conservatives, which was subsequently to change its name to the Conservative People's Party; the Left (*Venstre*∗ as it is still called) a moderate liberal party, especially close to the farming community, variously referred to in English as the Liberal Democrats or Social Liberals; the Radical Left, now completely divorced from the original Left Party, known in English as the Radical Liberal Party; and the Social Democrats. Thus the parties had taken shape after a varied and even confusing history over a period of fifty years, and Denmark had achieved certain political maturity.

∗ With this stabilisation of the parties the English equivalents for the various factions of the Left will hereafter be dropped; the Danish name of *Venstre*, free from the overtones which the word Left has in modern politics, will be used. The term Right, on the other hand, will be retained, because when an official change was finally made it was with a definite purpose in mind.

A Return to the Constitutional Issue

It was an old *Venstre* wish to return to the liberal constitution which had been replaced in 1866, and the new government under Klaus Berntsen, though more conservative in outlook than its predecessors, set about revising the constitution. In particular it looked into the role of the *Landsting* and suggested that in a case of disagreement between the two houses they should get together and vote as one. The difficulty, of course, was getting this new constitution through the *Landsting* after it had passed the *Folketing*. When the time came for new elections to the *Folketing* in 1913, no progress whatsoever had been made on this issue. The election results changed the balance of power in the *Folketing* completely: the Right had now only 7 seats and *Venstre* 44; while the Radicals had 31 and the Social Democrats 32. The time seemed to have come for the radical parties to share power.

All was not plain sailing, however, for although the Radicals themselves were willing to form a government, they did not wish to show any unseemly haste, while the Social Democrats, not being quite sure of the Radicals, and being more inclined to wait until they were in a position to form a government alone, preferred the Berntsen government to stay in office. It had gone to the polls on the constitutional issue and the Social Democrats were themselves interested in seeing the proposed amendment carried out. For a time the two majority parties argued that the government should remain at its post, while the government wanted only to resign, J. C. Christensen maintaining that the voters had given the majority to the radical parties and that therefore it was their right and duty to accept responsibility. The Social Democrats refused to form a coalition with the Radicals, but finally they promised to support a Radical minority government under C. T. Zahle, who had held office for six months after the Alberti affair.

The immediate concern was again that of a liberal constitution, and it was originally the new government's intention to lay before the *Rigsdag* the same proposals as had Berntsen's government. Yet it still remained uncertain whether, even if the *Folketing* passed them, the *Landsting* would not reject them again. The problem was further complicated when Christensen on his own account published some new proposals for a constitution, slightly more conservative than those of the Berntsen government, and suggesting that any future changes in the constitution should require a two-thirds majority in a general referendum. The proposals went counter to all that had been suggested so far, but they found favour among the Right and among more conservative members of the three parties which favoured altering the constitution.

In the event it was these proposals that formed the basis for the new legislation on the upper chamber. However, the proposal still had to go through the *Landsting* according to the constitution then in force. As it aimed at limiting the power of the *Landsting*, it was bound to run into opposition even though the leader of the *Landsting*, Deuntzer, was in favour of it. And indeed, the Right boycotted the debate, thus preventing a quorum. The only way forward now was to dissolve the *Landsting* and hope that the ensuing election would show a majority in favour of reform. This did in fact happen, so that the new constitution seemed assured of an easy passage when the new *Rigsdag* met on 20 July 1914. But before the necessary procedure could begin, the First World War had broken out and the constitutional question was completely overshadowed. Not for the first time, constitutional issues in Denmark were swept aside by external events.

Attention now turned to Denmark's international relations, with the aim of keeping the country out of the conflict which was obviously going to engulf most of Europe. Denmark was in the difficult position of being on good terms with all the belligerents, but while relations with Germany on the official level were good, there was a distinct anti-German sentiment in the population at large. The events of 1864 had not been forgotten, and emotions similar to those that had agitated for intervention in the Franco-Prussian War were widespread. The Germans were aware of this, and one of the worries of the Danish government was whether Germany in the final analysis would feel able to rely on Denmark's protestations of neutrality.

In the country as a whole, while war had been unthinkable, there was a feeling of approaching disaster: not merely a fear for the safety of Denmark as a country, but a sense that the world was witnessing the end of an era. After a period of unbroken peace and increasing stability and prosperity, upon which had been founded a civilised and increasingly humane society, Denmark found herself facing a catastrophe of unknown dimensions. Newspapers of the day tell plainly of the confusion in Copenhagen, while Jacob Paludan, in his novel *Jørgen Stein*, shows how the news of the assassination in Sarajevo broke on a typical upper-class dinner in the Danish provinces. On a different level there was the contrast between the widespread anti-militarism in certain circles in Denmark and the desire for revenge in others, a combination which was subsequently to have its effect on public morale.

The Immediate Effect of the War

Because of the loss of Schleswig and Holstein in 1864 and the ensuing repressive measures which had periodically been enforced by Prussia against Danish sympathisers in the former duchies, there was no doubt where the sympathies of the Danish people lay in 1914. Official policy was to keep out of the conflict, but there was some heartsearching in official circles in case the German government should have such doubts about the Danish will, or ability, to avoid taking sides that they might decide to invade. As long as the war was fought on land Denmark was of little significance, but in any naval hostilities she would hold the key to the Baltic, a position which in the old days had been an enviable one, but which has since on more than one occasion brought her into conflicts she would rather have avoided. Consequently, on this occasion the government went to considerable lengths to convince the Germans of Danish intentions, proclaiming strict neutrality and promising not to call up the security forces, although the navy was put on an alert and the sea forts manned as well. It should be noted that the British government had dropped a hint to Denmark that she should not rely on assistance in the event of an attack. The Danes had to do as little as possible and hope. Indeed, Edvard Brandes, the Minister of Finance, warned the people against demonstrating feelings at variance with the country's official policy of neutrality.

The first difficulties arose when Germany started mining the Langeland straits, south of the Great Belt, and put indirect pressure on Denmark herself to mine the Great Belt. The Danes were afraid that if they failed to do so, the Germans would lay their own mines and then establish shore posts to guard them. Consequently after lengthy consultations the decision was made to mine both Belts and the Sound. King Christian X sent a telegram to his cousin George V informing him of the move, and received the reassuring reply that Great Britain understood Denmark's difficult position. The Danes also informed Germany that any attempt to break through the minefields would be considered a breach of Danish neutrality, and that it would be communicated to other belligerent powers.

The trade situation was more complicated. A large proportion of Denmark's foreign trade was with Great Britain and Germany — about 60 per cent of Denmark's agriculture exports went to Britain, 30 per cent to Germany — and a difficult balancing act was needed if trade was not to be seriously interrupted. Moreover, Denmark was dependent on trade, especially with Britain, for her supply of raw materials. At the same time it was in the belligerents' own interests to continue trade with Denmark — Britain because of her agricultural imports, Germany because of her desire to use Denmark and Danish ports for the transit of goods from America. In this peculiar situation — both the warring nations were in a position to damage the other by cutting off Danish trade, but by doing so they would also hurt themselves — an arrangement was made by which Germany promised for the time being not to interfere with Denmark's exports to Britain, and Britain allowed American goods to be imported into Denmark provided that certain of them were not re-exported to Germany. Restrictions were immediately placed on some of these goods, but before the export of horses was prohibited in November 1914, some 80,000 had been sent across the frontier, and fortunes made in the process. Nor were these to be the only ones made in Denmark during the war.

However, during the first few days of August 1914 most people were less interested in making quick fortunes than in ensuring the safety of such money as they then possessed. There was a run on the banks and a demand for gold, which the National Bank was by law forced to pay in exchange for paper money. That law was very quickly changed, apparently only for a while, but in reality for good. Even silver money became scarce and the National Bank was given leave to issue paper money for amounts down to one *krone*. At the same time food prices soared, by as much as 30 to 100 per cent in the space of a few days, and it became apparent that the government would have to do something to ensure the reasonable distribution of food and to keep prices within tolerable limits. The argument that high prices would themselves ration food was correct, but it overlooked the fact that everyday commodities such as rye bread and potatoes were put out of the reach of precisely those people who were most dependent on them. As a result of the rapidly deteriorating situation the *Rigsdag* passed on 7 August a law giving the government very wide powers to regulate trade; to enforce maximum prices on goods; and to ensure a fair distribution of them. As a result of this new Act, the government was empowered to interfere in fields which had traditionally been outside its control. Here as elsewhere the old order was changing, for although these measures were only to be temporary, they were in fact the beginning of something new and permanent. The government was also required to act on the insurance question. With the outbreak of war, shipping had come to a standstill for fear of submarine attacks and minefields. Insurance companies refused to accept the increased risk, and thus the government was itself forced to accept a liability for compensation in the event of loss through hostilities. And losses there were — 236 Danish ships went down through submarine activities and 38 were mined in the course of the war.

The decision to help to insure shipping was taken by the new government Special Commission acting in conjunction with representatives of trade and commerce, a method of working which was to become more and more common during the war and to bear fruit in the years to come. From it came the realisation that by giving the representatives of trade and commerce some say in taking important decisions, their sense of responsibility also grew, and an increasingly close co-operation was fostered between the government and representatives of various branches of national life, including the trade unions. Responsible co-operation between these various parties has since stood Denmark in good stead and brought about a sense of working together for the common good rather than working for sectional interests at the expense of others.

However, a sense of responsibility was not common to all sections of the community, and some of its members set about the task of earning — and losing — large fortunes overnight. As Denmark was neutral, and had her imports more or less guaranteed, she was able to produce many goods which the belligerent powers wanted to buy. In particular Germany began importing great quantities of Danish goods, and at one time bought some 50 per cent of Danish exports. Not least among these was tinned stewed meat (goulash), and so great was German demand for this that the traditional Danish quality was in some cases alarmingly reduced. The sale of low-quality goods became almost symbolic of the age, which has become known as the goulash age, and the profiteers as the goulash barons.

The lack of competition from abroad, where all efforts went towards fighting and where manpower was scarce, and the demand for Danish goods from former competitors caused a remarkable drop in Danish unemployment figures. The percentage in the years before the war had varied between 6 and 13; but after an initial rise from 8 per cent at the beginning of the war, it fell to that figure again in 1915 and then even dropped as low as 5 per cent in 1916. Shares rose and there was widespread speculation in them. Denmark had for the first time in years a surplus in the balance of payments and ready money was plentiful among many sections of the population. The resultant rise in prices, however, led to hardship among those who had a five-year agreement on wages, workers and employees of state and local authorities. Counting 1914 as 100, the retail price index rose to 136 by 1916, but the workers were still bound by an agreement signed in 1911, and despite some slight adjustments by some firms, their standard of living fell. In the new agreement of 1916 a cost of living bonus was agreed, though this still did not reach the 1911 standard, and discontent was only to be expected among those who found themselves so severely restricted, while others were fast becoming rich.

The government found itself having to play an increasingly active part in regulating the day-to-day affairs of the Danes. More and more prices were fixed. So, in 1916, were rents, which were threatening to rise at an alarming rate and hit the already battered lower-income groups. The Statistical Department began gathering information on prices and costs, and on this basis it became possible to work out an accurate cost of living index, according to which it has since become customary to regulate wages and salaries, a system which has certainly led to difficulties, as it has had a direct inflationary tendency, but which has helped to avoid much industrial discontent.

The Constitutional Issue Solved

The difficulties occasioned by the war contributed, however, to reaching an agreement on the constitutional problem. A new willingness to compromise was evident and the Right ceased to block the progress of the constitutional reform in return for certain concessions on voting procedures. Its following throughout the country was fair, though scattered, and thus it had little chance of significant representation in the single-seat constituencies. Consequently, in order to maintain an influence corresponding to its total strength, it wanted proportional representation. In the end a complicated system was devised, with proportional representation in Copenhagen and 93 single-seat constituencies throughout the rest of the country, but with 23 supplementary seats spread throughout the country to be filled in proportion to the votes cast. Another concession to the Right was the decision that one-quarter of the new *Landsting* members should be elected by the outgoing *Landsting* and that any subsequent alterations to the constitution should be approved by 45 per cent of the electorate in a referendum.

Once these concessions were arranged, the remainder of the new constitution was plain sailing, providing for a lowering of the voting age for the *Folketing*, in stages, from 30 to 25, while the voting age for the *Landsting* was raised to 35. Women were also given the vote and made eligible for the *Rigsdag*, as were the lowest-paid workers. The new constitution gave Denmark, true to her predominant democratic sentiments, a much more progressive form of government based on universal suffrage. The right to free schooling was made statutory, but likewise parents were entitled not to send their children to school, provided that they ensured an acceptable standard of private tuition for them.

The new constitution was ratified by both houses, after which arrangements were made for a general election. By common consent, and with an eye to possible breaches of Denmark's neutral position in the heat of the debate, no election campaign was held. The new *Rigsdag* was elected and immediately ratified the new constitution, which received the King's signature on 5 June 1915.

According to the Constitutional Act, the new constitution did not come into force until one year after receiving the royal assent, and this period could be extended by legislation if necessary. Again with a view to avoiding the dangers of an election contest, the date was in 1916 postponed for a further year, largely thanks to the efforts of the newly formed Conservative People's Party, an amalgamation of the old Right and the Free Conservatives. It was a natural union and one which has lasted up to the time of writing, but it was scarcely a case of the same old party under a new name. The old Right had realised that it needed to base itself on a broader popular appeal and sought to become the party of the middle classes, aiming at freedom from government invervention on the one hand and at a system of protective tariffs, to safeguard Danish industry, on the other. At the same time, with the Danish security forces reduced to 35,000 men, it placed defence high on its list of priorities. On the basis of this programme it was hoped to appeal to a wide section of middle-class opinion and, perhaps, even to take some support from *Venstre*; or perhaps to co-operate with that party in opposing the related principles of the Radicals and Social Democrats.

While the desire to avoid controversy had been a contributory factor in solving the constitutional crisis, wartime conditions helped in the solution of a further problem. Steps were now taken towards a thoroughgoing reform of the Danish legal system. The judiciary and the executive were finally separated, and the principle of public trial by jury was introduced. Prior to this the executive and judiciary had often been one and the same thing — for instance, mayors were appointed by the Crown and their functions included those of both chief of police and magistrate. Thus what from a modern point of view was another anomalous situation came to an end and further democratisation of local government was duly promoted, as mayors could now be elected instead of appointed by the Crown.

Conditions in Denmark during the first two years of the war had been surprisingly good. Prices had risen, though government measures had maintained some stability. Denmark had fallen into debt, but earnings in the country as a whole had been good enough to make higher direct taxation feasible. A form of supertax on high incomes was introduced as was a tax on stock-exchange trans-actions — on the principle that it was here that many fortunes were being made as a direct result of the war. Nevertheless, Denmark had always been in a difficult position because of her need for overseas trade, and when in January 1917 Germany designated a number of areas as danger zones for shipping, the problems were considerably increased. They were intensified yet further when Great Britain demanded that a percentage of neutral ships carrying coal from British ports should sail for the Allies. In order to ensure sufficient supplies, 200,000 tons of Danish ship-ping were put at the disposal of the Allies for this purpose. Some-thing of the significance of these moves for Danish shipping can be seen from the fact that 33 ships, totalling 26,000 tons, were lost in

April 1917 alone, and still more the following month. After this ships sailed in convoy, using neutral waters as far as possible, and losses were considerably reduced. Nevertheless, total losses during the war amounted to 282,000 tons and 667 lives.

Further complications arose when the United States declared war on Germany in 1917, for now, as a belligerent power, the USA was less inclined to export fodder and industrial raw materials to Denmark if there were any possibility of re-export to Germany. Consequently Denmark soon experienced a shortage of raw materials and animal foodstuffs: imports fell to half their normal size and prices started to rise quickly. In July the retail price index was 155 and a year later 182. Even these indices were only held at this low level through government price control, and wholesale price indices rose faster, reaching 302 by July 1918. It was no longer possible to allow goods to regulate themselves through prices, and so rationing was progressively introduced through 1917, while other measures were taken to reduce the amount of fuel used on lighting by closing restaurants and theatres earlier than usual. Gas was cut off for several hours daily and people learned to cook their food by means of 'hay boxes': food was brought to the boil by means of gas and then placed in a box packed with hay, which kept it hot sufficiently long to finish it off. Special cookery-books were prepared to promote cooking by this method, which was also used during the Second World War. To some extent the difficulty of importing fuel from overseas was offset by increased imports from Germany.

This increase was due rather to commercial than to political reasons, but the public suspected pro-German sentiments among some members of the government, first in P. A. Munch, then in Thorvald Stauning, the first Social Democrat member of a Danish government, who as one of three 'control Ministers' had part authority over wartime measures. Stauning attended a meeting in Stockholm of a peace movement which was backed by Germany but not by the Allies, and therefore came under suspicion. Despite demands for his resignation, he refused to go.

There were also other reasons for suspecting a pro-German policy in Denmark. Because of the difficulties of trading with Britain and the USA it was obvious that trade with Germany had to be stepped up. Special credits were arranged to enable firms to do this. At the same time, however, a historically more significant move came from the need to boost inter-Scandinavian co-operation. Exports of agricultural goods were increased to both Norway (independent since 1905) and Sweden, and in return Denmark received saltpetre for artificial manure from Norway and industrial products and raw materials from Sweden. Mutual suspicion, long a feature in the relations between the Nordic countries and a legacy of the Swedish wars and the methods by which Sweden had acquired Norway in 1814, were by no means allayed as yet, but the first step had been taken on the road to Nordic co-operation and integration.

Under these conditions the Danish national debt grew considerably, reaching 420 million *kroner* by 1919. Increased taxation, including a new and very heavy tax on alcohol, again helped to cover it, but the need for a reduction in government expenditure was also apparent, and this accounted for the decision to reduce the security forces still further: first to between 23,000 and 24,000 men in 1917 and finally to 20,000 in 1918. This number was obviously not sufficient to cope with any major invasion, and it was doubtful whether anything more than even a token resistance was contemplated by the government should the occasion arise.

The goulash age of the first two years of the war continued more or less unabated, despite the economic difficulties in which the country found itself. Money was still in plentiful supply and profiteering was still rife. Even though an order was made restraining the amount of profit made on each transaction, the object of the law was avoided by increasing the number of middlemen between factory and retailer, thus forcing retail prices ever higher. Suspect companies were formed, holding companies with subsidiaries and subsidiaries of subsidiaries, so that it was easy to falsify accounts. It was therefore simple to persuade willing and naïve speculators into investing large sums of money. Profits in rural areas, too, were made, and a general fever for spending and investing money spread throughout the farming community. Many of the investments in modern equipment were sensible, but much of the capital was borrowed without any thought of repayments and the possible difficulties which might be facing farmers at a later date.

Yet the workers were not doing quite so well out of the apparently buoyant conditions, despite increased cost of living payments intended to maintain the standards they had been used to before war broke out. Unemployment was rising and reached the record figure of 18 per cent in 1918. Little wonder that the workers' thoughts turned to more violent means of demanding their rights, now that they had the example of the Bolshevik revolution in Russia and other revolutionary movements within Europe before them. In contrast to the sober and responsible efforts of the trade unions — whose freedom of action was partly circumscribed now the Social Democrats were partners in government — the syndicalists came into their own, fomenting wildcat strikes and threatening sabotage. In 1918 they began organising major demonstrations in Copenhagen and on one occasion they set about sacking the stock exchange, symbol of the society they hated. They were not truly representative of the workers, but were rather symptomatic of vocal minority groups taking advantage of lethargy to get their way. Nevertheless they succeeded in gaining control of some trade unions. The official unions reacted by pushing up their wage demands, in the hope of winning back support among the dissidents, and the employers, only too eager to avoid any greater conflict, gave in easily. They too had taken account of events abroad and wanted to avoid similar developments in Denmark.

It was under these conditions that elections to the *Rigsdag* were due to take place. The previous ones had been in 1915 and according to the old constitution a parliament's life was three years. Accordingly it was decided that the new constitution should come into force immediately before this election. The Radicals, the governing party, and the Social Democrats, who had supported them throughout, entered into an election pact outside Copenhagen, where the system of proportional representation was not favourable to them. The remaining parties fought alone. The election result, however, was not decisive enough and the Radicals and Social Democrats had a majority of only four over all other parties. In the event the Radicals formed a minority government with Social Democrat support, the opposition now being based on the two old rivals, *Venstre* and the Conservatives.

In 1917 Denmark had sold her West Indian colonies to the United States. Now the government was faced with another problem concerning Danish overseas possessions. Iceland, it will be remembered, had been left to Denmark after the loss of Norway in 1814, but was now seeking independence. Denmark adopted a conciliatory attitude and came to an agreement for a personal union in which citizens should enjoy equal rights in both countries, and in which laws concerning both should be passed by a special committee consisting of an equal number of representatives from Iceland and Denmark. One of the clauses in the agreement was

that in 25 years Iceland should have the right to complete independence if she desired it and could show this desire by a referendum in which at least three-quarters of the votes should be
positive and at least three-quarters of those eligible took part. No
one could then foresee that when the 25 years had elapsed, contact
between Denmark and Iceland would be severed by another major
international conflict.

The Wartime Atmosphere and its Literary Expression

The signing of the Armistice in November 1918 brought general
relief to Denmark, even if the country had not been directly
involved in the war, and the security forces were almost immediately disbanded. Yet the activities of the syndicalists, who
continued to organise strikes and demonstrations, brought worries
enough. A general strike, intended as a protest against an
eighteen-month sentence for the syndicalist leader, was a near
fiasco, though a largish demonstration did take place in a revolutionary atmosphere. The genuine demonstrators were joined
by others intent on trouble, and Copenhagen was a city of turmoil
for a few days before order was eventually restored.

The atmosphere in Denmark had undergone a remarkable
transformation during four years of war. The years immediately
before 1914 had certainly been a period of change and renewal,
but the transformation had been an orderly one, reflecting the give
and take of an ordered society. Now, under the shadow of the
Russian, and later of the German, revolutions, Denmark itself was
seething, and the future looked bleak. The old values had gone
and no one knew what had replaced them, so that there was a state
bordering on moral confusion in the country. One of the best
impressions of this is to be found in Jacob Paludan's *Jørgen Stein*:

> The thunder was rolling in the south for the fourth year.
> People has already had a long time to accustom themselves to
> the thought that the civilisation to which they belonged had
> been built on sand. Many had difficulty in understanding. But
> new broods appeared and had their most receptive years
> marked by the knowledge that war was possible, and that it was
> indeed taking place. For them the word took on a new, natural
> sound; it was no textbook word, but ordinary everyday reality.

Without any surprise at all the young people saw the publication of a work entitled *The Next War*, and cut open its pages in the light of the stinking carbide lamps which in many places had to replace electricity, which was in short supply, and paraffin, which had entirely disappeared. The future held no danger of boredom; this war, it appeared, was even now to be thought of as a grand, educational dress rehearsal. And accustomed as they were to war, their minds could contain the thought and their nerves stand it.

The older generation had more difficulty. Most of them would have denied that the individual, thoroughly civilised citizen engrossed in his daily paper could possibly have retained any vestige of barbarism. Certainly there was some virtue in the courage which impelled a man to defend his country's frontier, but in this massive world-engulfing cataclysm it was soon forgotten who was guilty and who the injured party . . . These elderly people had to learn in the afternoon of their lives that they had been sleep-walking in the forenoon. It was like having settled comfortably in a sunny vineyard only to discover that it was a nest of vipers. The concept of Man, the concept of Culture, had to be understood and defined anew — but they were far beyond the age when their brains were supple enough to form a new view of life. The older generation became in a strange way much older in these years; in some strange way they moved out of context — like false teachers who have to turn their heads away on being shown up. . .

Between the two generations, the dethroned and the acclimatised, there lived a third — the generation which had just had a taste of the era before 1914, its atmosphere and its spirit, its faith in unchanging values.

It was as a member of this third generation that Paludan was writing, for he was looking back at the war from the early 1930s — and thus could scarcely be considered a wartime author. Indeed the war played singularly little part in contemporary literature. How could it, when Denmark was not taking part? And yet it was a period during which some of the Danish authors who have achieved international fame were producing their best work. Johannes V. Jensen was engaged not on depicting modern events, but on writing his epic *The Long Journey*, in which he produced a poetic version of the descent of man, from the Ice Age to the discovery of America. It does not pretend to be a scholarly work, but within a framework of Darwinism incorporates inspiration from such diverse elements as the Bible, *Robinson Crusoe*, and Hans Christian Andersen's *Fairy Tales*. The theme of this large work is Man's ability to adapt himself to his surroundings and then conquer them, and it ends with Columbus moving towards the New World. Ultimately it is a question of Nordic expansionism, the Nordic spirit as the vehicle of progress, for it is the Scandinavians who originally brave the advancing cold of the Ice Age and adapt themselves to it, as it is the Scandinavians who, as the Cimbrians, move southwards and form the stock from which Columbus comes. From a scholarly angle it is easy to pull this epic to pieces, but as a work of poetic inspiration it possesses great beauty and power. Prior to this, in the years before the war, Johannes V. Jensen had written his *Stories from Himmerland* (the part of Denmark from which he originated, and from which it has been surmised the Cimbrians also stemmed) and his *Myths* (these latter being an attempt to express profound truths in short compass). In his movement towards myth Jensen was ahead of his time and in harmony with subsequent trends in literature outside as well as inside Denmark. As a poet, too, he made an original contribution to his country's literature, showing the same linguistic innovation and conciseness of expression as in his prose work.

At the other end of the political scale was Martin Andersen Nexø with his novels of proletarian life in Denmark: *Pelle the Conqueror* (1906–10) and *Little Ditte* (1917–21), the first showing Pelle growing up as the son of a farmworker in Bornholm, moving to Copenhagen, and becoming engaged in the socialist movement there, the second a more sentimental novel about a proletarian girl who is ill-treated by society.

Nexø was continuing the realistic tradition from the nineteenth century, and he continued to do so until his death, though he employed it more and more as the vehicle for his communist ideas. These two early novels, however, represented the height of his achievement, and only in parts does he here show any sign of a non-literary intention in his work.

Yet literature was beginning to change, and even though it did not reflect the war directly, in the shape of novels or plays dealing immediately with the conflict, the breakdown of the social order was reflected in the emergence of new and apparently less ordered forms. These were the work of poets singing in praise of modern civilisation, expressing their love of the twentieth century, with its violence, its terror, and its power. Foremost among the younger writers, the Expressionists, was Tom Kristensen, a poet who was born in London and wrote of these themes with greater perspicacity, as well as greater poetic insight and mastery of the language, than anyone else. In a poem such as 'Atlantis', he talked of the need completely to break down society in order to build up a new culture, while his novel *Havoc*, written a decade after the end of the war, is probably the most penetrating analysis in Danish literature of the demoralisation which the First World War brought about, the sense of frustration at being kept in the wings to watch the great events taking place in Europe at large.

Colour had been one of the major ingredients in the new Expressionist poetry. The new school of painters also emerged at this time and, under the general influence of a tempestuous age and under the particular impact of French painters, also produced works of new colours and new forms, breaking down traditional lines and traditional uses of colour. Sigurd Swane embarked on a series of atmospheric scenes such as 'The bend in the road', with its creation of a landscape shimmering in the heat. His portraits, too, exploit his ability to create an impressionistic landscape, and it is typical of him to place his model against an outdoor background. Harald Giersing, influenced by pointillism, cubism and fauvism, shows a further move towards abstraction, though he still works with recognisable contours in paintings in which a subtle mixture of blues and greens predominates. Vilhelm Lundstrøm went a good deal further towards abstraction, possibly affected by the sense of a loss of fixed values resulting from the First World War. Later, however, he returned to a simpler form of stylised realism in which he made a bold use of colour.

While new colours and forms were emerging in literature and painting, new sounds, new sound colours, were making themselves heard in the music of Carl Nielsen, who betokens a complete break with the late Romantic music which had been the vogue hitherto. Each of his symphonies explores new ground, and indeed each of his major works represents something new and exciting in sound combinations and in musical structure. Yet this tempestuous writer is often referred to as being typically Danish, an appellation immediately most suited to his songs, the simplicity and melodiousness of which are in direct continuation of Danish song tradition without being a slavish imitation of it.

Carl Nielsen is the giant of the period, and most other composers of the day, whether they were experimental in their approach, or whether they continued and built on the Romantic tradition, are only of modest significance. In recent years, however, another striking composer, Rued Langgaard, has emerged from obscurity and is becoming increasingly recognised. Langgaard was no late Romantic, rather of the stamp of Hindemith, but his energies and abilities were at the time totally overshadowed by Carl Nielsen, and he spent much of his life in the provinces as an organist at Ribe. It is consequently no surprise to discover him as a prolific composer of organ music, but in addition he wrote cantatas, a great deal of chamber music and no fewer than sixteen symphonies, some on a large scale.

There are many ways of looking at the years from 1900 to 1918. They can be regarded nostalgically as an age which saw the end of old values and the civilisation which had reigned, basically unchanged, for several centuries; or as the dawn of something new, something expressive of great power. The passage from Jacob Paludan's *Jørgen Stein*, quoted above, expresses all this in powerful terms, as it struck the people of the day. Yet whichever way one looks at the period, it was surely one of rapid, almost explosive, transformation in which not only society underwent a change and showed a new potential, but in which all branches of art followed suit. Traditional forms persisted and indeed persist until this day, but alongside went a longing for experiment, a willingness to cope with new forms and to look at art, and thereby at life, with an openness which had scarcely been there before. It is possible to talk of the advent of something epoch-making with Romanticism in 1803, or with Naturalism in 1871, but the general embarkation on untried literary forms, of which Tom Kristensen was perhaps the most outstanding representative, meant a striking and equally intense literary revolution. While Romanticism had brought the liberation of the individual, and Naturalism had introduced a new philosophical basis for literature, the results in each case had been readily related to what had gone before. Now, the move from Impressionism to Expressionism had meant the abandonment of an attempt at reproducing something approaching objective reality, and the surrender to complete subjectivism. The old realism had gone with the old society on which it had been based, and in Denmark as elsewhere everything was in a state of flux.

6 1918–1930: THE FIGHT FOR STABILITY

The Return of North Schleswig

Although Denmark had not been engaged in the war, the country was very interested indeed in the changed pattern which was bound to emerge in Europe after the end of the conflict. The Schleswig-Holstein problem began to raise its head again, not least because of the zeal with which Germany had gone about suppressing Danish sentiments before the war and even more so during it. Those of military age in the border area had been called up into the German army, as indeed was only natural, but it was less natural that these unwilling conscripts had been forbidden to speak or read Danish, or to write home in that language. Such measures were scarcely likely to help the German cause in the area, and some troops with Danish sympathies took the opportunity to cross the border when home on leave. Pro-Danish politicians had also been arrested for various lengths of time and had only been released when consenting to refrain from working for the Danish cause. Further complications had been caused by the fact that children of parents who had opted for Danish nationality but remained in German territory were in practice stateless, as German laws would not grant nationality to children of foreigners, while Danish law denied Danish nationality to children born abroad, even if they were the offspring of Danish parents. As a result of an agreement with Germany in 1916, these children were in fact given Danish nationality, but the resentment smouldered still.

The collapse of Germany, especially when one of the expressed objectives of the Allies was the right of people to choose their own nationality, provided an obvious chance to return to the thorny problems which had existed since the loss of the duchies in 1864. Yet there were different views in Denmark as to how this should be done. The majority, including the government, believed that the border should be revised according to the wishes of the local population, to be ascertained by referendum. The historian H. V. Clausen had for years made a village by village examination of

116

national attitudes in the border area, and could say with a fair amount of certainty where the border would be drawn in this event. One of his conclusions, however, was disturbing: the city of Flensburg, the largest city in central Schleswig and once a centre of Danish sentiment, would be lost, thanks to a thorough Germanisation over the half-century it had been under German rule. Consequently there was a movement to have Flensburg included in Denmark in any border revision. There was also the historical approach, giving rise to the opinion that the border should revert to the Ejder and that Denmark should regain control of the entire duchy of Schleswig. There was a good deal of support for this attitude, very reminiscent of the old National Liberal stance, but there were fears that more trouble would ensue in the future if this solution were adopted. Finally, after a lengthy debate in the *Rigsdag*, it became official Danish policy that a revision of the border should be made on the basis of a referendum. On the other hand, as Denmark herself had not been engaged in the war, she could not make demands as part of any peace treaty, and it was obvious that requests for frontier revision should come from inside Schleswig itself, as did in fact happen.

The final decision about a referendum lay with the Allies, and attention in Denmark turned to the question of how to formulate a policy which would be acceptable to them. After a period of disagreement and discussion, the decision was reached to divide into two zones that part of Schleswig which might be thought to want a return to Denmark, the northern zone corresponding closely to the part which Professor Clausen had deemed to be Danish in sentiment and a second, southern zone, in which the position was doubtful. The northern zone, excluding Flensburg, was to vote as one unit, while the second zone should vote parish by parish. Flensburg was to vote separately.

Demands were made for Flensburg to be incorporated into Denmark irrespective of the result of the referendum there, but the Danish government maintained its original stand and refused to work to this end. The referendum finally took place on 10 February in the northern zone and 14 March in the southern zone. In the north the vote was three to one in favour of Denmark, while in the south the ratio was almost exactly the reverse, with the exception of a few villages. In Flensburg itself 27,081 voted for Germany against 8,944 for Denmark.

Even now there were elements in Denmark who felt that it

might still be possible to win Flensburg with a different government in Copenhagen. When a Radical deputy and one of the Social Democrats joined the opposition on this point, there was a stalemate in the *Folketing*.

A change in government led to little change in policy, and a new administration under N. Neergaard worked for the implementation of the referendum result and for internationalisation of the southern zone, by which was meant that the zone should be turned into a free state and removed from both Danish and German jurisdiction. These objects were never achieved, but first the northern zone was put under Danish control, then the parishes in the southern zone which had voted for Denmark. The final incorporation of northern Schleswig into Denmark took place through a law passed in the *Rigsdag* on 25 and 26 June 1920, and was given effect as from 15 June. A period of festivities followed, during which the King made his famous crossing of the old border on horseback — and a promise was made not to forget those Danes who still lived in German territory. As a further safeguard for the permanent status of north Schleswig the treaty contained a clause saying that sovereignty could not be transferred again without the sanction of the League of Nations.

Feelings continued to run high between the two communities in the border area for many years; indeed, it is only in recent years that they have subsided somewhat. In towns with a divided community, it was not the done thing for Danes and Germans to consort together, for the Danes to go to the German theatres and cinemas, or for the Germans to attend the Danish ones. By means of German schools in Denmark and Danish schools in the German border areas, attempts were made by both sides to foster and, if possible, develop their own culture in the country of the other. The Second World War did not help matters, nor did the resettlement of refugees from East Germany in Schleswig and Holstein after the war. So far, the Danish argument went, the Danish language had been largely understood and Danish culture appreciated in those areas, but the advent of new settlers from the east without any basis for the understanding of either, meant the suppression of Danish culture. And this was at first attributed to the desire of the Federal German government to intensify the movement to Germanise the region. The fact that this thinly populated area was admirably suited to resettlement was apparently overlooked. But with the passing years, strong feelings and tension have eased and a new spirit of co-operation has asserted itself between the two peoples. There is probably more stability on the Danish-German border now than there has been for centuries, and the Schleswig-Holstein problem appears finally to have been solved.

Labour Troubles and Economic Problems

Meanwhile, the question of the return of north Schleswig to Denmark, although the one uppermost in many people's minds, and the one with most international perspectives, was by no means the only problem facing Denmark after the war. As has been seen, the war ended to the accompaniment of syndicalist stirrings within Denmark itself, and the inconclusiveness and dissatisfaction within the labour market continued. The problem demanded a solution. It was in the interests of neither the offical trade unions nor the employers to allow the situation to slide into the grasp of the syndicalists, and so the search for a solution was an eager one. Nevertheless, strikes were widespread, and particularly damaging ones took place in the docks, coping with the flood of trade after the war, and in the building industry, where an effort was being made to ease the housing shortage. All this was happening at the same time as wages in real terms were not only catching up with pre-war levels, but actually passing them. The 100 points of 1914 reached 148 in 1920.

Attention was turned from wage levels, which, with the cost of living arrangements, could to some extent look after themselves, to the length of the working day. The introduction of the eight-hour day came in 1919, first in the civil service and then in Copenhagen and other local authorities, while in May negotiations between the employers' and workers' organisations in a joint committee led to the acceptance of the eight-hour day for all sections of industry, though not for seamen and farmworkers. This arrangement was to take effect from January 1920.

Also in 1919 came the introduction of important legislation concerning land ownership. The original law on smallholdings of 1899 had been revised in 1914 and 1917, but still worked essentially on the same basis of a state loan which had to be repaid, albeit at a reasonable rate of interest. As a consequence of the general increase in prices, not least in the price of land, it was becoming more and more difficult for would-be smallholders to finance purchases even on these conditions. So the government proposed legislation which would radically alter the entire basis on which land was to be provided for smallholders. Instead of selling the land to them, the idea was to lease it to smallholders for an indefinite period. The smallholder should pay no deposit, but should pay interest of 4½ per cent on the value of the land he worked, the value to be revised at intervals in the light of current prices. In other words, if the value of land rose, he would have to pay more; if it fell, he would be liable to less interest. The buildings he put up on the land would be his — and the state would be prepared to make advances for this purpose. All equipment and livestock would be his to sell at any time.

The question of how to provide the land necessary for the projected reforms was simpler to solve than might at first seem likely. Most parsonages in Denmark were well provided for, a situation dating from the day when the pastor had depended on the land for his living. This land actually belonged to the state, and it was decided to requisition it — though where pastors were still working it, the property should only go to the state with a change of incumbent. In addition there was still a good deal of entailed land dating from feudal times, and this, too, it was decided to take over, as indeed was expressly provided for in the constitution. Tenants were entitled to buy the freehold for 20 or 25 per cent of its value, depending on the exact terms of the entailment, but the state was to take over one-third of each estate at its market value. This would both ensure the availability of land for the new purposes and also provide the state with funds to finance the scheme. The proposals were passed, despite some misgivings: *Venstre*, for instance, was reluctant to introduce a new form of leasehold and was more eager to extend individual ownership, which had been a source of encouragement to farmers in the past.

These developments had taken place against a background of economic crisis — the aftermath of war. Trade had been slow to pick up and Denmark was still suffering from the effects of the blockade of Germany: there was still a shortage of goods in the country and the regulation of prices was still necessary to avoid inflation. Developments in world trade were also against her. Although there had been a surplus during the war, and thus apparent prosperity, Denmark had allowed stocks to run down, and now had to replenish them at current prices. This she was forced to do at a time of rising prices, while she was obliged to sell her agricultural produce at a low rate. As had happened before, and was to happen again, she had been caught between her two main trading partners, Germany and Britain. Germany could not yet afford to import, while Britain did her own price fixing — and Denmark had little choice but to put up with it. At the same time the speculation of the war years still continued, and this resulted in a further running-down of financial reserves. It was hoped that Denmark could become a centre for trade with the Baltic lands as soon as they were in a position to start trading again and consequently enormous quantities of goods were imported into Denmark to be stored for further use. There followed a financial deficit and the *krone* fell to as little as 48 per cent of its face value. The consequence was inflation, with soaring prices — taking 1914 as 100, the price index rose to 182 in July 1918, 211 in July 1919, and 242 in January 1920. Little wonder that the government felt the need to maintain some control of prices, and little wonder, too, that there was discontent among the workers, although their wages were now linked to the cost of living and the effect of rising prices thus minimised.

By March 1920 there was a general malaise in the country: a combination of the desire to have the Flensburg problem solved in a way satisfactory to Danish interests; a general dissatisfaction with the government's handling of the Schleswig question; discontent with the country's economic situation; increasing tension between worker and employer, which had led to the warning of an imminent lock-out. Within the *Rigsdag* there was near stalemate, coupled with the desire for a revision of the electoral laws before a new election, a suggestion opposed by *Venstre*, who stood to suffer most from any change. There had been intrigues, details of which are still not known, to have the government dismissed and replaced by a caretaker government of specialists who would introduce new electoral legislation and then arrange for a new election. Finally, on 29 March, things came to a head.

The King sent for Zahle, the Radical Prime Minister, and demanded that an election should be held immediately. Zahle refused on the grounds that there had already been too many elections, that the electoral law was on the point of being revised, and that this would result in yet another election in the near future. By way of reply the King dismissed the government without asking Zahle to continue in office until the election. When, in order to avoid immediate trouble, the King was persuaded after all to ask the Zahle cabinet to continue for this short period, Zahle refused, and so a government of specialists, not politicians, was appointed, with the object of arranging an election.

In doing this the King was within his legal rights, though he certainly acted contrary to the spirit of the constitution, and the reaction among the Social Democrats and the working population was immediate and uncompromising. A meeting of the Social Democrat Party and the trade unions led to demands for the reinstatement of the Zahle government, failing which a general strike would be proclaimed. The ultimatum was given to the King on the evening of the change of government. He rejected it, and the unions went on to make preparations for a general strike, due to start on 6 April, a strike, moreover, which had a political rather than an economic objective. The combination of what appeared to them as a right-wing coup and an approaching lock-out seemed to smack of conspiracy aimed at the working classes. A statement issued on 29 March made clear the workers' demands, but as so often happens in comparable situations, the immediate demand for the reinstatement of the Zahle government was coupled with a demand for improved working conditions. After demanding the recall of the *Rigsdag* and the calling of elections, but no longer the reinstatement of the government, a further proclamation continued:

> At the same time, however, the situation of industrial conflict must be resolved, and lock-out notice must be withdrawn and the repeated demands of the Trades Union Association must be carried out — including the start of negotiations between the organisations, the ensuring of cost of living increases in August, and the start of negotiations concerning the right of the workers to participate in management.

These aspirations were far removed from the political question of which government was to be in power, but they were indicative of the increasing strength and ambitions of the unions, and also of their fear of being weakened by the combined efforts of the Right. Whatever the intentions of their opponents, the Social Democrats were no longer willing to have the idea of government by the people endangered. Although the Radicals sympathised with the aims of the Social Democrats, they did not approve of the means they proposed to adopt — as indeed was also the case with some of the more moderate Social Democrat leaders themselves.

No one at this stage could see what might happen. The Social Democrats, supported by the Communists and other extreme left-wing elements, arranged demonstrations in Copenhagen, and there were real fears that a revolution might take place. There were certainly calls for a republic. The police were thought not to be sufficient to control the situation if violence ensued — if indeed they could be relied upon — and some troops were called in from outside Copenhagen in case of trouble. It was obviously esssential that the government should go, and the King was finally persuaded that in order to save the situation he should appoint a fresh caretaker government consisting of men approved by the political parties after mutual consultation. They should, moreover, be men who had had nothing to do with the moves which had given rise to the crisis. After long and difficult negotiations it was announced on Easter Day that a government was formed and that the *Rigsdag* was to be recalled immediately after the Easter recess to pass the new electoral legislation. Elections would then be held by 22 April at the latest. At the same time the threat of a general strike was withdrawn and the crisis was resolved. As a by-product, the trade unions achieved most of what they were demanding from the employers.

This Easter crisis, as it had become known, opened many perspectives in Denmark and had a far-reaching effect. It was generally greeted as a triumph for democratic principles, and no attempt has since been made by the sovereign to interfere with the elected majority principle in government. Yet it could not be denied that the government in the final analysis had been brought down not by the *Rigsdag*, which the Prime Minister had refused to recall, but by the pressure exerted by the Social Democrats — in other words, by extra-parliamentary activities. The Social Democrats were proud of their achievement, but the remainder of the population had a different perspective in this newly-discovered power, and they were to show their disapproval in the elections which all parties had been clamouring for and which were now based on the new compromise electoral law.

The swing to the Right which resulted from these elections was the culmination of many factors. There was the fear of left-wing agitation and the strike threat, aggravated by the fact that a dock and transport strike did take place, since the unions concerned were under the leadership of syndicalists who refused to be bound by the compromise agreements. There was also a reaction against the emergency powers which had been adopted by the Radical government during the war, powers which many had deemed socialist in essence, not least perhaps because the Radicals had had the tacit support of the Social Democrats. In the event, however, the Social Democrats won an increased number of seats, 42 against their former 39, though the left-wingers of the party were routed. It was the Radicals who suffered most severely, their numbers being reduced to 17, the smallest of the majority groups. *Venstre*, the Social Liberals, were the real victors, increasing their representation from 44 to 48, despite the fact that the supplementary seats no longer worked in their favour, while the Conservatives also went up from 22 to 26 seats. The small Industrial Party was left with 4. This put a completely new complexion on the new *Rigsdag*, which now had a clear majority of moderate to right-wing members. There was nevertheless no question of a *Venstre*-Conservative coalition, not least because the farming community, represented by *Venstre*, had not yet forgiven the dictatorial régime of Estrup, whose successor the new Conservative People's Party was. So in fact a government was formed similar in principle to the preceding one: Neergaard formed an administration with the tacit support of the Conservatives and carried out a purely *Venstre* policy, though taking care not to antagonise the party on whose support he ultimately depended. His immediate concern was to put an end to the dock strike which was damaging national interests, and so he gave protection to volunteers who were prepared to work in the docks. The Social Democrats and trade unions were not enthusiastic, but on the other hand the strike was controlled by their opponents, the syndicalists. An end to the strike would be an end to the syndicalists, and so the Social Democrats looked the other way. The strikers were duly defeated and the syndicalist movement in Denmark disappeared from the scene.

Denmark Joins the League of Nations

The desire for elections in 1920 had been strong and there were to be plenty of them. The reunification with north Schleswig called for a modification of the 1915 constitution and this could only be done with the consent of two consecutive *Rigsdags*. So accordingly the new *Venstre* government introduced the amendment and carried it, after which the *Folketing* was dissolved and fresh elections held in July. The new *Folketing* again carried the amendment, as did a referendum which took place in September. Finally a new election had to be held on the basis of this amendment which gave representation to the population of north Schleswig. This final, enlarged *Folketing* saw *Venstre* maintain its majority with 52 seats — though only because of support in north Schleswig — closely followed by the Social Democrats with 48.

With its liberal views on the economy, the new government set about dismantling the wartime controls, including rationing, which was abolished in 1921, though not including rent control. Yet it was unable to make any significant reduction in taxes because of the financial burden of the reunification of north Schleswig, where the economic position was disastrous. In fact taxation was gradually increased and new taxes on luxury goods and a restaurant tax were introduced in 1922.

Together with the other neutral countries, Denmark had been invited by the victorious powers to join the League of Nations and had decided to do so in common with the other Nordic countries. It had seemed natural to accept the invitation, as membership of the League appeared to offer some sort of security to a small country, and Denmark had long suffered from being a small neighbour without any significant support abroad. Germany was certainly no longer a menace after the war, nor was Russia after the 1917 revolution, but there were plenty of influential Danes who even at that time foresaw that Germany would re-emerge as a dominant power in Europe. This latter feeling was one of the reasons why there was such widespread support for a Danish-German frontier based on the principle of nationality, as this would diminish the validity of possible future demands. At the same time Danes sensed that joining the League of Nations, which was so far essentially the instrument of the victors, meant sacrificing Denmark's traditional policy of complete neutrality. There was a definite conflict of principles and interests here, but the decision was made to abandon neutrality and to rely instead on a form of collective security, a stance which has been Denmark's ever since. The decision was made despite doubts in some quarters as to how much security the League did in fact offer.

Closely connected with membership of the League of Nations

was the perennial problem of Danish military preparedness. The defence laws of 1909 were due for revision because they contained the clause stating that Copenhagen's defences would be dismantled no later than 1922. The fundamental positions of the four parties were unaltered, the Conservatives being most inclined to maintain a fair-sized military force, the Social Democrats holding to their traditional anti-militarism. *Venstre* was in favour of some military forces and although the party did not go far enough for the Conservatives, its proposals were carried. Military expenditure was to be limited to under 50 million *kroner* a year and the army was to be centred on Jutland instead of Zealand. Conscription was to be limited to 8,000 men a year, in addition to which 1,500 were to do two months' service in the militia. No one was happy about this arangement: the Conservatives wanted more; the Radicals wanted no more than a militia, the Social Democrats only a police force; but the Conservatives were not prepared to bring down the government on the issue and risk the opposition's ideas being put into effect. So *Venstre* had its way and even when the Social Democrats came to power in 1924 they were unable to put their disarmament policy into practice.

Venstre Government and Further Economic Difficulties

The hopes for a quick return to pre-war conditions, partly reflected in the election in 1920 of one of the parties most dedicated to the old standards, were not realised. Post-war speculation in buying produce with a view to re-exporting to the Baltic countries was unsuccessful and Denmark was left with vast unsold stocks and a large foreign debt. Prices on the world market began to fall, but as raw materials were affected before manufactured goods, Denmark was not immediately hurt. Yet her day came with a general fall in prices and the value of money. The wholesale price index fell from 390 in 1920 to 223 in 1921, and further still to 171 in 1922. Farmers who had borrowed money some years previously to modernise their farms were hard hit, although they were to some extent helped when Britain started importing in larger quantities. But for industry there was little compensation and no encouragement. Production fell by a third within one year, and unemployment reached unprecedented levels, rising from 6.1 per cent in 1920 to 19.3 per cent in 1922 after a brief period when it had been at 34.2 per cent.

Extraordinary measures were obviously called for to deal with hardship resulting from unemployment. Under previous social legislation workers were insured against unemployment in their own insurance societies, in practice normally administered by the unions, but unemployment benefit was limited to 70 days. In many cases it was used up, and in order to avert serious hardship the government created an extraordinary unemployment fund to help workers who could prove there was no possibility of employment for them. To the annoyance of the Social Democrats the government also insisted that workers so benefiting should have a control card regularly stamped. (The system was scrapped in 1927.)

Even greater discontent was caused the following year, 1923, when certain categories of workers for whom such help had been possible were declared to be no longer eligible because of the improved situation. An enormous demonstration was organised in Copenhagen, described as the biggest ever seen there — the procession is said to have taken two and a half hours to pass. But nothing was achieved. Nothing in fact could be achieved, because events were against the workers, and their political fellows had no influence on the government. As wages were linked to the cost of living, they fell, but more than that, the employers had to cut costs, which they did by forcing down wages still further, resulting in a real reduction in the standard of living. Where negotiations failed, resort was had to lock-outs, and where strike action was attempted, it was generally broken by the use of volunteer labour. A combination of these two expedients led to violence in Randers in 1922 which had to be put down by the use of infantry. A general strike was called there and it lasted a month, but the strikers had to yield in the end.

It would be unfair to argue that the *Venstre* government was not interested in the industrial workers, for it was perfectly well aware of their significance for the country's wellbeing. But it was in the field of agriculture that it made moves for improvements in the workers' conditions, and this was, of course, the mark of a party with rural interests at heart. *Venstre* had never liked the Radical government's bill making provision for state smallholdings in 1919, insisting that the desire to own land rather than lease it predominated in the country districts. And yet the new laws had achieved their aim in at least partially stopping the drift from country to town which had begun with the vision of higher wages.

Venstre was convinced that more young people could be persuaded to stay in the country districts if more land were made available, and so in 1921 it passed a new act providing for more state loans for those wishing to buy their own land, and these people were now enabled to buy plots big enough to live on without working for others. The two concomitant plans did much to stop the movement away from farming, although the percentage of rural workers continued to fall throughout the decade, dropping from about one worker in three in 1914 to one in four by 1930. Consequent upon this the mechanisation of farming, begun during the war, proceeded apace, and alongside the increasing number of smallholdings, on which the owner or lessee had to rely on his own strength and energy, the larger farms became mechanised and modernised.

Nor would it be fair to give the impression that *Venstre*, which had been inclined to leave society to look after itself and to avoid state interference, was indifferent to social legislation. Indeed at the beginning of the 1920s it introduced social legislation of some consequence which was also symptomatic of profound changes taking place within Danish society at the time. First, the principle of sickness insurance was extended to cover disablement insurance, an early and significant change which ensured a reasonable standard of living for those who were partly or entirely disabled. The amount of disablement pension was based on the degree of incapacitation, which was in turn determined by special tribunals. The funds were obtained in the same way as those for sickness benefits — though this insurance was compulsory, whereas sickness insurance was still voluntary — by contributions from the employee and the employer and the local authority.

Changes were also made in methods of welfare for the aged. The legislation of the 1890s had introduced the principle of old-age assistance, but it still smacked of the Poor Law and people were still loath to apply for it. Now an old-age pension was introduced as a right, and rates of pensions were laid down by the state and no longer left to the judgement of the local authorities. Provision was also made for housing the old when they could no longer look after themselves. Old peoples' homes began to be erected in impressive, if not elaborate, designs, and care was taken to avoid the atmosphere of the poor-law institutions. The idea was to remove any stigma attached to living in a home, as changing conditions demanded. With the drift from country to town families had less room to house their old people: in the country there had always been the possibility of adding a small room or building some sort of cottage for the aged, but this could not be the case in the towns. There the new arrivals found a community of flat-dwellers, and although the size and quality of flats were better than they had been at the beginning of the century, there was still no room to spare. Provision was therefore made for some form of communal accommodation for the old. From this a social pattern which is perhaps typically Danish has emerged, where it becomes more and more the natural thing that old people should live not with their younger relatives but in communities and be well cared for. Subsequently the trend has been to build special flats for them as well, so that they can preserve their independence.

The First Social Democrat Government

Social legislation and help to smallholders were not sufficient to save the popularity of the *Venstre* government in the financial crisis of the 1920s, and in the elections of 1924 the government was badly defeated. After the war people had turned to *Venstre* in the hope of something better; now in their disappointment they turned not to the Radicals but to the Social Democrats, who had never held power before even though Stauning, now chosen to be Prime Minister, had been a Minister in the Radical government after the war. In the same year the first Labour government was elected in Britain, at a time when the Social Democrats were already in power in Germany and had achieved power in Sweden.

Stauning, who at fifty was acknowledged by all to be an outstanding politician, started on a programme designed to achieve the support of the Radicals. He talked of improvements in the existing social legislation, of educational improvements rather than reform, of medical and dental care for schoolchildren. But all this had to be preceded by the strengthening of an economy still in dire straits. The *krone* was at 62 per cent of par and measures had to be taken to strengthen it. The government made two major proposals: that it should introduce import restrictions; and that there should be a once-and-for-all wealth tax on all estates of 50,000 *kroner* and more. The Radicals successfully opposed this second suggestion, while their support for import regulations was of no avail, as the opposition majority in the *Landsting* rejected them. A law on land value taxation was thus the sole measure passed to alter the country's economic framework.

All-party agreement was vital before the obviously necessary action could be taken. In December 1924 it was agreed that the National Bank should back the *krone* at 65 per cent of par and gradually increase its support, if necessary by means of foreign loans. The government would at the same time increase taxation and start paying off its own debt to the Bank, which would thus be enabled to withdraw some paper money from circulation. This process worked — indeed it worked far more quickly than had been foreseen, as foreign investors were quick to pour money into Denmark and bring the *krone* up to 92 per cent of par within just over six months. It reached par within the year, and by 1 January 1927 the *krone* was again exchangeable for gold.

But this impressive result was only achieved at the expense of industry and agriculture which both suffered badly from increased prices. Unemployment, hitherto falling, rose again to 14.8 per cent, and in order to combat higher costs and diminishing profits, the employers tried to lower wages. The unions reacted sharply and there was a lock-out lasting from mid-March to early June. But the employers achieved nothing. By 1926 unemployment had risen to almost 30 per cent and remained on average just over 20 per cent throughout the year. In 1926, too, the effects of the situation became more apparent for agriculture, which also suffered from a series of extra difficulties, including foot-and-mouth disease and the imposition of import restrictions by Germany — again a symptom of how Denmark was exposed to the economic situation of other countries. It was clear that strong measures had to be taken and the government suggested a programme of direct aid to industry and agriculture, export credits, and a reduction of taxation. (A programme of public works was also suggested and, again, an extraordinary wealth tax.) The government threatened to resign if these measures were not adopted by the *Folketing*. They were not adopted. The subsequent election campaign, in which the Radicals and Social Democrats for the first time openly opposed each other, was the bitterest ever. The result was a slight but significant move to the right, *Venstre* and the Conservatives winning a small but sufficient majority over all the other parties.

Although *Venstre* was the largest party, it had no overall majority. But as Thomas Madsen-Mygdal, who was to lead

Venstre, refused to compromise on the party's liberal principles, a coalition was seen to be impossible, and so a *Venstre* minority government was formed, with conditional support from the Conservatives and Radicals. Its aim was to reduce state expenditure, by reducing civil service salaries, by reducing expenditure on social benefits, and by streamlining state services — for instance by combining the postal and telegraph services. With some modifications — mainly the decision to reduce civil service salaries by less than originally envisaged — these measures were agreed upon.

By 1928 some improvement was discernible in the economic sphere. Unemployment fell to 18.5 per cent, while a good harvest brought a breathing-space for agriculture. That year saw also a direct arrangement between the workers' and employers' organisations, providing for wage agreements to run for a number of years — an attempt to combat strikes and lock-outs.

Despite opposition to its liberal policies, the *Venstre* government stood firm and even embarked on what was called 'a doctrinaire liberal Act', Radical and Social Democrat opposition and Conservative reservations notwithstanding. The general aim of the bill was to allow the individual to follow his own conscience in the industrial situation, irrespective of pressures from his fellows and their representatives. He was to be entitled to work at a lower rate of pay than that approved by the unions if it so suited him. He was not to be forced to join a union against his will. Any kind of victimisation was to be punishable under the law. The Social Democrats were eloquent in their condemnation of the Act which they rightly saw as an attempt at undermining the principle of strength through solidarity.

Yet the government succeeded in forcing this law through because the Conservatives were not willing to vote against it. It was over defence that serious differences arose between the two parties. The Defence Act of 1922 needed revision, and attempts were made to reach an agreement with the Conservatives on this issue. The Radicals and Social Democrats were still arguing for different degrees of disarmament, while the Conservatives wanted increased spending on the armed forces. *Venstre* itself was divided, but the aim of the government was to reduce the scope of armaments while spending the same amount on them — this amount not being enough to carry through the present programme. Although *Venstre* indicated its willingness to consider a

modest increase, this was not sufficient for the Conservatives, and
negotiations between the parties broke down. As these had been
in private, there was no question of the government's resigning,
but the Conservatives decided to refuse to pass the budget — an
ironic gesture in view of what had happened in the 1880s — and
when their intention became known, the Radicals also abstained,
and *Venstre* was defeated by the Social Democrats alone. The
Conservatives had been aware of what might happen, but under
their new leader, Christmas Møller, they had decided to show
themselves as a party truly independent of *Venstre*, with whom
their constant and somewhat subservient alliance had begun to
identify them too closely.

Stauning's Return and Important Reforms

The Conservatives gained little in direct influence from this move,
and in the election following (30 April 1929) they slipped from 30
to 24 seats. The winners were the Social Democrats with 61.
Stauning led the new government almost as a matter of course,
and as a coalition of Social Democrats and Radicals it commanded
a majority of five. Its aim was a reform programme within the area
of general agreement between the two parties, touching on disarmament, social legislation, and reform of the criminal laws.

The armament question had been one of the main features of
the election campaign, and here there had been the usual division
of parties — Radicals and Social Democrats in favour of reducing
expenditure, the others against it. Now Social Democrats and
Radicals had their way, and the result was a reduction of 6 million
kroner a year, brought about partly by cutting the call-up from
10,000 to 8,000 a year and partly by increasing efficiency within the
armed forces. The result was a modest but efficient army, considered reasonable in an age which foresaw little danger of renewed war.

A marked change in attitude towards the treatment of criminals
was shown in reforms of the criminal law. The old principle of
punishment for punishment's sake had given way to the modern
concept of rehabilitation. The death penalty, in disuse anyway,
was abolished, as was imprisonment with hard labour. Instead
varying forms of imprisonment were introduced, while the
suspended sentence was used in a greater number of cases. More

suitable punishments for young offenders were also devised, and in general judges were given greater powers of discretion when dealing with criminals. This system has been the basis of Danish penal procedure for the past 60 years.

The other major reform intended by this government, which has also been the basis for all legislation until quite recently, was the social legislation, known as the Social Reform, introduced by K. K. Steincke, the Minister for Social Affairs. Both this and the penal reforms gave Denmark an aspect which even today is remarkably modern and which at the beginning of the 1930s must have been astoundingly so.

The Social Democrat Party had quickly learned to appreciate the virtues of moderation, and it has since retained this attitude. That it has had its rebels is quite obvious, but generally speaking they have had the courage of their convictions and left the party, which has thus for many years had the support of a very broad section of the population.

It was possible to introduce the far-reaching social reforms of the 1930s against a background of increased prosperity. For despite the economic and social difficulties of the 1920s, the overall picture was much brighter than the unrest and the unemployment figures seem to indicate. In the broader view, the difficulties had been concerned more with adapting to changed circumstances, and this had been achieved by means of widespread rationalisation both in industry and in agriculture. The drift from the farms had been offset by mechanisation, while rationalisation had served to make industry more efficient and to increase production. It also made for the creation of large firms and semi-monopolies, though this tendency was not as widespread in Denmark as in other countries. Consequent upon improved industrial efficiency, durable consumer goods made up an increasing percentage of exports, though Denmark was still predominantly a country exporting agricultural produce. However, the trend towards more industrial exports had begun and agriculture's share fell from 90 per cent to 80 per cent — mainly to Britain, which took about 60 per cent of Denmark's exports, but only provided some 13 per cent of her imports. Workers in employment earned good wages and their purchasing power was back to that of 1920. There was a feeling of affluence, despite the 15 per cent unemployment which still existed.

In general, Denmark in the 1920s had undergone the same sort of social transformation as had characterised most of Europe, the move into the modern age with its motor-cars, its radio, its aeroplanes. (In 1922 Danish Airlines opened their first regular route.) It was the age of hiking and cycling, of sport and dancing. It was also the age of popular education when, partly to counteract the nineteenth-century, Christian-patriotic influence of the folk high schools, the Social Democrats organised the Workers' Educational Association and attracted many pupils who studied not only general subjects but also politics and social problems. The sex age had also dawned and the subject was discussed openly for the first time, while inhibitions began to dissolve and the divorce-rate increased.

The old society was irrevocably gone. The move away from the stable conditions — as many saw them — from before the First World War and into the much more demanding situation of the mid-twentieth century was a difficult one for many Danes. For some, things were moving too fast; for others, in particular those who felt that the country had been left out of the mainstream of developments through its neutrality during the war, it was a case of catching up and committing themselves to progress. For the out-sider it must be seen as the time when the forces leading to the emergence of Denmark as a humane and affluent modern state were beginning to gather strength.

1930–1939: ECONOMIC CRISIS

The difficulties which Denmark had experienced in the 1920s were
largely independent of the world situation, and thus when the Wall
Street crash came in October 1929, the Danes were not over-
anxious about the consequences. It was expected to be a short-
term crisis which would pass. But in 1930 it reached Europe, and
when Britain left the gold standard in 1931, Denmark had to
follow suit, despite the fact that 1930 by and large had been a year
of prosperity. Some firms now went into liquidation, but this was
only a beginning, and the numbers grew throughout the following
years. By 1933 unemployment had reached the unprecedented
level of 43.5 per cent, though during the summer of that year it fell
back to 21 per cent. In this year Steincke's Social Reform came
into force and the plight of the unemployed, who previously had
had to exist on poor-aid when their unemployment insurance ran
out, was to a great extent mitigated. The stories of the unemployed in Denmark are like those from elsewhere and tell of the
hopelessness and desperation, the queuing up for the dole, and the
hardship and humiliation of looking for a job. Demonstrations
organised in Copenhagen were in some cases put down by the
police, by methods not always gentle. Jobs were so scarce that
employers attempted to take only those who would accept less
than the union rate, and such terms were often accepted.

The state stepped in with plans for public works, and work
camps were set up for the unemployed. Ten were built in all, but
they were regarded with some misgivings, as they smacked too
much of forced labour camps, though they were far from being so
in fact. Another way of alleviating distress was to provide free
periods of residence in folk high schools, an experiment of some
interest as it brought a completely new class of pupil to the
schools. Many were not interested in learning and felt themselves
in a different category from fee-paying pupils, but others resented
their situation less and profited from it:

Askov gave them a warm welcome, and probably all found new
courage, a new self-reliance, so that they were subsequently

135

able to create a new and worthwhile existence for themselves. But it was not always easy to be an unemployed man at a high school. We hardly ever had any money at our disposal, and at Askov this was more obvious than at the Workers' High School, because many of the pupils had plenty of pocket money. For instance, I could not go home for Christmas because I could not afford the journey. But that led to my spending Christmas with the Principal and his family, and it was the best Christmas I had experienced for many years.

Thus one unemployed man remembered Askov, the biggest of the high schools.

Yet not everyone from the country districts 'had plenty of pocket money'. Agriculture suffered as much as any other part of the economy, though the difficulties created for farmers were very different from those in the towns. The hard times appeared in rural areas earlier than in the towns; by 1931 the price of corn had been halved, and this was followed by similar falls in the price of dairy produce. At one time it was said to be cheaper to use butter for lubricating machinery than to buy proper grease and oil. Farm after farm had to be auctioned: in 1930 there were 324 such auctions, and the number rose to 1,214 in 1931 and 2,043 in 1932, falling back to 1,332 in 1933. It is, however, still true to say that even in 1932 the total only represented about one per cent of Danish farms, so the number of farmers who actually went bankrupt was relatively small. Much higher was the number of those who just scraped through. The fall in prices for cattle was catastrophic. Pigs fetched so little that a system of rationing production was introduced, and piglets were regularly slaughtered at birth and thrown on the rubbish heap or burned.

In 1932–33, before we came to an agreement with England on pig supplies, I remember that when I had to sell young pigs, which I had made a speciality, I once had to sell twelve for 48 *kroner*, and I had to deliver them in Terp, about 20 kilometres away from home. I can still remember that there was a thirteenth, and I made sure of smuggling it in to get rid of it. They weighed about 40 pounds each.

This was one man's experience, and it appears to have been typical.

With the difficulties of the farmers themselves came problems for their suppliers, and in 1931 the government made an arrangement to help those who could not pay their debts. Ten million *kroner* were earmarked, and the idea was that the state should pay the creditors 20 per cent of the sum owing, provided that the creditors were willing to give a receipt for the whole sum. Conditions were so bad that most were only too willing to go along with the arrangement. For their part the farmers were pleased with the respite, but many felt that they still owed the money, and with the arrival of better times paid off the remainder of the original debts.

In providing help of this kind, the government showed itself aware of the farmers' difficulties. It knew, too, that the farmers saw devaluation as the only real solution to their problems, a course that would help them to export their surplus produce. Yet, confronted by British complaints against the high rate of imports from Denmark, it could not accede to these demands, reasonable as they might have seemed, especially as Denmark was only taking a very low percentage of British exports. An effort was made to sell more British goods in the country and a British exhibition was arranged and opened by the Prince of Wales in September 1932. It was a success, but not sufficient to galvanise Danish importers, and the feeling remained that more could be done. After all, with 99 per cent of Denmark's bacon exports going to Great Britain, together with 72 per cent of her butter and 85 per cent of her eggs, the government was loath to lose áccess to the British market. The Foreign Exchange Office, created in 1932 to control all foreign trade and issue import licences, therefore showed itself more willing to grant licences for imports from Britain than from elsewhere.

There was widespread dissatisfaction with the foreign currency restrictions, which to many seemed to lack cohesion. By and large the Conservatives supported the idea of restrictions, but it was anathema to *Venstre*. So, to clear the air, the government called elections for November 1932 in which it increased its representation by one, while *Venstre* lost five seats.

New regulations concerning import control were now agreed, and the government was then able to discuss a trade agreement with Britain. During 1932 Britain had twice increased import duties, and Danish goods were affected. First Ramsay MacDonald's National Government completely abandoned free trade principles and put a 10 per cent duty on a whole range of goods including dairy produce, but not bacon. At the same time Empire goods continued to be imported duty free. These new arrangements came into force in February and were followed by the Ottawa Agreements on Imperial Preference according to which Britain increased the duty on butter and eggs to 15 per cent, while expressing an intention to reduce bacon imports. As a consequence Denmark was asked to reduce by 20 per cent bacon shipments to Britain, virtually the only market for these exports.

Britain was, of course, in economic straits as dire as Denmark's and the imposition of duties had to be accepted. Yet it was a heavy blow for Denmark. At the same time, Britain had expressed willingness to negotiate with foreign countries once the Imperial Preference Agreements came into effect, and Denmark was quick to seize her chance. Within less than a month talks were in progress and an agreement was reached which, if not ideal, did at least limit the damage for the time being. Britain agreed not to increase further the duty on dairy produce and fish, and not to impose a duty on bacon. In return Denmark acceped a quota arrangement for bacon which kept exports at their 1929–31 levels; while provisions were made for minimum quantities of other Danish exports if any sort of quota arrangement should be required in the future. For her part Denmark was to give certain privileges to British exporters of industrial goods and some foodstuffs, while arrangements were 'noted' concerning other British exports, especially those of raw materials for agriculture. Denmark also agreed to buy 80 per cent of her total coal imports from Great Britain. The agreement, which was for three years, was probably as much as could be expected under the circumstances. It did not give the Danes absolute security, as there were numerous escape clauses, but it did mean that they now had a clearer picture of their prospects than before, and could take steps to keep production within the limits imposed on the country as a whole.

The negotiations with Britain began in December 1932 and the agreement came into effect in April 1933, but during this period Denmark was faced with what some saw as the greatest industrial crisis of her history. As a result of the general fall in prices, the employers began to demand a 20 per cent reduction in wages on the expiry of the national wage agreements in January 1933. This, they argued, would be in the workers' own interests, as it would enable the employers to keep their prices low and so to increase production. But the unions were not prepared to see any reduction and consequently the employers gave notice of a lock-out from 1 February. Despite exhortations from the government, both parties refused to try for a compromise solution, and with the prospect of a vast increase in the already widespread unemployment, the Social Democrat government decided to legislate to ban all strikes and lock-outs for a year, and to extend the previous wage agreement for the same period. Both parties to the strike were opposed to legislation, while Conservative and *Venstre* politicians were able to point out that the proposed standstill would be to the immediate advantage of the workers. The Radicals would rather have seen some form of permanent arbitration tribunal set up, but decided not to oppose the government. At this stage *Venstre* started to argue that devaluation would ease the situation, helping exports and thus improving the country's economy, and forcing up prices in a wide range of goods, thereby weakening the arguments in favour of a reduction in wages.

Now the agricultural interests joined in the debate, and both large and small farmers made demands for measures to improve their lot. They desired an alteration in the system of taxation, and some form of protection, and although in their joint declaration they stated that the 'normal buying power' of the *krone* should be maintained, it was obvious that they really wanted devaluation. This now became a main object of *Venstre* policy, whatever the cost to the negotiations with Britain.

The difficulty was for the political parties to arrive at any sort of consensus to get a bill through the *Rigsdag*. At times it appeared that no agreement was possible and fears were expressed that Denmark's entire political structure was in danger. Finally in a last effort to reach a compromise, Stauning invited a number of the leading politicians from the Social Democrat, *Venstre*, and Radical parties to his home in Kanslergade. With only short breaks for refreshment they went on for eighteen hours before producing an outline agreement in which it was possible to fill in details during further negotiations. The main give-and-take occurred between the Social Democrats and *Venstre*. In exchange for a devaluation of just over 10 per cent, leaving the rate at Kr. 22.50 to the pound sterling — a devaluation grudgingly accepted by Britain as New Zealand had just devalued by a similar amount — *Venstre* had agreed not to oppose the Social Democrat proposal to ban strikes and lock-outs for a year. Other points settled in what became known as the Kanslergade Agreement were a reduction of taxation on farms, the starting of a number of major public works — including the building of Europe's longest bridge, the *Storstrømsbro*, between Zealand and Falster — and the unimpeded progress of Steincke's Social Reform. In addition the state was to buy up a total of 150,000 head of cattle for destruction. *Venstre* was not happy about the move from free trade, but a change of heart had been forced on the party by circumstances. With the advent of a Conservative government in London there was no real alternative but to look to Denmark's immediate interests and accept state interference in agriculture. For the Social Democrats the acceptance of state interference in industrial bargaining had also been a bitter pill to swallow, and so the Kanslergade Agreement has been seen as a turning-point in the history of twentieth-century Danish politics. It was, indeed, an historic occasion: the negotiations took place on the day Hitler came to power — 30 January 1933.

Partly as a result of the agreement and partly owing to further developments in the administration of the country, unemployment fell in 1933 to about 20 per cent, where it remained until the end of the decade, mainly because production began to look up after the lowering of the bank rate to 2½ per cent and money became cheaper. It even became possible to convert earlier loans at high interest rates, which helped many private individuals fighting to stave off bankruptcy. At the same time the Foreign Exchange Office did much to stimulate industry. Primarily, it distributed foreign exchange, thus forcing Danes to buy from countries to which they exported in significant quantities — Britain especially. But it was also in a position to refuse funds for certain imports, when it was deemed reasonable for Denmark to produce such goods herself. In this way industry was persuaded to look for new products and to be self-sufficient, and so an increase in the labour force was necessary. This led to a significant reduction in the import of finished goods, accompanied by a noticeable increase in the import of raw materials. Throughout the 1930s the Foreign Exchange Office exerted a decisive influence on Danish economic policy. A Foreign Currency Council was thus established on which most branches of industry were represented. This led to renewed co-operation between government and industry as well as the more effective organisation of industry into what amounted to pressure groups.

Thus the early 1930s saw the emergence of much more wide-spread state control of everyday life than had originally been envisaged, more perhaps than many people wanted. It had come about because the problems facing the country were too big to be solved by any less an agency than the state, which had to accept increasing responsibility for the wellbeing of each sectional interest. The Social Democrats bore the chief responsibility for carrying through this move, although it was not altogether to their liking. Nevertheless, it was done by state control, not by nationalisation. The state did not take over industry, but it took upon itself to direct it in so far as the prosperity of the country was concerned, leaving day-to-day running and ownership in private hands. In the social field, state direction was implicit in Steincke's Social Reform, which laid down more stringent rules than had existed before and took away from local authorities the rights they had previously enjoyed to decide for themselves the amount and form of help needed. The new social legislation was firmly based on close co-operation between state and local authority. In conjunction with this, taxation was used to bring about a redistribution of the country's financial resources. Taxes, indirect and direct, were increased, accounting for some 15 per cent of earnings.

Steincke's Social Reform, more of a rationalisation of social legislation than complete reform, was implemented not only because of the need for extra unemployment benefits in a difficult year, but as part of the general settlement constituting the Kanslergade Agreement. Steincke had for years worked in the social sphere and fought hard for his measures, and because of the need to reach agreement on as many matters as possible, he was able to keep his bill intact, despite Conservative opposition.

The result was a thorough tidying-up of Danish social legislation, which then remained basically unaltered for some 40 years. It introduced social service as a right rather than an act of charity, and was symptomatic of the increasing humanitarian ideals of modern Denmark.

The lot of the Danes was quietly but surely improving; but in Germany humanitarian ideals were being brutally cast aside. This could not be a matter of indifference to the Danes. They were well aware of fresh German demands for the return of north Schleswig, since the Dano-German border was a direct result of the Versailles Treaty, a main target for Nazi hatred. To make matters more complicated, some unrest did exist in the region, which had suffered more from the depression than other areas. (There had been five times as many enforced auctions of farms there as elsewhere.) The German minority fastened on economic discontent to urge a return to Germany, not least as agricultural reform there seemed to offer better prospects than in Denmark. The main pressure group among Danish agriculturists, known as the LS (*Landbrugernes Sammenslutning* — Agriculturists' Association), which was later to show Nazi leanings, was active in north Schleswig and was open equally to Danes and Germans. The latter made the most of their opportunity. Hitler, for his part, insisted that they should obey his orders, and Nazi organisations were formed in north Schleswig, as indeed elsewhere in Denmark, though their activities were to some extent limited when Denmark prohibited the use of military-style uniforms anywhere in the country. This prohibition was aimed not only at Danish Nazis but equally at other uniformed political organisations.

Anti-democratic tendencies were evident in the Denmark of the early and middle 1930s. Youth organisations attached to the major political parties were acting in para-military style, while numerous small anti-democratic parties sprang up. The Danish National Socialist Party was formed under Frits Clausen, but although it wanted to put up candidates for the *Folketing*, it was not able to gain the necessary 10,000 signatures to take part in an election. Nevertheless, the party whipped up numerous street demonstrations. How widespread anti-democratic tendencies were in the country as a whole, it is difficult to estimate, for they had little practical effect either then or later. Certainly the Danes would have nothing to do with the anti-semitism of the Nazis and accepted the small Jewish community in Denmark as an integral part of the Danish population. Anti-semitic gibes in Danish Nazi publications probably lost the party more support than they gained.

Anti-democratic views were not, however, wholly on the right, and indeed it has been suggested that the Nazis and neo-Nazi movements enjoyed a measure of support because of a communist threat. The Social Democrat politicians felt themselves threatened by the communists, while the unemployed were also showing signs of being receptive to the arguments of Marxist agitators. At the other end of the scale, left-wing intellectuals also joined the communist cause, often from the conviction — according to one of them — that this was the only way to stop fascism.

This polarisation of extreme views was a danger to the country's political system, but Stauning's government steered a careful course throughout and avoided any major splits. It was helped by the increasing number of votes polled by the Social Democrats in successive elections, which resulted in the highest Social Democrat vote ever in 1935, when the party gained over 46 per cent of the votes. This percentage has never been surpassed or even equalled since.

With gains such as these the Social Democrats now set their sights for the first time on winning a majority in the *Landsting* in the 1936 elections. In a hard-fought campaign, the opposition painted a grim picture of what would happen if the Social Democrats were to govern without any sort of check being put on them. The party only needed to win three extra seats, and when the counting was done, they had secured two of them. All that was left was the seat for Bornholm, and here there was a tie. The result had to be determined by drawing lots and the Social Democrats won, thus giving the party, in alliance with the Radicals, an absolute majority in both houses for the first time.

The problem of defence immediately exercised the new independent Social Democrat-Radical government. Traditionally, both parties had been in favour of more or less complete disarmament. The argument was that as Denmark would not be able, come what may, to withstand an aggressor for long, there was no real point in spending money on defence. During the period of optimism in the 1920s, defence expenditure had indeed been reduced; but now, in the 1930s, when optimism had given way to pessimism, and when Germany was emerging as a powerful and warlike nation once more, Danes began to think again. The old argument of futility was, of course, still as valid or invalid as before, but the spectacles were no longer rose-tinted. As early as 1933 a leading Social Democrat politician had described Denmark as a beautiful residence built by the joint efforts of the farmers and the workers, adding that 'the workers would be foolish not to secure and defend their house if thieves broke in'. This speech betokened a change in the Social Democrat attitude, and the following year Stauning himself argued that the time was not ripe for unilateral disarmament. He was supported by *Venstre* and the Conservatives, and by 1937 there was agreement between the parties that the defence budget must be increased to 45 million *kroner*.

Denmark was in a very difficult situation as far as foreign policy was concerned. The country had accepted limitations on its traditionally neutral policy by joining the League of Nations and accepting the clause on sanctions only after some hesitation. Now the Danes began to comment on the impotence of the League of Nations. In October 1933 Hitler had withdrawn from the League and flouted its principles by rearming, and subsequently by reoccupying the Rhineland — to the accompaniment of nothing more than protests from France and Great Britain. A visit to London by Stauning decided him that Britain would not be able to offer protection in the event of an invasion. After seeing the continued decline of the League during the Abyssinian crisis, Denmark, together with the other former neutral nations, reasserted her old neutrality. She had to try to protect her future as far as possible by not getting at cross-purposes with Germany.

Denmark therefore adopted what looked like an ambivalent position in European politics. Although she had a seat on the Council of the League of Nations at the time, she abstained from voting when Germany was condemned for reintroducing conscription. And later, in 1937, when there was a good deal of agitation from the other Scandinavian countries and from the opposition in Denmark for a Nordic defensive treaty, Stauning, anxiously aware of Germany's watchfulness, rejected the idea in no uncertain terms. It must be remembered that Hitler was not prepared to accept the 1920 Dano-German border as binding and Denmark had the examples of the Rhineland, Austria, and then the Sudentenland, to convince her that north Schleswig was in very much the same category, with plenty of Germans demanding to go 'heim ins Reich'. Thus when, in 1939, Germany reacted to President Roosevelt's protest about the Führer's conduct in Europe by offering non-aggression treaties to all the Scandinavian countries, Denmark was the only one to accept. There was little alternative, as Germany was on the doorstep, and a refusal would almost certainly have been regarded as an unfriendly act. Denmark had little confidence in the treaty, but felt some need for support in her attitude on north Schleswig, and Germany specifically promised not to change the frontier by force. Possible discussion on the border problem was not, however, ruled out. For her part, Sweden refused a treaty because it implied a break in her long-standing neutrality, and also, it was said, because she was afraid that such a treaty would in practice limit the freedom of the

Swedish press to comment on the German situation. The Danish press was already limited in this respect. Germany had made representations about the bad press she was receiving, and the government had therefore asked editors to be careful in their treatment of German affairs. It was Denmark's hope that as a result of this very circumspect behaviour towards Germany, the country would once more be able to remain aloof in any future war which might come, and as part of this hope had managed to have written into the treaty with Germany a clause giving her the right to trade with third countries in the event of war. Legally, then, Denmark, would still be able to trade with Britain if war came.

While Denmark had been concerned to secure her external position, there had been some internal recovery from the catastrophic situation at the beginning of the decade. It had come first to industry, thereby occasioning a good deal of discontent among the farming community who had sought some form of relief by organising itself and putting pressure on the government. In this the LS movement played a leading part, and helped to organise a massive demonstration of farmers in Copenhagen in 1935. A deputation waited on the King, but although he received it, he referred the members to Stauning. The government was unable to give them the help they asked for, including a further devaluation, and they tried to apply pressure by organising a dairy strike and withholding the foreign currency they earned. Their moves were not very successful, though they had the support of the opposition parties, who threatened to refuse to pass the foreign currency regulations when they came up for renewal. It was under these circumstances that the government held the 1935 elections which gave it an increased majority. 'Stauning or chaos' had been the cry, and the country chose Stauning. He became a father-figure in Denmark, a symbol of national unity, and it was his policy to govern the country for the good of all, not for any purely sectional interests.

Even with its new *Landsting* majority the government did not set out on a path of radical socialisation, but continued on its previous course: state control but not state ownership. And the state set out to control the unions and workers as well as the employers when necessary. Stauning aimed at close co-operation with the unions, but knew that this was possible only if they would accept that differences must be settled by negotiation. The effort was largely successful, especially when it was decided that the official arbitrator could put his suggestions for compromise solutions to all the unions concerned, in the knowledge that their majority verdict would be accepted by the remainder. The system of compulsory arbitration was so well developed in the 1930s that industrial disputes on the whole were settled in a civilised, responsible manner which avoided head-on collisions between parties in dispute. And the unions did take notice of the country's economic situation, not least by withholding wage-claims when prices started to rise and by thus ensuring that unemployment did not rise with them. In fact for a time they accepted what amounted to a 7 per cent drop in living standards, though wages did begin to rise again by the end of the decade.

The end of the thirties was not a period of great reforms, though changes were made in laws concerning apprentices, while the right to one day's holiday for every month worked — in practice a fortnight's holiday a year — was made statutory. Old-age pensions were made payable at sixty, thus helping many old people without work and persuading others to give up their jobs in favour of younger people, many of whom were still unemployed. As local authorities in Denmark derive their income from direct taxation (which had come to mean that the richer the town or district, the lower the percentage of income tax), a law was also passed which sought to distribute the tax burden more evenly amongst local authorities. The state was now trying to control a situation which had developed as a result of people moving into towns with a lower tax percentage.

The constitution also came in for scrutiny. The position now there was a Social Democrat majority in the *Landsting*, was very different from when the *Landsting* could be relied on to act as a brake. Suggestions were made for adopting a single chamber system, but instead a new constitution was suggested in which the *Landsting* was to be chosen by direct vote, in much the same way as the *Folketing*. The suggestion was approved by the *Rigsdag* and an election held in April 1939 so that, according to the constitution, a new *Rigsdag* could vote on the same bill. The Social Democrats lost a large percentage of their votes, but the new *Rigsdag* voted for the constitutional amendment. Then the suggestion had to be put to a referendum, where it had by law to be accepted by at least 45 per cent of possible votes. It received only 44.46 per cent and was thus rejected, to the great disappointment of Stauning. The advent of war in September prevented any more constitutional moves being made and it was not until 1953 that the present constitution was finally adopted.

In areas outside the immediate political arena, however, other changes were taking place, putting Denmark in the vanguard of European developments and at the same time showing the workings of the social legislation which attempted to play its part in all walks of life. The birthrate was falling and the fear was expressed that this would have catastrophic results in the 1970s. In an effort to stem this trend moves were made in two completely different fields. A bill was passed in 1937 to ensure regular visits by health visitors to mothers with small children, in an effort to cut the infant mortality rate, then one of the highest in Europe. It also became possible for families with three or more children to receive grants towards the cost of housing — either loans to build or subsidised rents.

On the other hand, in a decade when open discussion of sex had become more common, and when traditional moral concepts were being increasingly questioned, a move of a completely different kind was envisaged and to some extent carried out. Abortion was becoming a social problem, and although the existing law prescribed strict penalties for illegal abortion, more and more cases were coming before the courts and were either dismissed or resulted in a light sentence for the offenders. Since the law was obviously falling into disrepute, it was suggested by a government commision that legal abortions should be granted not only in cases of rape or for health reaons, but also for 'social reasons', i.e. if the birth of another child would have any seriously detrimental effect on the financial position of the woman concerned. Despite the prevailing liberal attitude, the suggestion of abortion for social reasons brought a storm of protest, and the clause was dropped before the bill was finally passed.

In making these provisions, the state also felt obliged to help in other ways any mothers, especially unmarried ones, who were in need. As a consequence the Council for the Unmarried Mother (*Mødrehjælpen*) was established to help mothers make the best of what in some cases was a bad job. A law was passed giving illegitimate children the right to bear their father's name and entitling them to inherit from him. This legislation, very advanced for its time, was a clear indication that Denmark was moving away from traditional social and moral concepts. The welfare state was extending its influence to people in need whatever the cause, and trying to do away with hardship without seeking to know or to determine the rights and wrongs — a demonstration of the egalitarian principles of the government in power. This particular move was made easier by the fact that neither of the government parties made any pretence of maintaining Christian principles. They were both expressly humanist in approach and thus could easily ignore the standpoint of an earlier age, still being observed in countries with a Christian, or theoretically Christian, government.

The same egalitarian principles also prompted the government to introduce a new Education Act, the aim of which was to improve the quality of schools and to bring their standards into line. Previously a distinction had been made between those children who went through a primary school and those who went on to 'middle school'. Now, in an effort to give equal opportunities to all, the middle school was made a part of the primary school. Some middle schools led, however, to an examination whereas some, known as examination-free middle schools, did not. At the same time moves were made to improve school standards in country districts, sometimes by combining several small schools into one larger one serving a wide area.

Literature in the Twenties and Thirties

The 1920s produced a literature which was the natural continuation of the immediate post-war works mentioned in the last chapter, works which reflected the disillusionment of the post-war generation, even though they may have been written ten years or more after the end of the war. Tom Kristensen and Jacob Paludan dominated the scene, Kristensen first and foremost in his poetry, but also in novels such as *Life's Arabesque*, a fantastic piece about a revolution in Copenhagen. It is, like the Expressionist poems which Kristensen was writing, unrealistic in its portrayal, but its political import and its disillusionment are real enough. Kristensen's most important novel, *Havoc*, was not published until 1930, a bitter book about men without a view of life, in which the main figure has to destroy himself by drink in order to build himself up again. Though published in 1930, it is still a novel of the 1920s.

The same is also true of Jacob Paludan. His major work, *Jørgen*

Stein, is a novel of the immediate post-war period, but it was published in two volumes as late as 1932 and 1933 — again a part-bewildered, part-disillusioned look at the generation. It also came as the climax to a series of novels looking critically at modern social developments. In other novels from the twenties, *Birds Around the Lighthouse* (1925) and *The Ripening Fields* (1927), Paludan takes other aspects of modern civilisation — technical progress, Americanisation, the emancipation of women — and dislikes them all. The works of both Kristensen and Paludan have not dated as social criticism of fifty years earlier has dated. They are full of dynamism and treat problems which are akin to, if not the same as, those which preoccupy many modern writers.

But as the literature symptomatic of the twenties continued to be written in the 1930s, that typical of the thirties had begun in the twenties. In 1928 a novel appeared in a completely different genre, *The Fisherfolk*, by a young writer called Hans Kirk. Kirk was a Marxist, and his novel, which tells of the successful efforts of a small fishing community to settle in a new part of the country, is a 'collective' work in which the group rather than any individual predominates. At the same time, in showing how the group of fisherfolk who belong to the Evangelical Inner Mission have a dynamic faith which they manage to impose on the more liberal and tolerant local inhabitants, it can be seen as a picture of the workings of a communist cell in a non-communist society. The genre was attempted by many other leading writers of the 1930s, some of whom have emerged as the most important Danish novelists of this century, though in most cases not because of their 'collective' novels. As may be expected, however, the pervading theme in the novels of the 1930s was the social problem, and the solution posed was normally that of some form of socialism, whether revolutionary or not.

Yet the traditional picture of the grey, disillusioned literature of the 1930s is only partly true. As early as 1924 the clergyman Kaj Munk had written his ten-act play *An Idealist*, intended as an examination of the personality of Herod whom he saw as an idealist with the wrong ideals. It was a monstrously long play, yet one of indisputable dramatic effect. Its approach to melodrama was to recur elsewhere in Munk's production: the dead woman brought back to life and rising from her coffin or the smashing of the bust which proved Christ to be a Jew, while the discoverer walks out and marries his Jewish secretary. Munk deals with current and yet timeless problems, and deals with them from a Christian point of view. There is a certain ambivalence about him. For instance, there is just a chance that the diagnosis was wrong and that the girl was not dead, and when Professor Mensch smashes his evidence and yet marries a Jewish girl, he seems to be eating his cake and having it. Munk is ambivalent, too, in his attitude to contemporary dictatorship. Like many others, he was an admirer of Mussolini, though less so of Hitler. When the Germans invaded Denmark, however, all ambivalence disappeared and Kaj Munk stood out as an uncompromising patriot, using his pulpit to denounce the Germans, until the Gestapo one night dragged him from his home, shot him, and left his body in a ditch.

Among the other more colourful figures of Danish literature in the 1930s was Karen Blixen, whose *Seven Gothic Tales*, appearing under her pseudonym of Isak Dinesen, was published in the United States in 1934, the first of a series of books in which story-telling and the imagination took the place of hopeless descriptions of a hopeless reality — a brilliant exercise in escapism. More realistic, indeed intensely realistic, was her autobiographical book *Out of Africa*, published in 1937, in which the aristocratic Danish coffee-farmer produces a glowing description of contemporary Kenya accompanied by a penetrating and understanding analysis of the African mentality.

It has happened before that those writers whose work has had lasting significance have in fact been untypical of their time. This is true of the 1930s. The men who wrote, perhaps most accurately, of their own day, overlooking the deeper problems of humanity and existence beyond the struggle to keep alive, are scarcely read nowadays. Those who while in some cases being aware of the reality around them looked beyond it, still occupy a place in the national consciousness. In the 1930s such figures were Martin A. Hansen, H. C. Branner and William Heinesen, who in the following decades were to become something different, able to rise above the immediacy of their surroundings.

Art also made its contribution to the social discussion of the day, and the paintings of Aksel Jørgensen show a new degree of social awareness with their portrayal of prostitutes and drinkers and the socially deprived. This new realism in art was, as in literature, accompanied by a wave of Expressionism, for which the inspiration came from Germany. The chief exponent of this was Jens

Søndergaard, whose use of colour was far more radical than that of his immediate predecessors, and whose portrayal of both town and country is deeply subjective and suggests the contrast between urban hardship and rural idyl.

As the most abstract of the arts, music was less able to play an active role in the social debate. Nevertheless, in their markedly anti-Romantic approach the composers of the time surely reflected the mood of the day. Jørgen Bentzon, a pupil of Carl Nielsen, was like his fellows in literature and the visual arts influenced by German Expressionism. His work consists largely of chamber music, but he experiments with larger orchestral works and a single opera.

The 1930s had been a time not of promise but of debate and struggle. By the end of the decade Denmark had begun to emerge from the economic crisis which the country had faced since 1929, and unemployment had sunk to about 9 per cent. Yet it was becoming increasingly obvious that the future held problems of a completely different dimension.

8 1939–1945: DENMARK IN THE SECOND WORLD WAR

When war broke out in September 1939, there could be no doubt where the sympathies of the Danish people lay, but neither could there be any question of their acting on these sympathies. The only hope lay in remaining strictly neutral and carrying out the tightrope act performed 25 years previously, a hope which had been encouraged by the non-aggression pact with Germany and its express guarantee that Denmark would be able to trade with other nations provided commerce with Germany was continued. In practice, however, it was much more difficult to maintain this position, as Germany was more self-sufficient than before and therefore less interested in maintaining unbroken trade links. Germany also gave evidence of her singular disregard for treaties and arrested several Danish ships on their way to England, though when a strong protest was made, they were allowed to proceed. Subsequently Germany did nothing during the early stages of the war to prevent Denmark from trading with Britain, though this trade was not without its physical dangers, mainly because of mines off the British coast. By March 1940 6 per cent of the Danish merchant fleet had been lost.

Nor, it must be admitted, was trade with Britain particularly lucrative. While the price of foreign goods rose, and while insurance premiums on freight reached unprecedented levels, thus contributing to rising prices, Britain introduced price controls immediately on the outbreak of war and refused to increase payment for Danish goods. The fact that sterling had been falling in value made the situation more difficult for Denmark who received less for her exports than had previously been the case. For a time the *krone* was allowed to fall with sterling, but on 1 September 1939 the decision was made to tie the *krone* to the dollar instead of the pound. Thus, in relation to other currencies the *krone* was stabilised, but in relation to the pound sterling it was overvalued, and Britain was still Denmark's main customer. Accordingly, negotiations were started with a view to increasing the price paid for Danish exports, and after long and difficult

152

bargaining an increase was agreed at the cost of Britain's curtailing the quantity of imports — a doubtful advantage for the Danes. On the other hand, Britain acknowledged their right to continue exporting to Germany in the same proportion as hitherto, and so it looked as though Denmark's precarious position might be maintained. But whether the agreements with the two belligerent powers would in fact have enabled Denmark to steer a neutral course must remain a matter for conjecture. The agreement with Britain was signed on 2 April 1940. A week later, Denmark was under German occupation.

The real reason for the occupation seems to have been not so much a desire to take over the country as the need to secure Denmark as a stepping-stone for the occupation of Norway. Norway was of strategic importance to Germany because of her indented coast, which would provide excellent bases for the war in the Atlantic, and also because Norwegian waters were being used for the transport of Swedish iron ore from Narvik. Britain and France had plans for dealing with the Norwegian situation and even mined Norwegian waters. Fearing that Britain and France might occupy parts of Norway so as to stop the transport of the iron ore on which Germany depended (the intention until Finland's surrender to Russia on 12 March 1940 after the winter war robbed the Allies of the excuse to intervene in the North), Germany decided to move first. To begin with, the Germans acted on the assumption that only Jutland needed to be taken, but finally the decision was reached that the entire country should be occupied.

Ironically, Denmark was warned of what was about to happen. Admiral Canaris, the head of German Intelligence and a leading if shadowy figure in the anti-Hitler faction, seized the opportunity to humiliate the Führer by allowing news of the impending invasion of Scandinavia to leak to the Dutch military attaché in Berlin. By this route the news reached the Danish ambassador, who sent it straight to Copenhagen on 4 April. Although it caused a stir and was followed by a number of emergency meetings, it was not really believed. The Danish government was aware of the country's dangerous situation, but was at the same time afraid of antagonising Germany by taking any step which might look like military preparation. Even as late as 8 April, when German ships were known to have sailed in the Baltic, and when a long column of troops was known to be moving northwards towards the Danish frontier, no mobilisation was carried out, though the armed forces were in a state of alert. The army chiefs would have liked to mobilise, but the politicians hesitated until it was too late. At 4.00 a.m. on the morning of 9 April, the German ambassador in Copenhagen — who had known that something was brewing, but was not fully informed — asked for a meeting with the Foreign Minister and delivered an ultimatum. The invasion had already begun. Denmark was merely to be used as a base for German troops, but would otherwise be left to look after her own affairs. If the German terms were not accepted, Copenhagen would be bombed. By 6.00 a.m. the government had capitulated. There was little choice, and the only object in prolonging resistance seemed to be to convince the outside world that Denmark was not pro-German, but did genuinely want to resist.

There was, for the time being, no question of Germany's taking over the Danish government or of replacing the lawful government with one of her own choosing. Within limits, which in the course of time became increasingly constricting, the Danes were able to continue to run their own country, and the day after the occupation the two main opposition parties, the Conservatives and *Venstre*, were invited to join a national administration, which they did — though only on condition that Stauning should publicly acknowledge that it was the old ministry which was responsible for capitulating. One of the first questions which had to be negotiated with the occupying forces was their demand that any Dane caught spying or engaging in other actions damaging to the German forces should be subject to German jurisdiction. The Danes fought against this demand and they were successful in their policy of evasion, although they had to appoint a Danish 'state advocate' to deal with all such matters and to demonstrate that they had saboteurs firmly under control. In this way the courts and police remained under Danish authority for the first years of the Occupation. But military establishments came, as a matter of course, under German rule, and bases were built to carry out air raids against Britain. The Danish army was not disbanded, although no call-up was effected between April and November 1940. Such arms as there were were kept in Danish hands, and the training of officers continued.

As far as possible, the Danish authorities continued to function in their normal manner. German requests for direct contact were rejected, and the arrangement was made that all contacts should be through the Ministry for Foreign Affairs. The Danes as a whole maintained a correct and dignified attitide, co-operating where necessary in order to avoid a direct confrontation with the occupying power and the inevitable taking-over of authority which would result from this. A more or less voluntary censorship was imposed on the press and radio, and political demonstrations were forbidden. This latter measure appeared to be a move towards appeasement, though in fact it was aimed as much at preventing the Danish Nazi Party from demonstrating as at anything else. This sort of move appeared to be based on a will to co-operate, but was in fact intended as obstruction, a typical manifestation of the non-violent opposition throughout Denmark during the Occupation.

Despite a Conservative suggestion that some sort of agreement should be negotiated to define the exact limits of sovereignty, the other parties in government refused this, arguing that it would be better to deal with each problem as it arose, rather than risk a further, legally defined limitation, which Germany could ignore at will. The government, and in particular P. Munch, the Foreign Minister, preferred to argue each case for as long as possible, and only to give in when it became inevitable.

Meanwhile, the Danish people as a whole, although they maintained their dignified stance, felt that they had been let down badly by the politicians. There was widespread disillusionment with the way in which their chosen representatives had behaved, a feeling exploited by the Danish Nazi Party and also by the LS movement, who for different reasons wished to see the end of democratic government. Although the LS movement was not fundamentally Nazi, there were certain affinities, and the two parties began to join forces in their demands for a new start. Despite the ban on demonstrations, the Nazi Party organised one in Roskilde and an even larger one in Copenhagen, both of which were put down by the police without any intervention on the part of the German troops.

Nevertheless, the increasing agitation put new pressure on the government which was afraid that the Germans might make use of the opportunity to install their own puppet régime. It was not forgotten that the Danish Nazi Party had its own 'leader', Frits Clausen, though his calibre does not seem to have been such that the Germans seriously thought of letting him take over the government. Under these conditions Stauning and his Ministers decided on a government reshuffle, and it was suggested that experts should be drawn on from outside the *Rigsdag*. In particular there was a widespread desire to see the back of Munch, who was made into something of a scapegoat. Party politics were officially abandoned and a committee set up to iron out differences in outlook, and finally a composite government emerged including three non-parliamentarians, of whom Erik Scavenius, a former Foreign Minister, was by far the most important and controversial. Stauning remained Prime Minister — another example of the extent to which the Danes were allowed their head within their own country, remembering the Nazi attitude to Social Democrats.

Scavenius was scarcely a collaborator in the sense usually given to that word, but he was willing to go further in co-operation with the Germans than his predecessor Munch had been. What he was aiming at was to gain the confidence of the Germans by co-operating with them where possible, and thus maintaining the government in Danish hands. He foresaw that any other policy might well lead to the handing-over of power to extremists, or at the very least the forced inclusion in the government of members of the Danish Nazi Party. It was an audacious policy which almost went wrong at the outset. On coming into office he produced a document outlining the government's attitude to the occupying power, and ending with an expression of admiration for the German military victories and of Denmark's readiness to find her rightful place in the emerging new Europe. The Danes were incensed by such a declaration, but the Germans were far more impressed by this apparent change of heart than could have been foreseen. On 18 July, 1940, ten days after the formation of the new government and the publication of the document, they enquired whether Denmark would be interested in negotiating an economic link with Germany immediately rather than wait until the end of the war. Again Scavenius took the audacious course of answering in the affirmative, expecting months of delay before negotiations became a reality. Once more matters took a dangerous turn when on 30 July Germany suggested a customs and economic union, the broad principles of which could be worked out within five days or so, and the details within a couple of months. A reply was requested for the following day.

There was nothing for it but to continue upon the course adopted, and Scavenius persuaded his fellow Ministers to accept the suggestion of negotiations, which began on 5 August. It had been understood all along that Germany should have the dominant position, but what emerged as soon as the negotiations began was that this was less a question of a merger than a takeover bid.

German currency was to be valid in Denmark and the Danish *krone* gradually to be phased out: Germany was to negotiate all trade agreements with foreign powers and all current Danish trade agreements were to be ended. All trade barriers between the two countries were to be removed and Danish indirect taxation and duties brought into line with those in Germany. There was also a clause giving Danish and German citizens equal rights in both countries. This was a treaty which Scavenius would never be able to get accepted, and when this was pointed out to the German negotiator, his reply was merely that Denmark was free to refuse to negotiate, but that terms offered at the end of the war were likely to be less favourable. When the terms of the offer became known in Denmark there was almost unanimous resistance, even from the farmers, who stood to gain most from open access to the German market. However, the situation was eased by the opposition of German business and farming circles, who did not want the well-organised Danish farmers to compete in Germany, and so it became relatively easy to break off negotiations.

Although it is possible from a distance to see the point in Scavenius' policy, it was not easy for the Danish people at the time to see it as anything but a betrayal. The effect of this was a reinforced Danish nationalism, some of whose forms had been seen before: Grundtvigianism, with its special mixture of patriotism and Christianity, took on a new significance, while patriotic songs were sung in large numbers. Another phenomenon was *Alsang* — a form of community singing at meetings which ran into their thousands. Although political demonstrations were forbidden, the regulations could hardly be stretched to people getting together for a sing-song — even if their numbers did on one occasion reach 74,000*. Thus a feeling of Danishness akin to the great Romantic patriotic upsurge in the nineteenth century had made itself felt in the country during the course of 1940, replacing the sense of despair and disillusionment which had come immediately after 9 April. There were no open demonstrations against the Germans, but they were everywhere politely cold-

*On 1 September 1940 it was estimated that 739,000 people gathered in groups throughout the country and all sang the same patriotic song at the same time.

shouldered or ignored. No one could be in any doubt as to where the sympathies of the Danish people lay, however ambivalent their government appeared to be. And as a symbol of the people's feelings, the King made it his practice to ride alone on horseback through Copenhagen every morning.

For their part, the German authorities sought to put more pressure on the Danes to co-operate, and a period began during which the Germans little by little encroached more and more on Danish sovereignty, making use where possible of the appeasement policy of the government. An undesirable politician, such as Christmas Møller, the outspoken leader of the Conservatives, was removed from his post as Minister of Trade, and then gradually eased out of political life altogether when he continued to work actively and openly against the occupation forces. Likewise the Minister of Justice was forced out, because he was prepared to see that justice was carried out according to Danish law and custom rather than according to Nazi wishes. The Germans then demanded that a section of the Danish fleet should be handed over to them — in breach of their earlier promises. The Danish authorities tried to prevent the handover, but failed to carry the day. However, they removed all guns from the ships, which were then towed out of Copenhagen to the accompaniment of flags at half-mast — by order of the King.

Various moves were made to replace the Stauning government, one by a group of non-party Danes, and one later by the Germans — though the Danish Nazi Party was in such a state of disarray that it was difficult to see how it could ever be entrusted with power. When Christmas Møller had gone, soon to be followed by Social Democrat politicians like Hans Hedtoft-Hansen (the future Prime Minister, Hans Hedtoft), an attempt was made to remove Stauning himself, but it failed. Nevertheless, in return the government had to introduce legislation to curb espionage and anti-German propaganda, and also to discourage propaganda against the Danish Nazi Party. Yet a surprising aspect about the situation in Denmark was that despite the German occupation, the press was largely free to say what it liked about Danish internal affairs, and it made the most of its opportunity. Even so, moves to limit freedom both of speech and action were now made. Certain crimes were removed from the jurisdiction of ordinary courts, partly in order to prevent the occupying authorities from overriding Danish laws when the verdicts and punishments were not what they wanted.

The general public became more and more dispirited with the constant moves to appease the occupying forces and began to lose confidence in their government. From their own point of view, the time had come to stop giving in to German demands. The question was how to do it, and what would be the result.

This feeling was encouraged by events in 1941. With the German invasion of Russia, the demand was made that Denmark should intern all communists. There was no question of negotiations on this issue, and however little it wished to do so, the government had to give in. Only thus could it ensure something approaching tolerable conditions in Denmark itself, and Ministers were aware also that if they did not do as they were told the Germans would do it for them, and the communists would suffer a much worse fate. Yet this was by no means the last demand made after the onslaught against Russia. Originally the Germans hoped that Denmark could be persuaded to take an active part in the Russian war. The winter war against Finland had intensified Danish dislike of Russians and of communists as a whole. But Denmark stuck to her policy of neutrality and refused. As an alternative the Germans persuaded the Danes to allow the formation of a Danish Free Corps to fight on the Eastern Front. It was organised by the Danish Nazi Party, but the press and radio were given instructions to accept propaganda on its behalf, while the military authorities were told not to prevent officers or troops from joining. In the event only about 1,500 joined the corps, which had to be complemented by members of the German minority in north Schleswig.

Still worse was to come, however, when later that year Germany invited Denmark to sign the Anti-Comintern Pact. By doing so Denmark would not in fact be taking on any new commitments, but the mere signature of the pact in company with Germany's allies seemed to be a step towards a full-scale alliance with the Reich. An attempt was made to decline the invitation, but the government was finally informed that a refusal would be seen as an unfriendly act, and that Germany would no longer feel bound by the earlier agreement with Denmark. Unlike other occupied countries, which were administered by the SS, Denmark was still within the remit of the German Foreign Ministry under Ribbentrop, and was eager to remain there. At the same time, Scavenius knew that Ribbentrop wished to maintain his authority over Denmark and so he was able to insist on four clauses being inserted in the pact which expressly stated that Danish adherence only obliged Denmark to take police action against communists within her own borders, and that under no circumstances was the country to be drawn into the war against Russia. With these express reservations the pact was signed.

Popular reaction was immediate, and a large demonstration was arranged in Copenhagen, in which many arrests were made. But this was a clear pointer to the true sympathies of the people, who were afraid of being dragged into the war on the German side. The demonstration itself led to nothing, except perhaps a clearer understanding abroad of the Danish attitude. It did, however, underline a stiffening resistance to the occupation. The communists reacted immediately by going underground and setting up an illegal press, and other groups organised illegal publications under such titles as *The Free Danes* and *Free Denmark*. The circulation of these publications grew rapidly and they attacked not only Germans and Danish Nazis but also the Danish government itself for being too willing to appease the occupying forces.

At this point, on 3 May 1942, Stauning, who had been failing for some time, died and his place was taken by Vilhelm Buhl, a politician who had been outspoken in his opposition to the Anti-Comintern Pact. It looked as though there might be an end to appeasement. Buhl was not nearly so ready to compromise as had been Stauning in his final months, but the real trouble, when it came, was caused not through any political clash, but because of a telegram which King Christian X sent to Hitler. The Führer had sent a congratulatory telegram on the King's birthday, to which Christian had replied, as had been his custom, with a brief 'Thank you very much'. Hitler saw this as an insult, and despite Danish protests that nothing of the sort had been intended, made preparations to strengthen the German hand in Denmark. The top German functionaries in Denmark were replaced by hard-liners, and the demand was made for a new government, including men closer to German ideas, under the leadership of Scavenius. Scavenius declined the offer, but when the only other candidate for the post who was acceptable to the Germans refused, he was in November 1942 forced to try to form a ministry; one, moreover, which was specifically intended to pass emergency legislation giving the government wide powers.

There was a general fear that Scavenius would form a much

more pro-German administration, but in the event there were no Nazi sympathisers among his colleagues, who included some non-parliamentarians but were mainly politicians. Emergency laws were passed, but did not include the death penalty, as the Germans had wished, and a clause was inserted to the effect that the powers lapsed on a change of government unless both houses of the *Rigsdag* renewed them after such a change. Thus there was no danger of the laws constitutionally passing into the hands of a Nazi-based government. The other great fear had been that Scavenius would be forced to pass special anti-Jewish legislation, but this he promised not to do, though he told his colleagues that he would try to avoid trouble on the issue by not promoting Jews to positions where they would be likely to upset the Germans. The general public had little liking for or confidence in Scavenius, but he was prepared to go only a limited way towards pleasing the Germans. So far Denmark had been spared the suffering of much of the rest of Europe, and it was his hope that he would be able to continue his policy in what were likely to be difficult months ahead: the fortunes of war had begun to change and it might well be that Germany would be more dangerous in defeat than in victory.

Yet the new German plenipotentiary, Werner Best, was still interested in maintaining tolerable relations with Denmark, as he believed this to be in the best interests of Germany. On the other hand, the military authorities under their new area commander, General Hermann von Hanneken, were in favour of clamping down on the resistance movement, now developing in strength and efficiency. More communists were arrested, some being sent to German concentration camps, while the Germans now went on to demand that certain categories of prisoners should be handed over to them if arrested by the Danish police. The Danes again complied, though when three Danes who parachuted into Denmark from Britsh planes were arrested and handed over, so many high-ranking police officers threatened to resign if they were executed that their lives were spared.

The great surpise in Danish political life came in 1943 when Best, to boost his co-operation policy, allowed the regular elections for the *Folketing* to take place. Local elections had already been twice postponed. The elections were allowed even though the result was a foregone conclusion, because Best wanted to have a *Rigsdag* which could pass valid laws. Moreover, it suited the

Germans to show that free elections were possible in German-occupied territory. No true election campaign was allowed, and the four major parties did not compete in any normal sense, calling rather upon the electors to vote for one of the parties in the national government as a symbol of their faith in Denmark and Danish policies.The response was heartwarming: 89.5 per cent of the electorate voted, an all-time record, and of these 94 per cent voted for one or other of the coalition parties. The Danish Nazi Party received a mere 2.1 per cent of the votes cast, the LS Party only 1.2 per cent. Neither did the communists achieve their aim of persuading people to hand in blank ballot papers: only 24,000 did so.

The election results, which broadly speaking confirmed the composition of the previous *Folketing*, were to make no difference to the cabinet, which was still to be headed by Scavenius. This was known from the start, and had been a condition insisted on by the German authorities.

If one of the intentions of this election had been to show that Dano-German co-operation was possible, the result was exactly the opposite of what was expected. This massive demonstration of national solidarity gave a new impetus to the resistance movement, which now became more accepted by the people as a whole and was also better equipped and organised, thanks to active help from Britain. It was apparent that Germany was going to lose the war, and Danes felt the need more and more strongly to demonstrate to the Allies that they were in no sense fellow-travellers of the Nazis. The thought of being classed as a German ally was repugnant, despite the appeasement policy of the government and however much easier life had been as a result. Consequently the resistance movement deliberately set about undermining government policy. Everyone was aware that an active resistance could lead to a takeover by the Germans, but whatever the implications of such a step for the immediate future, it was thought preferable to classification as a German ally. Together with a vast increase in the volume and effectiveness of sabotage, a wave of strikes hit the country, first in Esbjerg, then more violently in Odense and in other major towns.

As was to be expected, the government tried to stop the unrest, but its exhortations went unheeded, as did those of the unions and even of the King himself. This was wind in the sails of the German military authorities, who had all along wished to overrule Best's attempts at co-operation, and finally it was decided in Berlin that unless the Danes could put their own house in order, the Germans would have to do it for them. It must not be forgotten that the Danish army still existed, and further, that it was armed, and this factor was of some importance in German plans. Germany was afraid of an invasion in Jutland, which would find them with a built-in enemy army in their midst. They thus demanded that all weapons should be handed over, though the requirement was only partly met.

Finally, on orders from Berlin, Best demanded that the Danes themselves should declare a state of emergency; that assemblies of more than five people should be prohibited; that the death penalty should be introduced for sabotage; that a curfew should be proclaimed. Moreover, Odense was to pay a million *kroner* for an attack on a German soldier. This was the moment the resistance movement had foreseen for some time, the moment when no further appeasement was possible. The Danish government and the King, fully aware of the probable consequences, refused to comply, and waited for the German reaction. At the same time troops were told to offer no resistance if an attempt were made to disarm them, and a similar order was given to the navy.

The reaction was not long in coming. At 4 a.m. the following morning, 29 August 1943, the Germans introduced a state of emergency and took over full administrative powers. The plans for disarming the Danish army were put into effect, and though some resistance was made, it could not last for long. As for the navy, although orders had come from the political authorities not to resist, none had been given not to scuttle or try to slip away to Sweden. The commander-in-chief, Admiral Vedel, gave precisely these orders, and a large proportion of the fleet was either sunk or, where practicable, sailed to Swedish waters.

As on 9 April 1940, the Danes awoke on 29 August 1943 to find their conditions of life changed. All the measures demanded by the Germans a few days before were now a reality and the German forces were there to make sure they were carried out. Many prominent politicans and others thought to sympathise with the resistance were interned, though most were released within a few months. The army was likewise interned and soon demobilised. The press and radio were subjected to censorship of a much stricter nature than anything they had experienced before, and the censor was German. The period of appeasement was at an end, and what were known in Denmark as 'Norwegian conditions' seemed imminent.

Yet again, however, the worst was avoided. It was the intention of the German authorities either to have a new government appointed or to put in a purely German administration, and Best asked Niels Svenningsen, the civil service head of the Foreign Ministry, to put his proposal before the politicians. But the politicians were aware now that the time for negotiation had passed, and they finally said they were unable to form a government. The King refused to nominate a cabinet from outside the *Folketing*, as this would be contrary to the constitution. However, Svenningsen came to an arrangement with the occupying forces whereby the country was to be run by the civil service heads of department, who in fact issued instructions which had the force of law. Various of the leading judges had stated that if these instructions were contested in the courts, they would be considered legally valid. So for a period Denmark's civil service chiefs had both executive and legislative power in the country, a power which they in practice exercised in close consultation with the politicians. The main contact between the Germans and this new form of Danish administration was Svenningsen who brilliantly carried out his difficult task. Again it was a case of giving in to many of the German demands, but in some instances it was possible for the individual concerned to argue that something was outside his sphere of competence; in others the general instructions were issued by the Germans, while the working-out of details was left to the Danes. As a consequence the final draft was less inhumane than had originally been intended.

In one field, however, the German military now had a free hand. In what had for a long time been a contest between the Himmler and the Ribbentrop factions in Germany, the former had argued for the deportation of the Danish Jews. With the takeover on 29 August, these forces were now in the ascendant and orders were issued from Berlin that Danish Jews should be arrested and deported. Best, who knew that this was one thing the government had always refused to countenance, and who was aware of the probable reaction of Danes if it happened, fought against the plans, but was overruled. This same man who, as political leader of the German occupying authorities, was a target of general hatred, allowed his shipping attaché G. F. Duckwitz — himself an anti-Nazi — to leak the plans to both Danish and Swedish politicians. It became possible to warn Danish Jews of what was coming, and by the time the German arrests started, almost all had disappeared. Of the approximately 7,000 Jews in Denmark, only 472 were arrested and deported, and of these only 52 died in concentration camps. The remainder were hidden by friends and were then for the most part smuggled out of the country to Sweden in an operation which started on an amateur basis, but quickly became well organised.

Despite the relative failure of this action, it turned the Danish people even more against the Germans. It gave a new impetus to sabotage, which some sections of the public had so far viewed with disfavour, and it gave new impetus to the development of the resistance movement as a whole. The various groups hitherto making up the movement were combined under what became known as the Danish Freedom Council, which assumed, and by the population at large was given, something approaching governmental authority. In conjunction with London the Council set about organising an efficient underground army ready to co-operate with any invading forces and ultimately to be under the control of SHAEF. The Danish army, which had been interned on 29 August and released after the anti-Jewish action, made a welcome contribution to these activities, and while the majority stayed in Denmark, some officers went to Sweden to form a corps ready to take over when Denmark was liberated.

This more elaborate organisation stepped up efficiency in opposing the occupying forces, and acts of sabotage increased rapidly in both number and effectiveness. They encompassed everything from small supply dumps to major factories, and they also included the murder of any Danes known to be betraying resistance workers to the Germans. These informers were a great menace to the Resistance and there was no other way of dealing with them. For their part the Germans reacted by counter-sabotage, blowing up non-military buildings in Copenhagen such as the Students' Union and the Conservative head office. In the end Tivoli itself was devastated by fire. In retaliation for the murder of informers orders were given to the Germans, and more particularly to their Danish supporters, to murder chosen political figures and even innocent members of the population, Kaj Munk being the most famous of those who suffered in this way.

Such was the tension that on 25 June 1944 a curfew was introduced in Copenhagen from 8 p.m. to 5 a.m. every day, while assemblies of more than five people were once more forbidden. The reaction to this was immediate. On the following day the workers at Burmeister and Wain's shipyards stopped work at noon, in order, they said, to have eight hours of freedom before the curfew. The following day others followed suit, and the movement led to a spontaneous general strike in the capital. Martial law was introduced, but in the end, after stopping supplies of water, gas, and electricity; cutting off the city from the outside world; and preparing to starve the Copenhageners into submission, Best was persuaded to remove his terror squads from the streets and to allow a return to normal conditions. On hearing the promise of an end to the terror, the Danes resumed work, after one of the most spectacular demonstrations of national solidarity of the war.

Aware of the attitude of the Danish people and fearing — quite rightly — that the police were working hand in glove with the resistance movement, the Germans now decided that the police must be disbanded and deported. In September they struck; but, like the Jews before them, the police suddenly vanished, even if not with quite such success. Some 2,000 were arrested and deported before they could go underground, while the remainder made a useful addition to the resistance forces. From September 1944 to the end of the war, Denmark was thus without a police force of any sort, though local vigilante groups were formed to try to prevent the increasing and inevitable number of crimes.

By this time it was obvious that potential power in Denmark was divided between the politicians, whose function was now severely limited, and the Freedom Council. As a result of the popular strike in Copenhagen the two factions, who had hitherto had little sympathy for each other, recognised the need to co-operate and especially to come to some arrangement about the formation of a post-liberation government. Negotiations resulted in a decision to form a government consisting of nine politicians and nine members of the resistance movement, together with representatives of the Danes who had served overseas. Under pressure from Russia it was decided that no member of the new government should have been a member of the Scavenius administration. The Prime Minister was to be Buhl. It was hoped to avoid the conflicts which had arisen in other liberated countries, and which in some cases — notably Greece — had resulted in civil war.

There is no need to dwell here on the violence and bloodshed of the final months of the occupation. Suffice it to say that as the transport of arms from Britain increased, there was a highly organised and well-equipped partisan army in Denmark which set about sabotaging everything of use to the Germans. The railways suffered especially, when the Germans started transporting troops from Norway back to Germany, but factories and stores were severely damaged as well. Informers were liquidated in increasing numbers, and reprisals were made in a crescendo of violence and brutality. The Gestapo was active and successful in arresting leaders of the Resistance, and there was some fear that the movement might be entirely broken. These fears were, however, dispelled when the three Gestapo headquarters in Jutland, Copenhagen, and Funen were bombed, and most of the archives destroyed.

Fighting on Danish territory was expected but little ensued. There was some sniping in Copenhagen immediately after the capitulation, as Danish Nazi groups who felt they had nothing to lose were rounded up. Bornholm was the only part of the country where any serious damage was done. The German forces there refused to surrender to the Russians, although they were prepared to give in to the British. Consequently the Russians bombed Rønne and Neksø, causing both casualties and considerable damage, until the German commander was replaced by another senior officer who then handed over to the invading forces.

In many respects the Danes suffered less both nationally and personally from the effects of the war than did the people in other occupied countries. Until August 1943 the régime was tolerable and life could go on in many ways as normal. Thereafter things became more insecure. The fact that the government of the country, together with the police force, had remained in Danish hands, had helped to alleviate what could otherwise have been an unpleasant and dangerous situation. In the same way, food had been more plentiful in Denmark than in other occupied countries, and the farming industry had succeeded in maintaining a high level of production despite the difficulty of obtaining fertiliser and fodder. Thus, although food was rationed, it was possible to maintain a high level of nutrition. On the other hand, industrial products were in much shorter supply: although Germany provided a good deal of raw material necessary for industry, it was with a view to supplying her own war needs and the Danes had to be satisfied with what they could get.

This does not, however, signify widespread prosperity in Denmark. There was certainly a great deal of money in circulation, but at the same time Danish exports to Germany — for which a clearing account was responsible and for which the Germans often failed to pay — were far in excess of imports. As a result of the plentiful supply of money and the scarcity of goods, inflation set in, though it was brought under control by taxation, the encouragement of savings, and also by an increase in the exchange rate. It has been estimated that Denmark's economic situation in 1945 had fallen back to about the same as in 1930. It had not been an entirely cheap war for the Danes.

9   1945–1985: AFFLUENCE AND BEYOND

The Immediate Post-war Problems

The new government under Vilhelm Buhl, who had been Prime Minister once before but forced out by the Germans, was faced with many difficult tasks when it came to power on 5 May 1945. Although not appointed in accordance with the constitution, it had the stated aim of working within the constitution and returning to full constitutional normality as soon as possible.

A return to normality meant a thorough clearing-out of the backlog of the Occupation, the punishment of war criminals, and the restoration of some sort of balance in the country's finances. The state was left with a debt of some 8,000 million *kroner* at the end of the war, and at the same time it was known that great quantities of money had been earned by more or less legal means but never declared during the Occupation. Even before the liberation, the National Bank had arranged for banknotes to be printed, and thus it was possible to introduce these and invalidate old ones as early as 23 July 1945. The process of changing currency disclosed that something in the region of 2,700 million *kroner* had never been declared to the authorities. How much more was simply destroyed it is impossible to say. There was still too much latent buying power in the country, which was desperately short of goods, and a heavy tax was placed upon fortunes earned and saved since 1939, while a high percentage had also to be deposited as a loan to the state. These taxes went a good way towards paying off the debt which the state had incurred to the National Bank thanks to its guarantee for the money drawn by the Germans on their special account and never repaid. Much of this money had in fact formed the basis of the fortunes made, and so a sort of rough justice followed.

Another sort of rough justice was being done to the known collaborators and Danish Nazis from the war period. In all some 34,000 were arrested at one time or another, and some had to be punished. But laws had not been drawn up for this sort of situation, and so it was necessary to pass legislation allowing for the

169

punishment of war criminals. Discussion in the *Folketing* took in both the principle of introducing retrospective legislation and the demands for the reintroduction of the death penalty. Eventually, doubts were overcome, and retrospective legislation providing for the death penalty in certain cases was passed. Under these laws 78 were condemned to death and 46 actually executed.

This new legislation, passed in a short time when passions were high, was harsh indeed. Those found guilty of crimes faced a minimum penalty of four years' imprisonment and a complete loss of civil rights, which in practice meant the complete ostracism of anyone found guilty. For lesser offences a law was subsequently passed providing for more lenient sentences, leaving to judges the decision whether to condemn guilty persons to the loss of civil rights. However, being in effect emergency legislation, these laws did not provide for all contingencies, and judges often found themselves obliged to mete out harsher punishments than they felt were merited. In time they did in fact begin to give shorter terms of imprisonment, and the law had to be revised, while those condemned in the first outburst of zeal had their sentences reviewed and in many cases reduced. The Resistance was opposed to this clemency, and would have liked to see even harsher punishments, so much so that it even carried out a brief occupation of one of the prisons housing political prisoners, with the intention of itself ensuring justice.

The Resistance was dissatisfied not only with the treatment of war criminals, but in general with the return of the pre-war politicians and their policies, even though it had never formulated a political policy itself. And with the return of the politicians came a return of unemployment, though the politicians were not directly responsible for it. Whereas there had been the opportunity for work during the war, there were few openings for exports so far, and trade took some time in starting. As a consequence it was obvious that unemployment would increase. Dissatisfaction with the politicians came, too, from a new trade agreement with Britain, under the terms of which the Danes were to receive much lower prices for their agricultural produce than had been paid by the Germans. The agreed minimum of 4.18 *kroner* per kilo was also well below the price other countries were paying for Danish butter. But Britain offered an assured market for Danish produce, and as the prices agreed were minimum ones, the prospect of an increase seemed reasonable. It soon became clear that the liberation government could not last indefinitely, as it was a coalition of too many divergent views, from conservative to communist. During the summer of 1945 attempts were made to amalgamate the communist and Social Democrat parties, but the efforts led nowhere. By the autumn conditions were such that the only way out was an election, which was accordingly called for 30 October.

Election and New Groupings

It was probably a fateful turn of events for Danish political lfe that a general election was not called immediately after the liberation, for when it did come, people were tired of the wrangling that had inevitably followed the Occupation and were beginning to look more to the Denmark of the future than to the occupied Denmark of the past five years. Accordingly, although the election resulted in a change in the balance of political power, it was a quite unambiguous statement that Danes intended to remain on the path they had been following before the war. There was no re-thinking of the governmental system, which some of the Resistance had been hoping for.

Nevertheless, the election brought a striking leap forward for the communists, whose representation rose from the 3 seats of 1939 to 18. The reasons for this were manifold. Although the wartime government had been a coalition, it was dominated by the Social Democrats and they duly received their share of blame for the policies which had led to the Occupation and the state of affairs while it lasted. This had forced many of their more left-wing supporters into the commmunist camp, at the same time as the communists had received a good deal of public sympathy for their treatment during the Occupation, together with some reflected glory from the Russian war effort.

With this drift to the Left taking place, middle-class Social Democrats were leaving the party; because the party itself was moving leftwards, perhaps trying to steal some of the Communists' thunder by putting forward a far more radical and socialist policy than it had done under the moderate leadership of Stauning. The confidence which the middle classes had developed in Stauning's party was dispersed by the more openly class-based policies put forward by the new leadership under Hans Hedtoft-Hansen. Thus

the Social Democrats lost heavily in the election, their representation going down from 66 seats to 48. Moreover, the party as a
whole had lost the support of the Radicals, thanks to its more
extreme policy, which meant an end to the co-operation which had
for so long been a feature of political life.The Radicals now moved
more towards *Venstre*.

The moderate votes lost to the Social Democrats went mainly to
Venstre, which also picked up many former Conservative votes
both because of Christmas Møller's unpopular trade agreement
with Britain and his hard words about the profits made by farmers
during the war (*Venstre* was still a party based on the farming
community), and because of his refusal to work for a revision of
the frontier with Germany. He wisely maintained that the frontier
was fixed once and for all, but this attitude lost him much Conservative support. In fact, *Venstre* now stood as the *conservative*
party, not least owing to the attitude of its leader, Knud
Kristensen, who had demonstratively left the government when
Scavenius was appointed Prime Minister, and yet had stood out
against the extreme demands for vengeance after the Occupation.
He seemed to symbolise something immutable for the Danes, and
it was not unnatural that he was chosen as the new Prime Minister.
When the Social Democrats refused to form a government, the
choice fell upon *Venstre*, the second largest party in the new
Folketing. The Conservatives and Radicals both refused to join,
but promised their support, and so 1945, a year in which some
polarisation of votes took place, saw the formation of a government which, despite its name, was based on moderate conservative principles.

The new *Venstre* government under Knud Kristensen was
nevertheless a minority government, the first of several in the
immediate post-war years, none of which in the event proved to be
particularly stable. It used tacit Conservative and Radical support
to embark on a policy of reconstruction. The heavy taxation it had
to impose formed only a part of the efforts, largely successful, to
improve the country's economy. With its social-liberal outlook the
new government was also prepared to make a start on social
reform. A new law was passed providing for state aid for building
projects in an effort to ease the acute housing shortage after years
when no flats or houses had been built. This government also had
to negotiate on trade with Britain in an effort to win better prices
for its agricultural produce, and, when the attempts failed, it

introduced a system of support for agriculture which was further developed in subsequent years.

While the government, broadly speaking, ran into little opposition in its internal policies, it met difficulties in the external field, and these finally led to its downfall. The one question still sure of making Danish feelings run high was that of Schleswig. Although the liberation government had expressly stated that it considered the Dano-German border as permanent, there were plenty of Danes who saw their opportunity to move the border south once more, and voices were raised demanding an end to German rule in Schleswig. This coincided with a rapid growth in the pro-Danish voices in south Schleswig itself, partly perhaps as a result of the disastrous years they had experienced, partly as a reaction to the resettlement there of refugees from eastern Germany who threatened completely to swamp such Danish influence as still existed.

Knud Kristensen, the Prime Minister, declared himself in favour of making a change. If the wave of pro-Danish sentiment in southern Schleswig was genuine – and Danish supporters won roughly half the seats in local elections and seven in the Schleswig-Holstein *Landtag* — it could scarcely be denied the right to express itself in a referendum, though, added Kristensen, this should be at some time in the future when the immediate crisis was over. The matter was debated in the press and in the *Folketing*, and finally the British government, as one of the occupying powers, asked Denmark for an outright statement on what her wishes were, giving the Danes the choice of three alternatives: of exchanging the minorities on both sides of the border; of deciding the frontier on the basis of a referendum; or of moving the border without reference to the wishes of the people. The Danish reply was that Denmark would not herself demand a frontier revision, but that the population of southern Schleswig should be given the right to decide its own future.

Despite apparent agreement on this reply within the *Folketing*, certain members, including Knud Kristensen himself, continued to argue for a frontier revision, though Kristensen maintained that he was agitating for this as a private individual, not as Prime Minister, a point which led to his downfall. By adopting this standpoint he created so much personal opposition among the parties which wholeheartedly supported the moderate line of the reply to Britain, that the Radicals — never a party with pronounced nationalist tendencies — put down a motion of no confidence in him, and in October 1947 that motion was carried by 80 votes to 66, making a general election inevitable.

The Return of the Social Democrats

The paradoxical result of the election held on 28 October 1947 was a resounding victory for *Venstre*, but a government was formed by the Social Democrats under the leadership of Hans Hedtoft, as he now called himself. It was a minority government which was only enabled to govern with the help of the varying degrees of support it received from the Radicals and Communists. Accordingly, the Social Democrats were forced to temper the far-reaching programme which they had introduced in 1945 and carry out instead a moderate policy for which they could count on general support. Most important among the purely internal measures of the first Hedtoft government was a new Act which enabled the state to buy larger farms and estates as they came on the market, in order to provide more land for smallholders. This was in fact the continuation and culmination of a series of laws aimed at helping smallholders, which had begun with the first Smallholdings Act in 1899.

International Developments

Of greater international significance, however, was the fact that during Hedtoft's period in office Denmark finally brought about a complete reversal of her traditional policy of neutrality. Moreover, it was done by a government led by the Social Democrats, who were traditionally in favour of neutrality and disarmament. A step away from strict neutrality had in fact already been taken when the Danish *Rigsdag* unanimously decided to join the United Nations with the setting-up of that organisation in June 1945. It will be remembered that there had been doubts and reservations when the country had joined the League of Nations, and in particular the sanctions clause had caused apprehension. This time there were no such hesitations, and Denmark joined the United Nations without knowing the exact and final consequences of the move.

This was the time of the establishment of the International Monetary Fund and the International Bank, both of which Denmark joined as a means to industrial and financial recovery after the war. When in 1947 the Marshall Plan was launched, still more aid came to Denmark and the country seemed all set for recovery.

This period also saw the division between East and West becoming more and more painfully apparent, and although Denmark rearmed sufficiently to be able to make a modest contribution to the occupation of Germany, it was the government's intention to stay outside the two political blocs, in the hope of building bridges between them. The change in attitude came with the Communist takeover in Czechoslovakia in February 1948. Here was another small country which had attempted to remain neutral and build bridges being crushed by a major power. Finland, too, was subjected to Russian pressures and there were fears that a similar fate might be in store for that country, which was considered to be closely akin to Scandinavia, if not theoretically part of it. When the Brussels Treaty was signed between Britain, France, Belgium, the Netherlands, and Luxembourg in March 1948, founding the Western European Union — in theory a defensive treaty against a resurgent Germany — Denmark was not invited to become a party to it; but the three Scandinavian countries, on the initiative of Sweden, started negotiations aimed at instituting a Scandinavian defence treaty. Although there was plenty of goodwill, it proved impossible to reach agreement owing to the widely different views of Norway and Sweden.

At the same time the WEU powers, with Canada and the United States, were negotiating to widen WEU into an Atlantic alliance, the result of which was to be the North Atlantic Treaty Organisation. It was the hope of the Scandinavians that if they succeeded in formulating a defence treaty which kept Scandinavia outside both the major blocs the USA would help them with arms. The Americans, however, informed them that this was not to be expected, and when negotiations among the Scandinavian countries broke down, Norway decided to join NATO, and was later followed by Denmark, after Sweden had indicated a lack of interest in a bilateral defence treaty with Denmark. It had been a choice between complete isolation or a renunciation of neutrality, and the government chose the latter course. In doing so it had the support of the majority of the *Folketing*, 119 members voting to join NATO as against only 23 opposing the motion. Denmark insisted on regarding NATO as a purely defensive organisation, and although the Danes have been prompt in making their contributions, they have consistently refused to allow the country to be used as a base for long-range rockets which could be employed for offensive purposes, and have likewise and for the same reasons refused to allow atomic weapons to be stationed on Danish territory or to be flown over it. This applies also to Greenland, and when in 1968 an American B-52 bomber with atomic bombs on board crashed near Thule, there was considerable indignation at what appeared to be a breach of the treaty.

The Hedtoft government had been able to bring about a volteface in traditional Danish policy, thanks largely to the tactical position it enjoyed. Economic circumstances meant that Denmark was enjoying some prosperity at the beginning of 1949. Nevertheless, just as Denmark had come to realise the impossibility of staying aloof from the influence of the great powers any longer, so she was to realise within the year that economically, too, she was at the mercy of circumstances beyond her control. The change in the economic situation coupled with Hedtoft's attempts to cope with it brought the government down.

For the first two years after the war, Denmark had been in serious economic difficulties, having completely lost one of her main export markets, Germany, and experiencing difficulty in selling to the other, Britain. Because of its own economic troubles, the British government insisted on paying low prices for Danish goods, but demanded top prices for its own exports. A special credit was certainly made to Denmark, but by 1947 the Danish debt was so large that Britain had to put a stop to it. The Danes had therefore to accept more rationing than ever and the economic situation worsened, while a hard winter and a hot, dry summer in 1947, resulting in a poor harvest, did nothing to diminish the crisis. As Britain still refused to increase the price paid for Danish goods, the Danes for their part stopped all exports to Britain in September 1947, and sold instead to countries willing to pay the price they wanted. During the course of 1948, however, Britain declared herself prepared to pay more for Danish produce and the traditional relationship was re-established.

This was in itself a help to the Danish economy, but the real boost came from the Marshall Plan and the establishment of OEEC. Between 1948 and 1953 Denmark received $278 million in Marshall aid, most of it as a direct gift, so that the economy improved rapidly until September 1949 when Britain devalued the pound. Because of the close ties with Britain, Denmark was forced to follow suit, but the economy suffered. The difficulties were compounded the following year when the Korean War broke out and was followed by an increase in world, particularly dollar, prices. As a direct result of this and the general fear of another major war, Denmark agreed to spend another 400 million *kroner* on armaments and civil defence over the next two years.

Rationing had been largely abolished by this time, though import regulations were still in force. The government was pressed by *Venstre*, with its free-trade tradition, to liberalise commerce, and the pressure was increased from OEEC in December 1949. Faced with a very large trade deficit the government felt obliged to ask for powers to sharpen its trade regulations, but the *Folketing* refused to countenance such a move. For this reason a new election was called for 5 September 1950.

Internal Pressures

Venstre still seemed to be favoured by the electoral law, and so in 1948 the government had it amended yet again to ensure that the party only received its fair share of seats in proportion to the votes cast. *Venstre* thus seemed bound to lose seven seats in the 1950 election. In fact it lost 17.

Leaving the Communists aside, the overall result of the election was a tie — the Social Democrat-Radical group and the non-socialist group receiving 71 seats each; and after some negotiations, the Hedtoft government was reinstated with very little change. It was the Prime Minister's aim to deal with the economic situation in a manner acceptable to all parties, and in particular he meant to implement a defence policy with the support of *Venstre* and the Conservatives. General agreement to co-operate within the *Folketing* seemed likely. To everyone's surprise, the government fell within a week.

It fell on a technicality after an attack from an unexpected quarter. The tiny Single Tax Party had gone to the polls on a programme calling for the abolition of all remaining wartime restrictions and rationing. Emboldened by its own election gains, it called for the immediate abolition of butter rationing. With an eye to the need to export as much as possible, the government refused, but was then faced with a *Venstre*-Conservative compromise resolution calling for the end to rationing 'as soon as possible'. The government could not accept this either and when a division was forced, it lost by one vote. Although he could well have weathered the storm, Hedtoft announced his intention to resign both for personal reasons and also because he was not getting much-needed trade union support for his austerity programme.

It was the first time for forty years that a government on being defeated had resigned without calling an election. The first-ever *Venstre*-Conservative coalition succeeded it, previous *Venstre* governments having had only at most tacit Conservative support. The leader of *Venstre*, Erik Eriksen, became Prime Minister, with the Conservative leader, Ole Bjørn Kraft, as Foreign Minister.

The new government was still faced with the problem of strengthening the economy and continued the deflationary policies started by the Hedtoft government earlier in the year. There were increases in direct taxation, while a system of compulsory savings was introduced and then extended in 1951. Ministers would have liked to suspend the cost of living index, by which incomes were regulated, but the Social Democrats and Radicals were opposed to this, and the government, being in a minority, was forced to give in. On the other hand, a compromise was reached by which some of the extra taxes were excluded from the index. Despite vigorous complaints, especially from the farmers who felt they were being singled out to carry a heavy burden, the new taxes worked, and by the second half of 1951 the economic situation had improved. By the beginning of 1953 the large deficit of previous years had been turned into a healthy surplus and Denmark was at last able to comply with the OEEC requirements for liberalistion of trade between members.

A New Constitution

Although the minority government could count on Social Democrat support for much of what it proposed to do, the Radicals were firmly opposed to the foreign policy formulated by what became known as the Atlantic Pact parties — the Conservatives, *Venstre*, and the Social Democrats. There was thus always the chance that they might seize some opportunity to bring the ministry down. With such a possibility in mind, the government let it be known that it was planning a revision of the constitution, a subject long close to Radical hearts. From the start it had declared itself prepared to accept the single-chamber principle and had also pronounced in favour of reducing the voting age to 23. The Communists opposed the constitution as a whole because it contained a signficant clause allowing for some renunciation of sovereignty: 'Powers vested in the authorities of the Realm under this Constitution Act may, to such extent as may be provided by statute, be delegated to international authorities set up by mutual agreement with other states for the promotion of international rules of law and co-operation.' The main stumbling-block was, however, the question of voting age, and finally it was decided to put it to a referendum of all citizens over 21, which was the other age proposed. Next, the proposals were carried in both the *Landsting* and the *Folketing*, after which an election was necessary so that a new *Rigsdag* could also pass them. This also went without a hitch. In the referendum which followed, those in favour far outnumbered those against, but only 45.76 per cent of those qualified voted in favour, a mere 0.76 per cent above the necessary proportion. The majority approved 23 as the new voting age. The new constitution came into force on the traditional constitution date, 5 June, 1953.

The main innovation was the abolition of the *Landsting* and the introduction of a single-chamber parliament, the *Folketing*. In order to remove the obvious objections to a single chamber, however, provision was made for referenda to be held in certain circumstances on controversial legislation. Other provisions were made for the extension of the democratic system in Denmark, including the appointment of an ombudsman on the Swedish pattern. This was a special wish of the Radicals and although both the Social Democrats and the Conservatives opposed it, *Venstre* accepted the proposal, the wisdom of which has since met with general acknowledgement.

Appendixed to the Constitutional Act there was a short Act providing for the possibility of female succession to the throne. Not only was this innovation logical in a country with widespread principles of equality, but it also gave expression to popular sentiment. King Frederik IX, who had succeeded Christian X on the latter's death in 1947, and his wife, Ingrid of Sweden, had three daughters, Princesses Margrethe, Benedikte, and Anne-Marie, and there was a general desire to see the eldest named as her father's successor.

The 1953 constitution paid special attention to Greenland, which was made an integral part of the kingdom of Denmark with the right to send two members of parliament to Copenhagen. This far-reaching change meant a start on a complete revision of Greenland's social pattern which had remained almost untouched for centuries. Danish law was to be introduced to replace the local customs, and an attempt was made to improve the material lot of the Greenlanders and also to bring the benefits of modern industrialisation.

The earlier 1953 election had been called only to pass the new constitution; the second election, based on the new electoral law, took place before the constitution could be fully implemented, on 22 September. Together with the lowering of the voting age had gone an increase in the number of *Folketing* deputies, from 149 to 179; two came from Greenland and two from the Faroes.

One of the imponderables was the number of new voters, but the overall picture of Danish politics did not change to any appreciable extent. *Venstre*, becoming perhaps less exclusively associated with agrarian interests, made some gains, while the Conservatives lost a few votes. The Social Democrats made progress, which was outweighed by Radical losses.

Little Change in Party Constellations

Earlier in the year the Radicals had stood by the *Venstre–Conservative* coalition in order to ensure the passage of the constitutional proposals, but they now withdrew their support. Opposed in particular to the Conservatives and their foreign and defence policies, they were prepared to support a *Venstre* government, but *Venstre's* leader, Erik Eriksen, remained faithful to his new alliance with the Conservatives. At the same time, when it became obvious that the Social Democrats intended to form a new government, the Radicals, disliking that party's loyalty to NATO and the economic policies it would have to adopt, refused to enter a coalition, promising tacit support instead and thus again effectively holding a balance of power but without responsibility for government policy.

When the Social Democrats came to power, the economy was in reasonable shape, but unemployment was too high, and the government sought to reduce it by stimulating production. The result was a rapid overheating of the system and a new financial crisis. *Venstre* and the Conservatives refused to support the remedies proposed by the government, who thus had to adopt a policy which met the approval of the Radicals; in practice a cut-back on defence spending. In return the Radicals were prepared to support a strongly deflationary policy. This was not sufficient, but before further moves could be made, the Prime Minister, Hans Hedtoft, died in January 1955 and was succeeded by his Foreign Minister, H. C. Hansen.

Hansen continued as far as possible to follow his predecessor's policy, but in so doing began to lose working-class support. This occurred just at the time when the regular reviews of agreements between the unions and employers were due, and the negotiations now turned out to be protracted and difficult. By March 1956 no accord had been reached and strikes were called which gradually paralysed the entire country. However, when the strikes spread to petrol- and oil-workers, the government stepped in and passed legislation forbidding the strike in the petroleum industry. A general compromise agreement was drawn up by the offical mediator and accepted by the employers. Although the plan gave considerable benefits to the workers, they rejected it and continued to strike. Again the government acted and imposed the mediator's proposals on industry as a whole. The unions and workers were furious at this, feeling they had been let down by a government from which they might have expected more sympathy. The Communists thereupon began to fish in troubled waters, but just as they were showing signs of progress, the Russian suppression of the Hungarian uprising turned the tide against them once more. As in 1948 after the Communist takeover in Czechoslovakia, people reacted sharply to this show of force.

In the midst of these difficulties and those occasioned by the Suez crisis of 1956, the government turned its attention to some new, far-reaching social legislation. Although received by some 55 per cent of the population over the age of 65, the old-age pension was essentially intended as a help to those in need, and in addition it was generally considered to be too low. Thus the Social Democrats, with widespread support from the other parties, legislated for retirement pensions for everyone over pensionable age, coupled with supplementary benefits for those in need of them. Pensions were no longer to be seen as charity, but were now the legal entitlement of all citizens.

Three-party Government: a Time of Change

According to the constitution, an election had to be held in 1957, and by that time people were less interested in future pension benefits than in the urgent economic problems facing the country. The National Bank's foreign debts had almost doubled to 275 million *kroner* in the first five months of the year and were a welcome stick with which the Conservatives and *Venstre* could beat their political opponents, arguing that on a previous occasion they had managed to re-establish a healthy economy, and now was the time to do it again. It was a good argument and they certainly won some votes on it. But with 75 seats in all they did not win an absolute majority. Social Democrat strength now stood at 70, while the Radicals kept their representation at 14.

A completely new political situation had now developed, as the Radicals no longer held a balance of power. They were not sufficient to ensure a Social Democrat majority alone, nor were they prepared to support a *Venstre*–Conservative coalition. The single Tax Party had made considerable gains, but its support would not be sufficient to ensure a strong minority *Venstre*–Conservative government. The crisis was unprecedented and despite recent antipathies between the Single Tax Party and both the Radicals and Social Democrats, the outcome of negotiations was a coalition government based on these three parties, with H. C. Hansen as Prime Minister. It became known as the 'Triangle Government'.

There were protests from *Venstre* and the Conservatives at its formation, but there was little they could do to prevent what was, for the first time in many years, a majority government, provided the three partners could agree. They did agree, largely because of Hansen's sensitive and tactful leadership. Their first task was still to deal with the financial situation, and they were able to introduce stern measures without looking over their shoulders at the other parties. Moreover, they followed a far-sighted policy. Unpopular though it was, the government introduced a scheme for enforced savings, which took some 400 million *kroner* out of circulation. This was coupled with investment incentives for industry which were to have considerable effect. The opposition parties argued in favour of import deposits as being a more effective means of reducing expenditure, but they had no success. These new measures to save the economy were accompanied by a fall in world prices, so that industry was helped from two directions, and this change saw the start of a period of hitherto unknown prosperity in Denmark.

It fell to the Triangle Government to lead Denmark at a time when Europe was dividing into different economic units. The gradual movement towards Nordic co-operation which had begun before 1939 and was fostered by events during the war, had led to the formation in 1952 of the Nordic Council. This is in no way a supra-governmental organisation, but a conference of members of parliament from Denmark, Iceland, Norway, Sweden and, from 1955, Finland, who meet at regular intervals in the member countries. Specifically excluded from making suggestions relevant to either foreign or defence policy, the Council produced many useful ideas for co-ordinating internal legislation in the Scandinavian countries, and in 1954 its proposals led to the formation of a common labour market in Scandinavia. Passport restrictions were removed, first for Scandinavian citizens and subsequently for all others, while more recently Scandinavian citizens have been given access to social benefits in each other's countries. As has already been seen, negotiations in 1948 aimed at forming a defence union in Scandinavia came to nothing, but the success of the movement towards Nordic co-operation in other fields led to the idea of a Nordic common market.

However, events elsewhere in Europe overtook these plans for Nordic co-operation in the mid-1950s, when the EEC was being discussed. As she exported a large percentage of her agricultural produce to EEC countries, Denmark was faced with an uncertain future. So difficult and delicate was the situation that when Britain and Sweden took the initiative to form EFTA, Denmark was at first somewhat reserved, fearing that an economic war might result, with damaging consequences, whatever the outcome might be for others. On receiving assurances from the other countries that this was in no way the intention behind EFTA proposals, Denmark decided to take part in the negotiations, and subsequently became a member of EFTA. One of the immediate results of this process was the end to negotiations for a Nordic Common Market.

Once the coalition government had made up its mind on joining EFTA, it was able to proceed without difficulty. It was the strongest government for many years, and thanks to this position of strength and to a rapid improvement in Denmark's economic position, it was also able to propose and carry out a number of important social and educational reforms. The change in the economic climate after 1957 was partly, but not entirely, the achievement of this government. The fact that after 1957 the country considered it respectable to seek and take up foreign loans was a point very much in its favour. An immediate improvement in the balance of payments was the result, for hitherto Denmark had used a good deal of the money she had earned to pay off long-standing debts. At the same time foreign capital began to flow into Denmark, especially from the major American oil companies. Such a financial influx provided the means for capital investment in Danish industry. The sudden industrial boom furnished jobs for the sizeable force of unemployed, 10.2 per cent in 1957. Yet, as most of the early deflationary measures were still in force, internal buying power was for a time kept down, and most of the initial increase in production went to exports. For a number of years, then, there was a period of unprecedented wealth in Denmark, until in 1961 the economy became strained, and a fresh deflation was necessary.

Meanwhile, however, the government's social and educational reforms had been introduced. First, new building laws were passed. So far the state had been prepared to provide loans for buildings of certain categories, especially for flats, which were in short supply. Now a number of loan-giving institutions were set up and the state withdrew from this sector of the economy. Rents, which had been fixed since 1939, were partly freed, though the new and greater profits were in some measure recouped by the state through increased property taxes. The general effect of these new measures was a building boom, related to the now buoyant economy.

The educational reforms affected the schools system, so far based on seven years' instruction with selection for grammar schools at the age of 11 or 12. Those not selected for grammar-school education went on for a further two years in a secondary school but were to some extent stigmatised as failures. The new legislation of 1958 provided for universal comprehensive education for seven years — in practice up to the age of 14 — after which a pupil was free to leave school, to continue for a further two years on a voluntary basis, or to take a three-year course leading to the middle-school examination or, if desired, an extended academic course ending with the Student Examination. As the title suggests, the Student Examination gives access to one of the Danish universities.

With improved schooling thus available better opportunities for those who had previously been denied a full schooling and those who desired to further their technical knowledge were demanded, and these demands were met. Funds were also provided for those in need. The education explosion resulting from these reforms then began to create its own difficulties. A student examination automatically entitles its holder to a university place and the demand far exceeds the number of places available. To help cope with this situation, a third university was founded in Odense in 1964 to ease the load on the universities of Copenhagen and Århus, and since then universities have been established in Roskilde and Åalborg. The problem was aggravated by the traditional flexibility of Danish university education; an absence of fixed timetables meant that seven years spent at university was the norm and ten years by no means unusual. This system had clearly become unworkable, partly by reason of limited space and partly because the demand for scholarships and grants was becoming much more widespread. Although the practice of student loans is the norm in Denmark, it is obviously impracticable to provide students with money over an indefinite period. Accordingly new syllabuses were devised which would shorten the period of study and be more suited to the modern world.

Social services provided the Triangle Government's third sphere of reform. Although the changes did not all take place at one time, those started by this government and continued by its successor have been referred to as the Second Social Reform. The people's pension was really the beginning. Financial aid for the disabled carried the new ideas still further. Disablement benefits were increased in 1965 and those eligible received more than a people's pension — obviously on the assumption that people injured in road or factory accidents often had greater financial responsibilities than the aged and thus needed more help. Widows' pensions were also increased and brought into line with the general trend. These laws, taken together, have given practically every Dane freedom from fear of poverty or hardship, whatever sudden change may take place in his circumstances.

A Return to Austerity

The government parties could not be blamed for their high hopes when the next election to the *Folketing* came round in November

1960. The result, however, was a shock for everybody concerned. Of the three government parties only the Social Democrats did well, increasing their representation from 70 to 76 seats. The Radicals lost ground, going down from 14 to 11 seats, while the Single Tax Party was completely eliminated. Outside government there was an almost equal confusion, with *Venstre* losing ground and the Conservatives increasing their representation. At the other end of the scale the Communists lost all their seats, but they were replaced by a new left-wing group, the Socialist People's Party, under Aksel Larsen, the former Communist leader. An obvious polarisation had once more taken place in Danish politics, the three centre parties having fared worst.

The Radicals, it was decided, had lost a good deal of support because, though by tradition pacifist, they had agreed with the other parties in the *Folketing* on a new defence law earlier in 1960. They had accepted a military budget of 1,053 million *kroner* (rather less than the 1,400 million asked for by the NATO Commander-in-Chief, General Norstad), and this figure was in future to be tied to the cost of living — to avoid new and difficult negotiations brought on by inflation. On the other hand, they had successfully opposed suggestions that the country should be armed with atomic weapons and could reasonably claim that they had gone some way to standing by their principles. Nevertheless, it must be admitted that much of the party's support came from confirmed pacifists, who now looked elsewhere — to Aksel Larsen's Socialist People's Party. Larsen had been an able and respected leader of the Communist Party, and the Hungarian revolution had not dented his loyalty. Yet, he gradually came to work for a communist policy which would be less dependent on Moscow and more in tune with Danish life. In 1958 the party stalwarts expelled him and asked him to give up his seat in the *Folketing*. This he refused to do, and on being assured of wide support among his former comrades, he formed his new party which duly ran in the election. He refused to budge from his strictly socialist principles and thus brought a number of Social Democrats and Communists into his fold. As he was also a strict pacifist, he attracted the votes of sympathisers who would never have voted Communist.

Venstre had also had its troubles. Together with the Conservatives it had agreed on a joint election programme and also on a joint approach to tax relief. *Venstre's* financial spokesman,

Thorkild Kristensen, who reacted strongly to a programme with which he did not agree and which had been concocted in his absence, resigned from the party and stayed for the rest of the *Folketing* session as an independent *Venstre* member. In contrast to Aksel Larsen, he did not seek to form a new party, and he retired from active politics at the next election in November 1960. His action had, however, started a *Venstre* split from which the Conservatives and, presumably, the Independents, were able to profit. The explanation of the Single Tax disaster seemed to be that the party had relied heavily on the votes of defectors from other parties, who now reacted against its contribution to the previous government. It was assumed that the People's Socialists won many of their votes.

Whatever the reasons for this change in the composition of the *Folketing*, it was plain that fresh negotiations on the formation of a new government would have to start. They did not prove difficult, but again resulted in a break with tradition. The Social Democrats and Radicals were together one vote short of an overall majority, and this they found in the person of one of the two Greenland members, Mikael Gam. It had been customary that the non-Danish members — the Faroese, Greenlanders, and Schleswigers should keep out of internal Danish politics, but now the precedent of taking a direct part had been created, and Mikael Gam became Minister for Greenlandic Affairs.

The new government, headed by the Social Democrat Viggo Kampmann, who had succeeded Hansen, ran straight into trouble. During a period of boom and full employment, wages and salaries had tended to rise faster than had been allowed for in the regular round of national salary negotiations. Thus, when a new round came early in 1961, serious complications quickly set in and the unions demanded large increases. Consequently, there were strikes in the steel and transport industries as well as a strike by farmers obliged to pay their workers increases they could not afford.

On a different front the government was faced with a momentous decision. Britain announced in the summer of 1961 the decision to apply for membership of the EEC. Denmark decided to follow suit, and lodged an application, which was withdrawn after the French veto of the British application.

The question of whether or not to apply for membership of the EEC was thoroughly debated both in and out of the *Folketing*.

Account was taken of far more than the mere economic aspects of membership, not least of the possible effect on relations with the rest of Scandinavia. In putting forward this question, speakers and writers made plain how much stronger the sense of a Scandinavian identity had grown in recent decades. There was a feeling of Nordic culture and a fear that this might in some vague and indistinct way be threatened if Denmark entered the Common Market. The need for Nordic unity in any future expanded Common Market was clearly expressed by Franz Wendt, the General Secretary of the Nordic Council and himself a Dane: 'Only if the Nordic countries act as far as possible in unity can they defend their material and spiritual interests and play their part in implanting in the European community the ideals and the social concept which we in the North feel should be spread wide.'

The problems raised for Denmark by the establishment of the EEC and EFTA were clearly serious. The avoidance of a lasting split in Europe and the achievement of suitable terms with the EEC while herself belonging to EFTA became a major aim of Danish foreign policy early in the 1960s. From 1963 to 1966 this policy was under the control of Per Hækkerup, one of the most outstanding Danish Foreign Ministers of the present century, who won international respect during his period in office (1962–66). His successor, Jens Otto Krag, again followed Britain with a second abortive application to the EEC in 1967.

Wages and salaries had risen over the country by some 12 to 15 per cent during 1961, and pensions by 9 per cent, while production went up by a mere 7 per cent; such a dangerous inflationary tendency had to be countered. Tax increases on petrol and alcohol were not enough to put an end to it. Consequently, the government resorted to a 5 per cent purchase tax to take the heat out of the economy, though its proposals had to be modified drastically to take into account the objections expressed by *Venstre* and the Conservatives.

These measures were part of a comprehensive legislation introduced early in 1963, clearly the work of the government, but supported by a recommendation from a new body which it set up in the second half of 1962. An advisory body made up of representatives of the most important sections of the Danish economy had long been considered overdue in some quarters. The result was the creation of the Economic Council, consisting of representatives of the unions and employers' organisations, the banks, commerce and agriculture, as well as three professors of economics. The aim was to have enlightened discussions on any problem directly related to the economy. The Council had only advisory powers, but it had the right to initiate discussion without waiting for specific problems to be referred to it.

In December 1962 the Council recommended that all negotiations about incomes for 1963 should be conducted at the same time and a comprehensive solution worked out. This 'comprehensive solution' was in fact an incomes policy aimed at ensuring that wage, salary and profit rises should be kept within limits dictated by the national economy. *Venstre* and the Conservatives voiced opposition, but the government managed to force the plan through the *Folketing*, and it led to a major stabilisation of the economy in 1963. Apart from a compulsory savings clause, the solution allowed for limited rises for the lowest paid workers in 1963, accompanied by some improvements in pensions and social benefits. Larger increases were promised for 1964. Prices and profits were also regulated by law. Employers were thus carefully dissuaded from giving larger increases in 1963 than those allowed for by the law, as they would have to absorb the cost themselves and knew that they would have to grant more the following year. The state had clearly entered the field of salary and price negotiations. Conservative and *Venstre* opposition was silenced by the threat of an election. The People's Socialists could not be expected to agree.

The comprehensive solution not only offered the prospect of fresh increases the following year, but also promised legislation to introduce supplementary pensions for workers. All employees were to pay a proportion of their income to a private pension fund which was to be independent of the state. Not everyone in the country was to be included in the new Act to begin with, but it was extended to cover civil servants in 1965, and the idea then was to extend it further to include self-employed persons. This, too, provided not only greater security, but took a good deal of money out of circulation.

Although the government had thus managed to carry the *Folketing* with it through some fairly controversial legislation, it failed to gain necessary support for a number of bills on land reform. There were ten altogether; of these four were passed by the *Folketing* with Conservative and *Venstre* opposition. They aimed at preventing the sale of land to foreign citizens — of special significance if Denmark were to join the EEC — and also introduced some limitations on the rights of Danish citizens when selling land: in some cases the local authorities were to have first option on larger estates, while measures were introduced to secure land for smallholders whose plots were based on the original smallholder legislation and thus too small for modern conditions and ideas. *Venstre* and the Conservatives were vehemently opposed to what they saw as encroachments on individual rights, and when they failed to prevent the passage of the bill, they invoked the clause in the 1953 constitution by which the opposition of one-third of the members of the *Folketing* could lead to a referendum on controversial legislation. In the ensuing referendum the four bills were rejected by large majorities, and the government was forced to drop its plans. There was some doubt about whether the government would now feel obliged to resign, as it was obviously out of line with public opinion. On the other hand, there were fears of setting a precedent, by which any future government would be forced to resign on losing a referendum even if it had in fact carried the *Folketing* with it. This was a possibility scarcely foreseen when the constitution was drawn up and in the event the government did not resign. Some of the abandoned proposals were in any case no longer so pressing with the withdrawal of the application to join the EEC in January 1963.

Return to Social Democrat Minority Government

Because of the negative result of the referendum, there was an added interest in the statutory general election in 1964, but in some ways the result was a confirmation of what had gone before, despite the additional unknown factor of the increased number of voters since the reduction of the voting age to 21 in 1961. There was little change in the parties' representation, with the Social Democrats keeping their strength at 76. The Radicals, however, lost one seat and refused to join the government. There was no longer an overall majority, and when no other viable coalition was found, the Social Democrats, now led by Jens Otto Krag, decided to form a minority government.

The new government had to steer a middle course and, as before with minority governments, chose to legislate in such a way that one or other of the main parties would support a specific bill. With

Radical support insufficient and co-operation with the People's
Socialists out of the question some sort of *rapprochement* with *Venstre*
seemed to be called for. This was made easier by the inclusion in that
party of some members who could be termed left-wing and who
wished to see some form of co-operation with the Social Democrats. A
tendency to draw closer became apparent in 1964 after the British
Labour government broke the EFTA agreement and imposed a 15 per
cent duty on EFTA goods. Denmark was hard hit by this, and the
Social Democrats, who so far had been adamant in demanding that
Denmark should not enter the EEC without Britain, began to have
second thoughts. *Venstre* stipulated no conditions for joining.

However, dissensions within *Venstre*, leading to the resignation of
its two leading left-wing members, put an end to the honeymoon, and
there were rumours first of a union between the bulk of *Venstre* and
the Conservatives, and then of negotiations to find common ground
with the Radicals.

Despite party dissensions this particular session of the *Folketing* led
to significant new housing legislation. The rents charged for new
houses and flats had been constantly rising for years, while rents of the
older flats, some of them very large indeed, had remained stationary.
In an attempt to ease the situation for the occupants of new buildings,
an agreement was reached in the *Folketing* gradually to raise the rents
of the older houses. A proportion of these increases was to go to the
owners, another to maintenance and a third to the financing of new
buildings in an attempt to keep down costs in an inflationary situation.
Although a piece of legislation with attractions for the opposition
parties, it provoked bitter feelings among Social Democrat
supporters. Consequently, in the Copenhagen local elections of 1966
they suffered a severe defeat, the People's Socialists making gains at
their expense. The obvious swing against an unpopular minority
government persuaded Krag to call an election in November 1966,
well before the end of the statutory term. The result was one foreseen
— and feared — by many: the emergence of the Socialist People's
Party as a candidate for government coalition.

Left-wing Co-operation

The other, and perhaps the main, reason for the unexpected election
was the difficulties the government had encountered in its efforts to
reform the taxation system. The purchase tax on wholesale prices had

turned out to be insufficient, and the main question at issue was how to increase it without hitting trade too badly. Putting it on the retail price of goods was a possibility, but this suggestion was not seriously considered for long, and instead the idea of a value added tax gained ground. The general consensus was that this tax should be at 10 per cent, though *Venstre* would have liked to see a higher figure coupled with a reduction in direct taxation. In general the parties could not agree on the exact terms of the value added tax. The government's intention was to couple it with the introduction of the pay-as-you-earn system of direct taxation, which won increasing support from the electorate. With direct taxation as high as it was, there was increasing resentment at the large tax accounts which had to be paid ten months in the year. It was thus largely because of the inability to agree on VAT that the government decided to call an election on the issue of taxation at source, which was thought to be a vote-catcher.

But the attempt misfired and the electorate seemed more concerned with the effects of the unpopular legislation just passed than with the hope of things to come: the Social Democrats fell from 76 to 69 seats; the People's Socialists, who reaped the main benefit of dissatisfaction with the Social Democrats, doubled their representation to 20 seats. A coalition of the two parties thus seemed to be the obvious solution.

When it came to the point, however, the People's Socialists declined, largely because of opposition to Social Democrat foreign policy. So yet another minority government was formed, and this went ahead with plans for tax reform. In this it was supported by the People's Socialists, whose votes assisted the passage of bills. A value added tax of 10 per cent was to commence in July 1967, and from 1 January 1970 a system of taxation at source was introduced.

In practice the People's Socialists held a position comparable to that of the Radicals in previous years, a balance of power without the responsibility of government. They were not interested in provoking a fresh election, and so they supported the Social Democrats in their financial policy, whereas they had previously opposed it, and they showed signs of a compromise attitude on the EEC. But even now signs of a split began to emerge within the party, some of its members wishing to limit the area of co-operation with the Social Democrats, against the wishes of Aksel Larsen.

Hilmar Baunsgaard, Prime Minister from 1968 to 1971, argued

that this period of co-operation between Social Democrats and People's Socialists marked a change in Danish political tradition, in that the government was for the first time subjected to direct and intense influence from the extreme left. The Social Democrat government was effectively hamstrung by its allies, who were uncompromising in their demands for socialist legislation. It is not, therefore, surprising that the tacit coalition came to an early close. The subsequent decision to call an election in 1968 was supported by six of the twenty Socialist People's Party members of the *Folketing*, and this brought the disunity within the party to a head. On 16 and 17 December 1967 a conference of the twenty members took place and the six dissidents decided to leave the party and form their own left-wing party to be known as the Socialist Left. These six members had the previous day voted against a government decision to suspend payment of a cost of living-based wage, salary, and pension increase in order to stem the rising tide of inflation, while the remainder of the party had voted for the motion. The left-wing members felt that the Socialist People's Party as a whole was in danger of becoming a mere appendix to the Social Democrats, in contrast to many others outside the two parties, who felt that the People's Socialists had far too much influence in relation to their size.

About half the People's Socialist deputies now left the party and joined the Socialist Left, a split reflected throughout Denmark, even down to local committee level.

The People's Reaction

In the 1968 election the Social Democrats paid the price for their flirtation with the left and lost heavily. The following list shows a comparison of the election results in 1966 and 1968:

	1966	1968
Social Democrat	69	62
Radical	13	27
Conservative	34	37
Venstre	35	34
People's Socialists	20	11
Liberal Centre	4	0
Socialist Left	—	4

In 1968 participation was the largest since the war at 89.3 per cent, and the second largest ever (it reached 89.5 per cent during the Occupation). The socialist majority disappeared and *Venstre* lost its place as the second party to the Conservatives, a result fore-shadowed by previous developments. The Radicals, on the other hand, despite earlier Conservative protestations that they were no longer a party to be reckoned with, made an impressive comeback, presumably having gained a lot of the disgruntled votes previously given to the Social Democrats and People's Socialists. Whatever else this election could be said to show, it was a resounding repudiation of left-wing policies. A non-socialist government was now feasible and the outcome was a new three-party coalition, this time between the Radicals, Conservatives, and *Venstre*, under the premiership of the Radical Hilmar Baunsgaard. This government had the largest majority of any government since 1935, the three parties together commanding 98 seats of the 179 in the *Folketing*. Even the Stauning government in 1935, with its clear *Folketing* majority, had to fight a *Landsting* dominated by the opposition parties.

The new government inherited the perennial question of the balance of payments.

The 1967 deficit was the largest in Denmark's history, and had been seriously affected by the 7.9 per cent devaluation which followed on Britain's 14.3 per cent in November, a devaluation estimated to have cost Danish agriculture something in the region of 282 million *kroner* a year. This in itself was a sign of the difficulties inherited by the government, and to it can be added the rising unemployment figures, a very high interest rate, and, almost inevitably under these circumstances, many bankruptcies. The system of linking wages and salaries to the cost of living was having a spiral effect, and it was expected that wage levels would probably rise by about 13 per cent in 1969 to a level considerably above those of Denmark's competitors.

It thus became the ministry's aim to save money wherever possible and to hold consultations with industrial and trading interests to contain inflation. The ultimate target was to prepare a new economic advance, which the government felt to be well within the country's ability. On the other hand, despite the attractions of the EEC for one of the coalition parties, and despite some disillusionment with Britain's attitude to EFTA after the imposition of the 15 per cent surcharge on imports, there were no plans for a change in foreign policy, except that the government was interested in consolidating the Nordic alliance — a desire which was instrumental in opening negotiations on a possible Nordic common market, to be known as Nordek. In a broader field the hope was to work for a breaking-down of trade barriers within Europe, possibly by means of an enlarged common market including the EEC and such EFTA countries as wished to join it. Negotiations were to begin with Germany on Danish agricultural exports, which had been badly hit by EEC tariffs. In addition it was the government's intention to bring in educational reforms, including the introduction of a compulsory eight years at school, with a possible extension to nine and ten years. New social legislation was announced, and the government planned to widen support for the arts. Greenland and the Faroes were to be further developed and aided. The civil service was to be reformed, and the voting age lowered. It was doubtless a further sign of the desire for increased Nordic co-operation in a completely different sphere that Denmark in 1968 ordered a squadron of Swedish Draken fighters for the air force and took an option on a second — the first time that a NATO country had bought its fighters outside the NATO area itself.

In immediate action to stop the economy getting out of control the discount rate was raised from 6½ per cent to 7½ per cent, and on the 15 February 1968 a move was made to stop price increases. Firms were compelled to report projected increases to the Monopoly Control, and they were not, except in certain circumstances, allowed to implement such plans without permission. Likewise professional fees for services were pegged. The regulations remained in force until 1 November 1968. Wages were not affected, though when the biennial wage negotiations came up in February 1969 they were difficult and protracted, and at one time looked likely to lead to a general strike.

Political Change and Economic Reform

Meanwhile, the intention of containing the economy was not fulfilled. Boom conditions existed throughout Europe, and Denmark was carried along on the wave, despite government attempts to prevent this. There were rumours that Germany was going to revalue the *Deutschmark*, and thus Danish businesses sought to pay off debts calculated in *Deutschmarks* in order to avoid the obvious repercussions on the Danish *krone*. The immediate consequence was an alarming fall in foreign currency reserves, which by mid-May 1969 stood at less than a third of what they had been in January that year. The year was one of rapid expansion, with rising production and rising imports accompanied by rising wages and prices; consequently, 1969 saw a vast balance of payments problem, which showed no signs of being alleviated in 1970. A fresh series of drastic measures to improve the economy was introduced in 1970, but the government failed, as it had done in 1968, to persuade the trade unions to give up their rights to index-linking in wages and salaries, and this was now having a serious inflationary effect. Accordingly, VAT was raised to 15 per cent. The original intention of reducing taxation had come to nothing, and largely under the pressure of circumstances abroad the government had in fact been forced to go in the opposite direction and raise taxes.

Because of these unforeseen problems, the government was unable to carry out a number of the reforms it had intended. It did, however, bring about the amalgamation of local authorities, for which preparations had already been started in 1967. The existing authorities were too small and diverse to be able to carry the burdens of a modern administration, and so they were originally encouraged, and eventually obliged, to join together. By the time the law finally came into force in 1970, the number of local authorities had been reduced from 1,388 to 277.

This process was then completed in 1973 with the reorganisation of the administration of Copenhagen and surrounding areas. This was not done by the piecemeal creation of a single, vast local authority, but by the establishment of a county authority responsible for various fields of immediate significance to the whole area, such as hospitals, public transport and water supplies. One very tangible result was the organisation of the entire public transport network in the Copenhagen area, so that the city can now boast one of the most highly integrated and efficient systems in Europe.

More contentious, but probably equally significant in their way, were two other reforms introduced by the three-party government. In 1967 the law governing pornography had been liberalised by the Social Democrat government, and the publication of pornographic texts was now legal. This government extended the new law to cover pornographic pictures, though it was, and still is, forbidden to use children in the process. In both cases the argument was that adults should be able to decide for themselves what to see and read, and that they should not be subject to the dictates of the government of the day. A similar view prevailed with the introduction of free abortion in 1970; here the contention was that the mother-to-be was the only person to make the decision whether or not to have the child. This same government then introduced sex instruction in the schools as part of the normal curriculum. There was vocal opposition to all these measures at the time, but they have now become a generally accepted part of the Danish scene and are no longer the subject of debate. In particular, the large numbers of sex shops which suddenly sprang up in the centre of Copenhagen have largely disappeared as their curiosity value has diminished. Indeed, supporters of the new legislation said from the very beginning that this would be the case, and time has proved them right.

Meanwhile, by the time of the next election, in September 1971, there was a dual sense of disappointment with the government's performance. On the economic front it had manifestly failed to achieve what it had set out to do, though this was not entirely its own fault, while the reforms it had introduced had upset many of its own supporters, who now looked in other directions, not in-significantly to the new Christian People's Party and its outright opposition to the introduction of the new liberal laws. The election gave the coalition supporters a majority of one over the rest, but when the members for Greenland and the Faroe Islands were elected, only one from each of the countries remained neutral (as they had traditionally been), while the remaining one from each declared support for the Social Democrats, who were thus enabled to form a minority government.

This new government, under Jens Otto Krag, was immediately faced with two major problems. It had to bring the economy under control, and it had to make up Denmark's collective mind on the issue of joining the EEC now that Great Britain had again applied for membership in 1969. A decision on this was all the more urgent since the attempts to form a Nordic Common Market, Nordek, had foundered largely on Denmark's insistence that provision should be made in any treaty for possible incorporation into the EEC at some future date. In guiding the country in the face of these two difficult problems, the government was forced to rely on the support of the Socialist People's Party for its economic policy (which unexpectedly included import surcharges for two years) and on the non-socialist parties for progress towards the EEC — the Socialist People's Party being staunch opponents of such a move. In the event, each grouping was interested in not bringing down the government, and, minority government or not, it managed to carry out an intricate policy.

Negotiations with the EEC council of ministers began in June 1970, the main sessions taking place later in the year and being concluded by mid-1971. There was a clear majority for membership in the *Folketing*, with only the Socialist People's Party and individual members of the Social Democrats and Radicals being opposed. However, when the negotiations had been completed, it was decided that the final decision should be put to a national referendum. In the event, after a campaign of impressive proportions, the people's verdict was in favour of membership, some 57 per cent voting for and 33 per cent against. The Faroe Islands, already enjoying self-government, took no part in the proceedings and did not join the EEC; Greenland, however, was still an integral part of Denmark and, although the majority of Greenlanders voted against joining, it went in together with mainland Denmark. After also being granted internal self-government, Greenland, has, of course, since held its own referendum and subsequently withdrawn.

The opponents of membership used, and still use, a great many emotive arguments, many of which are based on a sense of Nordic solidarity. They have seen Denmark being dragged into a European sphere of culture alien to it, while their own Nordic culture they see as being under threat. The 'Nordic' argument has been one of great force, and the sense of a Scandinavian unity is, at least at a popular level, widespread and powerful. Nevertheless, negotiations between the Nordic countries on defence treaties and plans for a Nordic common market have tended to show overriding national differences. Adherents of Danish membership of the EEC have rejected this argument and they mostly emphasise the economic benefits to Denmark in joining, especially with Great Britain as a member. It was almost unthinkable that Denmark should remain outside while her two principal trading partners were full members.

With the pro-marketeers carrying the day, Denmark became a member of the EEC on 1 January 1973. The much-feared influx of other EEC citizens did not take place, and such guest workers as there are in Denmark have tended to come from outside the area, principally from Yugoslavia, Turkey and Pakistan. Nor has membership adversely affected the Danish social legislation, as some people had feared, while co-operation with the other Nordic countries has gone on unhindered. Denmark has even managed to maintain its place in two mutually exclusive passport areas!

Before Denmark became a member of the EEC, there had been radical and far-reaching changes at home. The day after the referendum, the Prime Minister, Jens Otto Krag, surprisingly announced that he was retiring from politics. He was replaced by the Deputy Chairman of the Social Democrats, Anker Jørgensen, a trade union figure who was relatively untried as a politician, and who had never before held office. Like his predecessors, he was faced with a problem of rising prices and wages against a background of worldwide boom conditions, and he was forced to seek the help of the People's Socialists in order to carry out a practicable policy. The People's Socialists were unwilling to make the required savings, and when the biennial wage negotiations took place, their result was seen to be highly inflationary. The left-wing bias of the government and its supporters was blamed for this, and consequently the right-wingers in the Social Democrat party broke away and formed their own party, the Centre Democrats. They had been in existence for only a month when fresh elections were held in December 1973. They won 14 seats, a clear sign of dissatisfaction on the part of the electorate with the government's way of tackling the chronic economic problems with which Denmark had been battling for so many years.

A still clearer sign was the support given to the other new party, the Progress Party, which won 28 seats and was suddenly the second largest party in the country.

The Progress Party was unashamedly a party of protest, and its founder Mogens Glistrup, had won his support very largely through his attack on the Danish taxation system and his subsequent promises of drastic tax reductions if his party were voted into power. One of his notorious statements was that he would abolish the Danish defence forces and replace them with an answering machine saying in Russian: 'We surrender. We surrender', to be used in the case of armed attack on the country. Glistrup had come into prominence through a television interview in January 1972 in which he said that although he had an income of a million *kroner* a year, he was able to manipulate the tax laws in such a way that he paid no income tax. He raised more than a few eyebrows by saying that tax dodgers were just as patriotic as the members of the wartime resistance. Glistrup was later to pay dearly for this interview when the Danish tax authorities went into his affairs, and after a prolonged court case he was sentenced to four years in prison for aggravated tax evasion, and precluded from acting as a solicitor henceforth. In 1985, the sentence served, he established himself as a tax consultant.

There were no fewer than ten parties represented in the 1973 *Folketing*, and of these, the well-established ones had been given an unambiguous vote of no confidence by the electors. When the new government was formed, it was led by Poul Hartling and was a minority *Venstre* government based on only 22 seats. It was faced with an entirely new situation, in which the old groupings were no longer valid, and in which the voices of the new protest parties had to be taken into consideration. It was also faced with the severe economic effects of the first oil crisis. The inflationary boom, stretching back to the 1960s, was at an end.

Crisis in the 1970s and 1980s

The 1973 election, and the emergence of the Progress Party, showed clearly that Danish voters were dissatisfied with the performance of their political representatives, and the move towards the newly founded Progress Party was more than a mere protest against heavy taxation, probably indicative of a yearning for a new direction in Danish politics. The established parties, however, refused co-operation with Glistrup and his colleagues (which would in any case have been a difficult task), and the Progress Party was excluded from negotiations on the formation of a coalition government. Consequently, when Hartling formed his minority government in 1973, he had to rely on the support of the new, smaller parties, the Centre Democrats and the Christian People's Party, though occasionally he had to look to the Progress Party for tacit support. The immediate tactic of the new government was to cope with the economic crisis by increasing taxes and, in particular, import duties. However, the consequent reduction in spending power accelerated the growing unemployment, and as a result direct taxation was again reduced — in the view of the Progress Party by too little, in the opinion of others by too much, too soon. The result was dissent amongst government supporters and the calling of fresh elections, by which time the deficit in public spending had become, and was to remain, a major problem.

Hartling had enjoyed general respect and he hoped to form the next government, but this proved impossible thanks to an unexpected distribution of seats in the other parties. The task fell to Anker Jørgensen, who managed to put together a Social Democrat minority government. He stood on the left of his party, but in fact he was unable to go much further than his non-socialist predecessor, and the need to find compromises that would attract the indispensable support of some of the other parties led him to carry out a programme not very different from theirs. The problems facing the government were the well-known ones: increasing unemployment coupled with rising prices in a time of recession, and the initial attempts to cope with this combination resulted in a growing budget deficit and an increasing balance of payments deficit. So a Social Democrat government which at one time had aimed to reduce VAT to 9.25 per cent was after a fresh election in 1977 forced to increase it to 18 per cent. At the same time the government aimed at greater control over the biennial industrial bargaining, and imposed settlements when strikes seemed inevitable, while a start was made to limiting the automatic indexing of wages and salaries, which had certainly avoided confrontation between employers and employed in a period of inflation but which in itself had contributed to that inflation.

In 1978 Anker Jørgensen broke new political ground by suggesting, and establishing, a coalition between the Social Democrats and *Venstre*, a coalition which few people really believed would work. The policy remained the same: VAT was increased to 20.25 per cent, and the new coalition maintained the same kind of incomes policy as its predecessor. By this time, however, it was clear that there were sufficient natural gas reserves in the Danish sector of the North Sea to be commercially viable. In a new effort to counter the effects of the high oil prices — and Denmark had so far been almost entirely dependent on oil — plans were made to switch to natural gas, originally importing it from Germany but subsequently making use of Denmark's own reserves.

As foreseen, the co-operation between the Social Democrats and *Venstre* was a difficult one, especially as *Venstre* wanted more stringent savings measures than the Social Democrats were prepared to countenance. By 1979 the situation became untenable, so elections were called yet again. This time the distribution of seats was such that the Social Democrats were able to form a minority government on their own. They turned now to a prices freeze, and although the government reintroduced a limited form of indexing, the basis was changed in order to prevent the rapid rises there had been in previous years. Most important of all, fuel costs were excluded from the prices on which indexing was based. The policy worked to some extent: foreign trade was brought into balance, but the overall balance of payments deficit remained, thanks to the interest payable on Denmark's foreign debts.

One of the government's intentions in order to reduce unemployment was to legislate to channel pension funds in what they saw to be a favourable direction. This suggestion met stiff opposition, and in order to clear the air Anker Jørgensen called new elections for December 1981. There was a good deal of suspicion of the government's intentions, and the Social Democrats lost ground. Nevertheless, with the support of the People's Socialists they made a fresh attempt to govern. Within months, however, their position had deteriorated, and they resigned, to be succeeded in September 1982, without a fresh election, by a coalition of Conservatives, *Venstre*, the Christian People's Party and Centre Democrats, with Poul Schlüter as the first Conservative Prime Minister of the twentieth century. It was the largest number of parties ever in a coalition in Denmark. The sudden emergence of the Conservatives was particularly surprising, for one of the features of the previous ten or fifteen years had been the volatile tendencies of the electorate, one result of which had been to vary the Conservative vote from as little as 5 per cent to as much as 25 per cent. The reason for the viability of the new government lay not only in the strength of the Conservatives after the 1981 election and the possibility the non-socialist parties thus saw for governing, but also in the fact that the Progress Party was also prepared to give a measure of support to it. The protest party was already in fact losing a good deal of the popular support it had originally had, though ironically it has lost more since it became less of a protest party and more like the other non-socialist parties, albeit retaining a generally more radical stance.

Poul Schlüter is an admirer of Margaret Thatcher, and his

government has followed the kind of trail already blazed by her, with drastic cuts in public spending, not least in the sphere of social services. Furthermore, taxation has been extended to certain areas, such as pension funds, which had hitherto escaped it, though the Social Democrats had been arguing in favour of taxing them for some time. A limit of 4 per cent was placed on wage and salary increases, and index-linking abolished. In October 1983 the government announced its intention of removing the balance of payments deficit within three to four years, and the budget deficit within six — though by April 1984 both had in fact increased. Another priority was the reduction of interest rates, and this has been achieved, thanks partly to falling international rates.

The government failed to muster a sufficient majority for all its proposed cuts, so elections were called for January 1984. There had been protests and demonstrations outside the *Folketing*, some of them violent, but the government had held firm and it won the day. Despite unemployment, which was at this time only rising slowly, it felt confirmed in its policy, not least because it could point to a growth of between 2.5 and 3 per cent in the economy in 1983–84, twice the European average. As a result of the 1984 election the government coalition overall was strengthened, though this was largely because of a large increase in Conservative votes, while the Centre Democrats lost significantly. So, outside the government, did the Progress Party, which in May 1984 actually split when some of its members broke away to form the Free Democrats. Since its re-election, the government has continued its stringent economic policy. This fact, helped by falling interest rates generally (a serious burden on Denmark with its enormous foreign debts) and lower oil prices, has brought a note of optimism into prognostications. The current account and foreign trade deficits have fallen, though it looks increasingly doubtful whether trade can be brought into balance by 1988 and the current account deficit eliminated by 1990, as the government had hoped. More important for the morale of the average Dane is the fact that unemployment at least seems to be falling, though a high level is expected to persist at least until 1990.

There are those who would argue that the present improvement would have come irrespective of the stringent financial policy and that it is not based on any secure foundation. The situation was questioned in September 1985 by Erik Hoffmeyer, the President of the National Bank. According to newspaper reports, Erik

Hoffmeyer warned the government that it will either have to raise VAT and indirect taxes by the end of 1985, or else interest rates will have to rise in 1986. If that happens, the task of keeping Denmark on its present course of modest progress will be in danger.

Politically speaking, Denmark underwent a radical and complicated transformation between 1945 and 1973. The old, apparently fixed party constellations changed and finally disintegrated. The Social Democrats, who once tended to rely on Radical support, moved closer to the left-wing Socialist People's Party, while the Radicals moved into alliance with the Conservatives and *Venstre*. A clear polarisation of view had taken place. Yet the voters' disenchantment expressed itself in 1973 in a completely new way with support for parties based on protest or on specific and limited policies — the Christian Democrats for instance, representing the anti-abortion lobby. Placed together in the *Folketing*, the new group of ten parties, with changed or unknown allegiances, spelled a new kind of uncertainty.

Structural Change

The social transformation was equally far-reaching. The way in which the Danes have been housed over the years could be taken as a symbol of social change and growing affluence. In 1945, after the Second World War, a majority of Danish town-dwellers lived in flats, houses being the domain of the more well-to-do. By the end of the period a vastly increased proportion of Danes (almost two-thirds in 1978) were living in their own houses, the minimum standards of which were strictly governed by law, and the minimum area for which was likewise regulated. These small detached houses sprang up often in the outskirts of towns with the advent of increasing numbers of motor cars. In 1953 three per cent of the population owned cars, but by 1973 the number had risen to 25 per cent. The movement from the inner cities took shape, and it was only with the revaluation of housing in 1966, which allowed the rents of the older flats to be raised and provided for subsidised rents for modern ones, that the inner city flats began seriously to be modernised to keep up with the double-glazed, centrally heated individual houses well away from the centre.

The new houses in the suburbs and small surrounding towns

were expensive, but the heavy mortgages could be managed on a double income, which is at least one of the reasons for the increasing numbers of women who started to go out to work during this period. And with the index-linked incomes in a period of rapid inflation, the large mortgages became less and less of a burden. Moreover, with the Danish system of loans, it was possible, even desirable, to take out second and third mortages to pay either for extensions and improvements, or simply to buy other consumer goods. The sixties and early seventies thus stand as a period of rapid expansion and rapidly rising standards of living. And increasing debts.

At the same time the growing numbers of cars and the ever-increasing affluence led to a growth in the number of summer cottages in the more popular coastal areas. To own a cottage in the country had long been the dream of city dwellers and the privilege of the well-to-do. Now, increasing mobility together with more freedom at weekends resulting from the introduction of a shorter working week led to the growth of large numbers of purpose-built summer cottages, to which their owners flocked at summer weekends. Those who did not wish to use them throughout the summer then saw them as a new means of income, by letting them out for periods to holiday makers.

It was not only the increased number of people travelling by car to work or to their summer cottages who were responsible for demands for more and better roads, but also the vastly increased amount of international commercial traffic. It was during this period that the first motorways were built, and it was now too that the new bridges began to make their appearance, notably the second bridge over Lillebælt, complementing the first built in the 1930s. The railways were improved, both by the acquisition of new and modern rolling stock and diesel locomotives to replace the outdated steam engines, but also by the construction of the new, direct route to Germany through Rødby and Puttgarden. The main airport at Kastrup was developed and modernised, but plans for an ambitious, entirely new one on the island of Saltholm, part-way between Denmark and Sweden were scrapped. The equally ambitious plans for a bridge across Storebælt and another across the Sound to Sweden have yet to materialise.

However, progress was not only limited to the growing demands of an affluent consumer society. That same society was to be looked after, educated, provided with hospitals and doctors, also to become the focus of attention of succeeding governments. One result of the changing social pattern was the increased need for facilities for taking care of small children while both parents were out at work, and greatly improved provisions made for nursery schools and daycare institutions were made throughout the period 1960 to 1975. Some 40 per cent of all children under two now attend daycare institutions while some 56 per cent of all aged between two and seven attend nursery schools.

The Danish social conscience dates back at least to 1849, when provision for help to those in need was written into the constitution, and more precise kinds of support were provided for in 1891 in the Poor Law which laid down detailed regulations for the provision of aid to poor people. That same year also saw the Law on Support in Old Age, providing for help for the elderly without their incurring civil penalties associated with poor-aid. In the following decades a good deal of piecemeal legislation ensued, and in 1933 the then Minister of Social Affairs, K. K. Steincke, introduced what was known as the Social Reform, which repealed all existing social legislation and replaced it with four simplified and comprehensive Acts covering general insurance, unemployment insurance, accident insurance and public welfare. For its time this was one of the most progressive pieces of social legislation anywhere, and the Danes were justly proud of it. The intention was to maintain the dignity of those being cared for, and not merely to provide for bare necessities, as had previously been the case.

The Social Reform and the way in which it was administered led finally to the demand for social security for all, a right which is written into the 1953 Constitution:

(1) In order to advance the public interest, efforts should be made to ensure work for every able-bodied citizen on terms that will secure his existence.

(2) Any person unable to support himself or his dependents shall, where no other person is responsible for his or their maintenance, be entitled to receive public assistance, provided that he shall comply with the obligations imposed by Statute in such respect.

These clauses have formed the philosophical basis of all subsequent social legislation, which originally developed as and when the need arose, and has subsequently been simplified and centralised. The old-age pension concept was no longer thought to be sufficient, and the demand was raised that there should be a pension for all, irrespective of income. Consequently, in 1956 the 'People's Pension' — a general retirement pension — was introduced, providing a minimum pension for those in the higher salary brackets. In 1964 it was decided to provide a full pension for everyone, irrespective of income, and this was put into effect in 1970. Sickness benefit was based on semi-independent sickness insurance funds ultimately related to the co-operative ideal and now plagued by bureaucracy. These, too, were streamlined in 1960.

In 1961 a new Welfare Act replaced the Steincke Act from 1933, and for the first time replaced the concept of poor-aid by supplementary benefits as of right for those needing them. At the same time the principle was accepted that the amount of help available should be increased, and that those needing assistance should not have their standard of living drastically reduced.

In 1970 a thorough review of social services was decided on in the light of the restructuring of local authorities. In 1971 the sickness benefit societies were abolished; health insurance now became the province of the local authorities, and the former flat-rate contribution was replaced by taxation based on income. Sickness benefit, however, only started after five week's illness, and an Act from 1972 stipulated that employers were obliged to pay benefit for that period.

The only area in which social security benefits were now based on the contributory principle was now, and has remained, unemployment benefit. It is still necessary to be a member of an unemployment fund (usually run by the trade unions) in order to be eligible for benefit.

The various forms of benefit available, however, were still administered by a number of different institutions, and it was therefore decided radically to overhaul and simplify the entire system. This was accomplished in the Social Security Act (*Bistandsloven*), which came into force in 1975 and provided for all social security services to be administered centrally in each local authority. The idea was that applications to a centralised social services office could result in applicants immediately being channelled to the relevant department or departments instead of being referred to individual, unco-ordinated offices. The system has been referred to as a social security supermarket.

This extension of social services ranging from daycare institutions to retirement pensions — and even to short-term benefits for the temporarily disabled — together with soaring prices became a significant economic burden on the country. The system was subjected to considerable criticism from the Right — and, to some extent, also from the Left, who saw ulterior motives behind some of the legislation. The Social Democrats, on the other hand, were eager supporters of the changes, which they saw as contributing to their ultimate goal of a more equal distribution of wealth. That the new legislation has gone some way to this can scarcely be doubted, but it has been pointed out that the extra taxation needed to maintain the system has also hit those less able to contribute, while the better-off have been better able to devise means of alleviating their own tax burden. Another criticism made of the radical reform programme is that it has led to an explosive increase in the number of civil servants administering it. Indeed, it has been suggested that the administration will have increased threefold over fifteen years.

The Liberal Society

In view of the constant improvement in material conditions until 1973, it might well have been supposed that society in the sixties and seventies would have been marked by general satisfaction and calm, the main complaint of many being the large proportion of their income that went in taxation. This was not, however, the case, and the period was in fact characterised by increasingly voluble discontent on the part of many young people who still saw their society as one of class division and inequality. And these young people chose to go their own ways in a society that was tolerant by nature and conviction.

Despite the social levelling out that had taken place during this century, Denmark was still in many respects socially conservative and stiffly middle class. During the 1960s the younger generation, brought up in schools where they were deliberately taught to question social structures and well-informed about what was taking place elsewhere, reacted against what they saw as stuffy conformism. Informal dress, such as jeans, became almost a uniform, while open-necked shirts replaced the bow ties which hitherto had been a striking feature of Danish dress. The use of titles, so beloved of earlier generations and sometimes taken to ridiculous lengths, was dropped; even the use of Mr or Mrs became less common — a change that happened more or less to coincide with the introduction of a centralised civil registration number! The divisive formal and informal forms of address, *du* and *De* (corresponding in principle to German Du/Sie and French tu/vous), were also largely abandoned; the informal *du* became almost universally *de rigueur* among the younger generation, and increasingly common among their seniors.

Family patterns, seen by the young as symptomatic of a former, unwanted bourgeois age, were broken down. Young people in Denmark had long shown a tendency to leave home relatively early and to rent their own rooms; now they went still further and many lived in extended families in communes, even in some cases going so far as to adopt — legally — a new, communal name. The first of these extended families settled in a large house on the outskirts of Copenhagen as early as 1967, and many others followed their example. Although such labels as group sex were attached to these experiments in living, and though established taboos were doubtless rejected in many cases, there was among the young a genuine attempt to create a new society with greater respect for individual needs and characteristics than they felt they had obtained in the more orderly society from which they had withdrawn.

In particular the extended family led to a greater equality among the sexes and, in many cases, a greater say for children. The 'family' decisions were often taken in family meetings, which all attended, and this pattern itself crept back into the 'ordered' society, being adopted by some, though by no means all, 'ordinary' families. The patriarchal structure of only twenty years before rapidly disappeared to be replaced by a more relaxed and flexible family pattern to which all members had to contribute now that there was no longer usually a mother at home all day to arrange things for the comfort of the other members of the family. The resultant increasing sense of family responsibility and the acceptance by individual family members that the larger unit, the family, was more important than the smaller, the individual, spread outside the family circle and has over the past twenty years or so become the broader social philosophy in Denmark. Although it is still theoretically possible to be an individualist, in fact there are widespread social pressures to conform to the new social pattern in which the individual must adapt more and more to the general needs of the community or group.

Meanwhile, the breakdown of the old family patriarchal pattern was not limited to the setting up of individual collective dwellings. In 1970 an extensive military barracks in Christianshavn, not far from the centre of Copenhagen, was evacuated by the military, and the following year it was taken over by groups of young people who settled there and gave it the name of Christiania. This was to be an alternative society, a state within a state, to which the young could resort if they were too much in opposition to established norms. In one sense it could be seen as a reaction against the affluent society. Unfortunately, because it was so big and to some extent outside the effective control of the law, Christiania attracted considerable numbers of unwanted drop-outs, criminals and drug addicts, not only from Denmark, but from the other Scandinavian countries, and still further afield. This social 'experiment' was thus in serious danger of going wrong, and for years there were threats to close it. However, an element of order has been restored and though it is still very much an *alternative* society, the situation seems to have been stabilised. Cynics argue that one reason for not closing Christiania is that it would be too expensive to rehouse the many hundreds living there.

Parallel with this went yet another group of young people who occupied condemned properties, often blocks of flats, which were standing unoccupied in Copenhagen and the provinces. This was done partly in protest against the shortage of housing which still persisted, and partly at the mounting price of rented accommodation. They won little public sympathy. However, like the other groups, they seldom resorted to violence. This changed, however, at the beginning of the eighties when a new generation of squatters emerged, a generation of a more aggressive kind. On one occasion the police had to resort to tear gas in a confrontation with this new breed.

Social change, however, was not limited to questions of family structure and ways of living. By 1968, to some extent inspired by events abroad, though before the major French student revolt, students in Denmark began to express their opposition to the existing structure in their universities. In particular they complained at the old-fashioned nature of the courses on offer, demanding new and more 'relevant' courses, and also protesting at the admittedly highly formalised 'professorial regime' in the universities. Copenhagen University was occupied, as was Århus, and the result was finally the most liberal university regulations in Europe, in which students had a right to one-third of seats on all committees, the other two-thirds to be divided between academic and administrative staff. The reforms went furthest in Århus, which is still the most radical of Denmark's universities. The quietest and relatively least affected was the University of Odense, founded in 1964, while the new Roskilde University (founded 1972) was in its constitution a product of the new thinking.

It was among students, too, that the modern women's movement first appeared, with the demand for equal status and opportunities for women. Apart from argument and discussion, the more militant of the increasing numbers of women supporting the movement — who became known as 'red-stockings' — resorted to more potent forms of action in the shape of demonstrations, women's communes and, in 1971, in the organising of women's camps on the island of Femø, where participants studied women's legal rights, media attitudes to women and the art of self-defence. The movement spread well beyond the limits of students and intellectuals, and came to encompass sympathetic women from all classes of society. One of their principal demands was equal pay, to which by 1973 the unions and employers' federation had in principle agreed. For whatever reason, the government looked on the ambitions of the women's movement with a certain benevolence, even going so far as to provide money in support of the first Femø camp. A commission was set up to study the question of equality between the sexes, and in 1976 a law was passed to enforce equality. The principle has thus been established, though there are still complaints that it is not in fact being carried out.

However, the movement has led to increasing awareness of the need for a new relationship between men and women, not least in the home, where there is an increasing tendency, side by side with the kind of family democracy referred to above, for the male members of the family to take on their share of the work which at one time was considered the province of the womenfolk.

Sexual equality has also had its effect on attitudes to marriage. For many years Denmark had one of the highest divorce rates in the world. The past twenty years have seen Danes take the next logical step and omit to marry. The phrase 'paperless marriages' was invented for couples living in a permanent but undocumented relationship, and this form of cohabitation became very widespread indeed. It is estimated that some 225,000 couples are now living together without being officially married, and that some 40 per cent of these consider the relationship to be a trial marriage. This development had an immediate but unmeasurable effect on the divorce rate, as the breakdown of such relationships is not registered, and it also had an effect on the (theoretical) illegitimacy rate. It no longer mattered and one effect of this, together with women's demands to keep their identity, was a law under which children are to be called by their mother's name unless a specific request is made for them to be given the father's surname. For their part, women in increasing numbers have kept their maiden names after marriage, or have, in well-established tradition, kept them as a middle name, by which they continue to be known. The result can be confusing, but it can almost be seen as a modern variant of the ancient naming practice of calling all children by their patronymics, which is still the rule in Iceland.

The eighties have seen a noticeable return to marriages, in the view of some as a symptom of a rather more 'romantic' tendency among the young accompanied in some ways even by changes in dress. In the view of others, these new marriages are dictated by tax advantages — though the tax laws have been revised to take account of changed social conditions. Whether they take place in church or town halls, however, the new wave of weddings does not appear to have any significance for the attitude of Danes towards church as such. Although official statistics still claim that 92 per cent of Danes belong to the Lutheran (State) Church, this means that 92 per cent of Danes have not bothered to sign out, and thus pay church taxes. A survey carried out by a research team from Copenhagen University in 1985 maintained that only 2 per cent of Danes go to church every week, and argued that Denmark is now the most 'de-Christianised' country in the world.

Christian or not, well-informed or misinformed, the younger generation of Danes has a broad sense of responsibility for its fellow men together with a willingness to express its views without hesitation. Following on the 1973 oil crisis came the great discussion of other forms of energy, and while Sweden, when it came to the point, decided on a programme of atomic power (and placed one power station closer to Copenhagen than the Danes like), Denmark hedged on the issue. Plans for atomic power were officially shelved in 1979, largely under public pressure, though partly because of the costs involved, and the government began instead to research seriously into other forms of energy, at the same time taxing electricity and subsidising housing insulation. While solar panels made their appearance, though without becoming commonplace, attention was in particular turned to wind power, and the windmill made its comeback. Modern windmills generating power for small numbers of houses or farms are now a common sight in Denmark, and windmill 'parks' are also making their appearance, providing power for larger areas. There are six such windmills grouped together on the island of Fanø, opposite Esbjerg, and another such park is situated on Ærø. So far, parks on the scale of those built in California (using Danish know-how and products) have not made their appearance in Denmark itself, but there are serious suggestions that such huge groupings of windmills will sooner or later become part of the Danish landscape. In an effort to encourage the private production of power in this way, the government has provided for a rebate of the tax otherwise paid on electricity.

With these, we have reached the Danish awareness of the environment. There is a widespread conviction in Denmark that action has to be taken now to protect the environment, and this awareness has established itself in the younger generation who are eager to limit the commercial exploitation of natural resources.They are also keen to limit the human intake of the chemicals used to increase production, turning their attention on the one hand to farming and nursery methods and on the other to more precise information on what goes into the food we eat, coupled with a programme of educating the general public about the dangers of the wrong diet. Such activities are not merely the preoccupation of a small group of fanatics: they are widespread, particularly among the younger generation, but also to an increasing extent among their seniors.

The Arts

The period since the Second World War has been one of rapid change and intense debate in Denmark. Social and political dogma have been questioned; the established patterns of family life have been redrawn; the relationship between the sexes has been subjected to scrutiny, as has, in particular in recent years, the role of women in society.

All this has made its mark on post-war literature, which stands as a close commentary to the more tangible changes which have taken place. Many of the most productive authors of the pre-war period were still writing when peace returned. Uncontroversial, in a political context at least, was Tove Ditlevsen, whose basically realistic short stories and novels continued an earlier tradition and reflected the social deprivation of the 1930s, though they can scarcely be seen as contributing to the social debate of the age. Towards the end of her life, in her patently autobiographical novels, Tove Ditlevsen did become more controversial, giving rise to the question of the extent to which living persons should be brought into what became known as 'confessional novels', and to what extent reality as seen through the eyes of the author should be veiled in some way. The 1970s saw a large number of such novels, though the vogue seems to have died down in the 1980s, to some extent, it is said, under the influence of a mock confessional novel written by Klaus Rifbjerg.

Rifbjerg has been the dominant figure in the Danish novel for many years, producing some two or three almost every year. Not all have been equally good, but Rifbjerg clearly has a talent for writing prose which is unchallenged in Denmark at the present time. He writes third person novels, is also able to project himself into a variety of characters, to identify with them and turn them into his own fictional writers, and through them to comment on contemporary society. He first came into prominence in 1958 with a study of young people in their development and social entanglements, entitled *Chronic Innocence*, clearly inspired by J. D. Salinger's *Catcher in the Rye*.

Also inspired by Salinger's novel was another of the most successful novels of the time, Leif Panduro's *Kick me up the Traditions*. After Rifbjerg, Panduro was one of the most widely read novelists of his day, a man with a distinct sense of humour as he looked at the society of his time and doubted its sanity. There is often a streak of madness in his characters, but ultimately it is they who are sane and society which needs attention. Panduro was highly successful with his plays for television, which often portray the problems and frustrations of the middle-aged (often lonely, middle-aged women who feel themselves superfluous), and his success seems to have been occasioned partly by the inventiveness with which he wrote and partly by the fact that his characters were living through situations and problems with which many of his viewers were familiar.

A more obviously intellectual writer is Villy Sørensen, profoundly affected by Kafka (as is apparent from his short stories) but also deeply concerned with the morality of the age. He expresses his views indirectly, often through the portrayal of other personalities — for instance Seneca, on whom he has written a long and penetrating study, but through whose life and experience of the Roman court a clear analogy is drawn with the present age. More directly, Villy Sørensen has taken part in public debate with the influential *Revolt from the Centre*, in which he and his co-author take issue with the Marxist ideas which have played a prominent role in Danish thinking over the past thirty years.

The 1970s and 1980s have seen the emergence of a group of young and energetic women writers whose ultimate views on society are as varied as those of their male colleagues, but who approach their subjects from a distinctly female point of view. In her early novels Kirsten Thorup is realistic in her portrayal of a family struggling for its standard of living after the war, but in her later publications, in particular her novel *Heaven and Hell*, she breaks with pure realism, and in her analysis of the generation of the 1970s moves towards a fantasy which is at times almost surrealistic. In her novels of the working classes Dea Trier Mørch is well within the realist tradition, writing with warmth and understanding of ordinary people and their private efforts and cares. For her part, Dorrit Willumsen concentrates on the battle between the sexes and in her novel *Marie*, based on the life of Madame Tussaud, she writes a historical novel aimed at showing how, with determination, a woman could win through in a male-dominated world.

The period has seen large quantities of experimental prose, but it is probably in poetry that the most successful experimentation has been made. Outstanding is Inger Christensen's *It*, a vast and complex poem of cosmic proportions, while of other writers the name of Henrik Nordbrandt stands out, both for his sheer poetic skill and on account of his questioning attitude towards the highly developed society of present-day Scandinavia. Nordbrandt spends much of his time in Greece and Turkey, and his views on the distribution of good and bad in the two parts of the world with which he is familiar stand in refreshing contrast to the generally established picture.

Until his death in 1973, Danish painting was dominated by Asger Jorn, an ardent admirer of Kandinsky, a pupil of Léger and at first clearly influenced by Miró and Klee. His abstract paintings often teem with tiny figures and details, but at times he uses a less intricate approach, resorting to vague, stylised figures aimed at conveying the message of apprehension and terror which is often implicit in his work. Thus, his 'The Right of the Eagle' consists of an abstraction of an eagle with a double head, peering Janus-like in opposing directions and furnished with sharp teeth in half-open beaks. In this way, the 'eagle' acquires an outline reminiscent of a mushroom cloud. Beneath it there are suggestions of apprehensive faces and eyes reflecting varying degrees of terror. In other paintings, too, Jorn reflected the atmosphere of his age, for instance in the desperate 'Stalingrad' with its message of the futility and meaninglessness of war, and 'The Fall of Hiroshima'.

Jorn sought spontaneous abstract expression for many of the moods he aimed to convey, and in this he was joined by other artists such as Carl-Henning Pedersen and Egill Jacobsen. These men, and others associated with them, have based themselves on a combination of colour and abstract form. Parallel, to this the sculptor Robert Jacobsen experiments in his wrought-iron sculptures with a combination of space and form.

Experimentation has been the keynote of much modern Danish music, with composers on the one hand being inspired and influenced by Carl Nielsen, and on the other trying to escape his influence and derive their impulses elsewhere. Seen from another point of view, it can be said that Danish music since 1945 has shown a dichotomy between Nordic musical and cultural tradition and influence from outside the North. Thus the presence of Schönberg and Webern can be sensed in the music of Axel Borup-Jørgensen, while Svend Schultz, the composer of a successful opera 'Autumn' (or 'Harvest' — Danish:'*Høst*'), Svend Westergaard and Leif Kayser clearly have their roots in earlier Danish tradition. Two younger composers, Per Nørgård and Ib Nørholm, seek to combine a Nordic awareness with avantgarde experimentation.

The arts in general are in a thriving state in Denmark, largely thanks to an enlightened government policy over many years. In 1961 the Ministry for Cultural Affairs was established with the express purpose of, among other things, fostering the arts and creating a public awareness of them. Three years later, the process was taken a step further by the creation of the State Foundation for the Arts, under which provision has been made for more art in public places, while funds have been made available for financial support for artists, musicians and writers. At the same time the concept of 'art' has been broadened to include not only the kind of art appealing to an intellectual minority, but to give recognition to more widely popular forms, including children's art. That the system should have its critics was inevitable, but it can scarcely be denied that it has helped create a widespread artistic awareness which together with the long-standing awareness fostered by the folk high schools has had a radical formative influence on the state of the arts and the public appreciation of them in Denmark today.

Denmark is, as the Danes never tire of proclaiming, a small country. What it lacks in size it has tried to make up for in moral influence abroad and public enlightenment and awareness at home. The problems facing a relatively small community (some 5,500,000 inhabitants) which is still to a very large extent homogeneous, are minute when compared with those facing the major countries in Europe or outside. It is not surprising therefore that, given a general willingness to pull together for the sake of the community as a whole, together with an impressive degree of public enlightenment, Denmark has for long been able to stand as a country with a striking respect for human beings as well as a notably high standard of living. This it has managed despite the economic problems, some of them self-created, with which it has been faced over the years. It is a country with an inventiveness and a determination to maintain its position. In 1985, with signs that the economy might at last be improving after the crises of the past ten years, one must assume that it will continue to tread the path which it has chosen for itself.

APPENDIX 1: THE FAROE ISLANDS

Although there are earlier accounts of journeys to islands north of
Scotland, which must be the Faroe Islands, the earliest use of the
name by which they are known today is in a manuscript of *c*. 1225,
where they are called Færeyiar. This name, probably meaning
Sheep Islands, is almost certainly a reference to the mildness of the
climate which allows sheep to graze out throughout the year, and it
has presumably also led to the Faroese national symbol — a ram.
The islands seem to have been inhabited from about AD 700 by
Celtic monks, and a certain Dicuil tells how they were driven out
by Vikings around the year 800. The Vikings then proceeded to
colonise the islands, either direct from Norway or indirectly from
the Scottish islands — in the view of some scholars, a few traces of
Gaelic words in the Faroese language seem to indicate this latter
course. On the other hand, the Saga of the Faroe Islanders
— historically as unreliable as most other sagas — tells how the
colonisation of the Faroes was carried out from Norway in order to
escape from Harald the Fair-haired, an assertion in agreement
with Snorre. The Saga also tells how the Faroes became Christian
in 1000, at the same time as Iceland, and how after a period of
complete independence they acknowledged, probably in 1035,
King Magnus the Good of Norway as their king, thus becoming in
effect a province of Norway.

However, an account from 1273 indicates that there was a
period of decline after coming under Norwegian rule, for now the
Norwegian king promised to send at least two ships a year to the
Faroes. It looks as though the Faroese, originally seafarers themselves, were no longer sailors, possibly partly because of the lack
of trees on the islands with which ships could be built. Trade with
the Faroes now became more or less a Norwegian monopoly, and
the changed status of the islands is also shown by the fact that
Norwegian law was extended to include them. Before 1300 the old
Faroese *Lagting*, which had so far enjoyed a legislative function,
had its role reduced to that of administering Norwegian law.
Norway's appropriation of the Faroes is also indicated by the fact
that the Hanseatic states were in theory stopped from trading

there in 1294, a privilege not restored until 1361. With the union between Norway and Denmark in 1380, the Faroes came under Danish rule together with all other Norwegian possessions, and were governed as a province of Norway.

Exactly what the legal status of the Faroes was during the early part of Danish rule is not certain, but there are indications in the reigns of Christian III and Christian IV that they were not considered as an integral part of Norway. The first completely unambiguous evidence of this, however, is the fact that Frederik III on becoming king in 1649 sent a deputation to receive the homage of the Faroe Islanders as distinct from the Norwegians. It seems that the islands, rather like Iceland, were considered as provinces within the kingdom, but not as part of the kingdom itself. Certainly by the seventeenth century the old connection with Norway had no longer any significance. The administration, hitherto based on Bergen, was moved to Copenhagen and the only real sign left of the Norwegian connection was the fact that the legal system continued to be based on Norwegian law.

From 1602 there had been a Danish trade monopoly in Iceland in the hands of the Icelandic Company, and in 1619 the Faroe Islands were included in this. It was not to begin with a state monopoly, but was leased to various people, perhaps the most notable and notorious being Christoffer Gabel. Gabel received the islands in fief in 1655 and was furthermore given a trade monopoly in 1662 which was to last for his lifetime and that of his son Frederik, in fact until 1708. The Gabels used their monopoly for their own ends, not for the good of the population, and the period of their governorship is generally considered to be one of the blackest periods in the history of the Faroes, one which has, incidentally, furnished the subject for one of the finest novels in modern Danish, *The Good Hope*, by the most outstanding of all Faroese novelists, William Heinesen. Upon the death of Frederik Gabel, the monopoly reverted to the state, which operated it more for the benefit of the Faroes themselves, more in the spirit of the monopoly operating in Greenland. This state of affairs lasted until 1856 and aimed at providing the islanders with their needs rather than at making a profit from the trade. None the less, it was in some ways a doubtful benefit, not least because of the refusal to allow trading anywhere in the Faroes but Tórshavn, and was doubtless largely contributory to the backwardness of the Faroese people and economy in subsequent years.

Like Greenland, the Faroe Islands should in theory have gone to Sweden along with Norway proper in the Kiel Peace Treaty of 1814. That this did not happen was partly because the Swedish negotiator was not sure of his historical facts, but also partly because Sweden was only interested in unifying the Scandinavian peninsula, not in acquiring distant territories. Thus any remaining sense of unity between the Faroes and Norway was removed, and the islands passed purely into Danish control, although Christian V's Norwegian law continued to operate there. Moreover, certain complications arose later in the century as Norway never acknowledged the provisions of the Treaty of Kiel and could thus lay claim to her old territories. The process of closer incorporation into Denmark continued, and the Faroese parliament, the *Lagting*, probably the oldest parliamentary institution in Europe, was abolished in 1816. Henceforth the Faroes were to be considered as a Danish *Amt* (county).

This move, coming at an economically unfortunate time soon after the Danish state bankruptcy, was perhaps symptomatic of the Danish attitude towards the Faroes in the nineteenth century. The Danes failed to recognise the individuality of the Faroe Islanders, who temperamentally were more akin to the Icelanders than to the Danes. Like them they had preserved their ancient culture in a purer form than those Scandinavian countries closer to the continent of Europe, while their language was also akin to Icelandic and far removed from Danish. Yet at the beginning of the nineteenth century this was lost on the Danes, who considered the Faroes as a colony or at best a province. Danish civil servants were overbearing towards the Faroese and refused to consort with them.The Faroese language was not officially recognised, though Danish never became the language of the Faroese themselves, as to some extent had happened in Norway. Poverty was widespread, partly as a result of the financial state of Denmark herself and her consequent inability to provide help for the Faroes. In addition the ancient custom of dividing up a farm between all one's offspring had led to gradual impoverishment of many families. Conditions deteriorated so much that from 1777 to 1856 only those who could afford to maintain a family were allowed to marry. In an attempt to alleviate distress, experiments were made to introduce deep-sea fishing into the Faroes, but they were an immediate failure. By 1840 it was being suggested that the trade monopoly should be abolished in an attempt to revitalise the Faroese people, but the

Rigsdag decided in 1844 to continue it. It was felt that to end it might bring more hardship to the population, but what was not realised was that free trade would have spurred them on to achieve more for themselves instead of relying on artificial trading conditions.

In that same year, 1844, a request was made to the Roskilde Assembly, in which the Faroes were represented, for an improvement in education facilities. There were in fact no schools in the islands, and instruction was given in the home by itinerant teachers. The result of this appeal was a proclamation on 28 May 1845 providing for the establishment of schools, though it received but scant support from the Faroese themselves. The schools were thought of as being Danish, not least because the language of tuition was to be Danish, and moreover the population showed little inclination to pay the taxes necessary to finance them. This was perhaps not surprising, considering the economic state of the islands, and the situation was aggravated by the unwillingness of parents to send their children to school. They wanted them to work instead. A new Act was therefore passed in 1854, leaving parents to provide for their children's education as they thought fit.

In 1850, the Danish constitution was extended to include the Faroes, although the Faroese people were not themselves consulted on this. They were now entitled to elect one member to the *Folketing* and one to the *Landsting*, although their numbers were only about half that required to qualify for such representation. However, the people did not see this as generosity but, becoming increasingly conscious of the depressed state of the Faroes and seeing a national awakening as the only solution, they elected a Faroese as their representative in both chambers in place of the Danish candidates who also stood. This was in itself a defeat for the Danish administration, made worse by the fact that although the *Landsting* member, Hendrik Wejhe, was a fairly conservative figure, the new member of the *Folketing*, Niels Winther, was a radical and outspoken Faroese patriot who immediately began to work for a status for the Faroes comparable with that of Iceland. For while the Faroes had been formally incorporated into the Danish kingdom, Iceland had successfully opposed a closer union. Winther aimed at more self-government in the Faroes, and in order to achieve this he had two immediate objectives: the reconstitution of the Faroese *Lagting*, with similar powers to those of the Icelandic *Althing*, and the end of the Danish trade monopoly.

The first of the objectives was quickly achieved, and the *Lagting* was reconstituted in 1852, though it was a purely consultative organ without the powers which Winther had sought. In fact it was more akin to a Danish county council than to the *Althing*, and the Danish *Amtmand* (Sheriff) and *Provst* (Dean) — the main representatives of the state and Church in the islands — were *ex-officio* members. This *Amtmand* subsequently made himself so unpopular that he had to be removed. The abolition of the trade monopoly took longer, but that, too, was achieved by 1 January 1856 after a unanimous vote by the *Lagting*. There was a feeling that a turning-point had been reached in Faroese life, and that without a trade monopoly the standard of living could be improved until it equalled that in the Orkneys and Shetland, two groups of islands with a Norse background and conditions of life roughly comparable with the Faroes.

Free trade did in fact quickly bring about an improvement in the Faroese economy, for whereas the monopoly had encouraged the wrong industries, under different trading conditions the people ventured into different and more appropriate fields. The increasing export of fish now became the basis of the Faroese economy and has since come to account for some 90 per cent of the Faroese national product. The first trawler was bought at the end of the nineteenth century and others followed, although it was not until 1934 that the first steam trawler was acquired. As late as 1939, when the Faroes owned ten deep-sea trawlers, they still used some fishing boats which were fifty years old and more. Even with improved equipment they still faced difficulties because of the refusal of permission to fish within Greenlandic territorial waters and because of the loss of the Spanish market for dried fish during the Spanish Civil War. Nevertheless, despite what was still a hard life and despite social legislation still far behind that of Denmark proper, the economy was soon capable of supporting a larger population. Instead of living on smaller and smaller plots of land, the people were now able to engage in profitable employment. Consequently, even with an increase in population from 8,922 to 15,230 by 1901 and 24,000 in 1930, the economy was able to provide for the people, and the Faroes did not experience the effects of mass emigration which were known elsewhere in Scandinavia, not least in Iceland.

After the abolition of the trade monopoly, attention was turned to education, which was still suffering from the unpopularity of the previous school legislation. In 1861 a secondary school was opened in Tórshavn, and three teachers were found capable of running it. The next step was the opening in Tórshavn in 1870 of a training college to provide the teachers necessary for a real expansion of education. However, the first real improvement came in 1872 when Denmark decided to support local efforts at establishing schools. The language of instruction was still in theory to be Danish, but in practice much of the teaching was done in Faroese, and this was made official in 1938. The main obstacle to a more rapid increase was still, for a time, the Faroese unwillingness to pay the necessary taxes. Finally, because of the Grundtvigian interest in the Faroes as a source of genuine Nordic culture, a folk high school was opened in 1899, but had little immediate effect until it moved to Tórshavn itself in 1909.

Meanwhile, along with improved living standards, the sense of national identity grew steadily until, to some extent inspired by the granting of independence to Norway in 1905, an Independence Party was formed under the leadership of Jóannes Patursson in 1906. At first it made slow progress, and by 1914 the Union Party, formed in opposition to it with the aim of maintaining close ties to Denmark, had the support of two-thirds of the *Lagting*. However, the Independence Party gained the support of the young, and by 1918 it had a majority in the *Lagting*. The *Lagting* itself was reformed in 1923 and given more powers. From then onwards all its members were elected, and the appointed members who had previously been a feature were removed. It could now elect its own chairman and the *Amtmand* could now take part in its deliberations but no longer vote. The Dean of the Faroes lost his seat altogether. The *Lagting* was now empowered also to choose its own representatives in the *Landsting* in Copenhagen. Although the Faroe Islands remained a county, their special position was now much clearer. Many Danish laws were no longer valid in the islands, and laws originating in Denmark but concerning the Faroe Islands were if possible to be passed by the *Lagting* before coming into force in the islands. In its turn the *Lagting* was empowered to make its own proposals for legislation.

Although the Danes thus gave increasing powers of internal government to the Faroes, they opposed any attempt on the part of the Faroese to express themselves as an individual nation. They had acquiesced in the use of a Faroese flag designed in 1919, but when it was officially flown at the Icelandic *Althing* celebrations in 1930 a protest was made and it was lowered. However, the Faroese had their revenge the same year during their annual celebrations on St Olaf's day, 29 July. The *Dannebrog* was cut down by nationalists to the chagrin of the Danish *Amtmand*, who walked out of the ceremony in protest. The flag was a point of irritation until the Second World War, when it was allowed by the British authorities in order to distinguish Faroese ships from those of occupied Denmark.

In a way the British occupation of the Faroes furthered the ultimate cause of Faroese nationalism, for the internal administration of the islands passed almost exclusively to the Faroese themselves. Regulations for administering the Faroes without the aid of the Danish authorities were passed in 1940, less than a month after the occupation began, and the *Amtmand*, after issuing a formal protest to the British forces, took over the powers hitherto enjoyed by the government in Copenhagen. Although their stay was formally an occupation, relations were good between the British forces and the Faroese population, who in fact found a great economic advantage in the situation. They traded in fish with the British, even transporting fish from Iceland to Britain when Iceland stopped the trade. 156 Faroese sailors lost their lives in this trade, a greater percentage of the population than was killed in Britain itself. For their part the British saw to it that sufficient provisions reached the Faroes. Under these conditions a second nationalist party, the People's Party, demanded independence and in 1943 could command a near majority in the *Lagting*. Britain refused the demand, arguing that this was a matter to be settled with the Danish authorities after the war. However, the Faroese flag was recognised, and the Faroes issued their own banknotes.

After the war there was no inclination to return to the *status quo ante*, and the temporary arrangements were allowed to continue until such a time as some settlement could be reached with Denmark. The Danes themselves expressed a desire to maintain their association with the Faroes, but agreed to independence if this was the desire of the people. At the *Lagting* elections immediately following this declaration, parties in favour of continuing the union were elected. Plans were made for a referendum on the independence question, but the results were confusing: 33 per cent voted for independence, 32 per cent for union, while the remainder either abstained or spoiled their papers. When a member of one of the two ruling parties changed sides on this issue, there was a majority of one in the *Lagting* for independence, which was proclaimed immediately. The opposition parties protested, and the Copenhagen government refused to grant independence on such a narrow and inconclusive majority. Instead, the *Lagting* was dissolved, and in the ensuing election there was a clear majority for maintaining the union with Denmark.

Nevertheless, there was an obvious desire for complete internal self-government, and this was granted in March 1948. Under the settlement the Faroe Islands were a self-governing community within the Kingdom of Denmark, entitled to send two representatives to the *Folketing* and one to the *Landsting*. This changed to two representatives in the *Folketing* after the 1953 change of constitution. The *Lagting* was given legislative powers in all matters concerning the Faroes alone, and whereas previously Faroese legislation should *preferably* be debated and passed by the *Lagting* before coming into force, now it was stated that it *must* go through the *Lagting* first. Moreover, the Faroes were now made into an independent customs area in which all duties and taxes were to be fixed by the local government. The Faroese flag was recognised, and the Faroese langauge was given equality of status with Danish.

While maintaining their links with Denmark, the Faroes have increasingly gone their own way. Although joining Denmark in EFTA until 1973, they chose, as was their right under home rule, to remain outside the EEC because of what they saw as a threat to both their culture and their economy. Since the Danish accession, however, the Faroes have entered into an advantageous trade agreement with the EEC, and since establishing a 200-mile fishing limit they have negotiated fishing and trade agreements with other countries.

Throughout the 1970s the Faroe Islands experienced boom conditions, and by the end of the decade they had one of the highest standards of living in Europe. At the same time, however, borrowing had been high, and with the stagnation of trade in the 1980s the country has been faced with severe economic difficulties.

Meanwhile, energetic efforts have been made to establish a truly independent Faroese economy — and the Faroese government has gradually taken over most of the spheres of administration

hitherto run and financed by Denmark, such as roads and communications, schools and hospitals. At the same time strenuous
efforts have been made to preserve and promote traditional
Faroese culture, in particular through the work of the Faroese
Academy, the mini-university established in Tórshavn in 1965. In
more recent times a Nordic House, financed by the other
Scandinavian countries, has opened in Tórshavn with the specific
object of promoting Nordic culture.

It might be expected that a tiny community which has been as
depressed as the Faroese would only have made a modest contribution to world culture, but in the field of literature the
nationalist movement did give rise to a new, dynamic and purely
Faroese literature at the end of the nineteenth century. A first
impetus to modern literature was given by J. H. O. Djurhuus,
whose grandiloquent poetry fuses Nordic and Classical
mythologies — a sensitive, if to modern taste somewhat
rhetorical, neo-romanticism. It was then left to Christian Matras to
go further along this path and establish a truly twentieth-century
means of poetical expression in work which covers the entire
spectrum from neo-romanticism to modernist, highly condensed
poetry reminiscent of the Japanese haiku, this latter written when
the poet was over 80-years old. In prose it was Heðin Brú and
Martin Joensen who, in novels and short stories reflecting everyday life in Faroese villages, established a Faroese prose tradition in
keeping with twentieth century literary expectations. While these
men together founded a Faroese classical literature, a younger
generation — Jens Pauli Heinesen in prose and Regin Dahl in
poetry — have sought to come to terms linguistically and tech-
nically with the international literature of the late twentieth
century.

Two Faroese writers, both, ironically, using Danish as their
medium, have achieved international recognition. Jørgen-Frantz
Jacobsen's early death from tuberculosis prevented him writing
more than one historical novel: entitled *Barbara*, it is available in
English translation. His second-cousin William Heinesen was, like
Jacobsen, born in 1900 and is now ranked among the most outstanding Scandinavian writers of the twentieth century; a man who
combines a tender but often satirical portrayal of life in Tórshavn
with cosmic perspectives, themes of good versus evil, life and
death, time and eternity, man's place in the universe. Although
theoretically concerned with life in the Faroe Islands, principally

in Tórshavn, his work is universal and completely accessible to readers without any knowledge of the Faroe Islands.

While instrumental music has played only a modest role in Faroese culture, painting has asserted itself as an important medium.The dangers inherent in the traditional way of life in the islands have made the Faroese people highly aware of the constant presence of death, and this has resulted in the sombre paintings of S. J. Mikines. At the same time the Faroese landscape and the quality of light peculiar to the islands have led to an array of impressive landscapes by Mikines, Ruth Smith, Jóannes Kristiansen and now by Zacharias Heinesen. An outstanding sculptor in the Nordic tradition is Janus Kamban, while Ingálvur av Reyni has gained an international reputation for his abstract paintings.

Furthermore, the Faroe Islands have made one outstanding but very different contribution to culture, in that they are now the only part of the world where the medieval chain dance or ring dance is still performed as a part of everyday life. The ancient ballads — a significant part of the Scandinavian ballad heritage — are still sung, and the dances performed much as they have been for centuries. The dancers form a chain by linking hands, and the dance is led by one man who sings the verses of the — often very long — ballads, while the remaining dancers sing the refrains. The monotonous rhythm of the dance is enlivened by the mime and expression of the dancers, of whom it has been said that they do not merely recite the stories of the ballads, but actually experience them. This kind of dance, to which some writers have ascribed cultic significance, is gradually losing its position in favour of modern dancing — English dancing, as it is known in the Faroes — but it is nevertheless still a living force in the islands and a symbol of the continuity of their old Nordic culture.

APPENDIX 2: GREENLAND

In 982 AD an Icelander known as Erik the Red, having accompanied his father into exile from Norway, fell foul of society and was outlawed for three years. He had heard rumours of a land to the west, and so he set out to find it, arriving on the east coast of Greenland. In search of a more hospitable shore, he followed the coast southwards and then westwards, where he found a fertile area around what is now called Qaqortoq/Julianehåb and settled for a time in what became known as the East Settlement. The following year he travelled further north and found the area known as the West Settlement near Nuuk/Godthåb.

Iceland itself was overcrowded at this period, and on his return it was not difficult for Erik the Red to entice more settlers to Greenland — hence his rather optimistic name for the new land — and at one time there were some 3,000 Norse settlers, occupying about 200 farms in the East Settlement and a hundred in the West Settlement. So many people were there that Erik the Red's son Leif (who subsequently sailed to America) was able to bring a priest from Norway in 999, while a bishop was appointed by King Sigurd the Crusader in 1126. With their Norwegian antecedents the Greenland Norsemen must obviously have felt it natural to receive their clergy from that country, although they did not acknowledge Norwegian jurisdiction. It was in fact 1270 before they did homage to the King of Norway and recognised him as their lord and master.

This action was largely the result of a decline in trade between Greenland and Europe. The narwhal tusks on which this had been based had lost their attraction for the Europeans, and consequently the trade gradually stagnated. By acknowledging the suzerainty of Norway and giving Norway a trade monopoly, the Norsemen hoped to improve their lot. The time coincided with a move southwards by the Eskimos — or Inuit, as their present-day descendents prefer to be called — who had hitherto had little or no contact with the Norsemen. As contact was made, they learned a good deal from them, but there are plentiful signs of strife as well as of peaceful co-operation. In the middle of the fourteenth century the West Settlement was wiped out by Inuit, and in 1379 an attack was made on the East Settlement.

Although Norway did make attempts to accept her responsibility and relieve the Norsemen of Greenland, she was in decline at this time and could offer little assistance. Finally contact died out and by about 1500 the Norsemen were left to their own devices. In 1540 some Danish sailors landed and found a Norseman lying dead on the ground. It is tempting to think that he was the last survivor of the Norse settlers, the last of a community which archaeological excavations and grave finds have shown to have suffered from malnutrition, disease, and debilities caused by constant intermarriage. Nevertheless, a thesis published in Copenhagen in 1969 examines blood samples of the Greenland Inuit and discovers similarities betwen the blood of Inuit in one region and that of the Icelanders, while Inuit from another region show similarities with some Norwegians. This seems to open up the rather less romantic possibility that some at least of the Norsemen were assimilated into the Eskimo population.

Despite the lack of communication, the Norse settlers were not entirely forgotten, and in 1721 the Norwegian-born Hans Egede decided to go there as a missionary and preach the Lutheran faith to the survivors (remembering that contact had been lost before the Reformation). He had persuaded the authorities in Copenhagen to help him on his expedition and they had agreed on condition that his mission should be linked with a resumption of trade between Denmark and Greenland. He found only Inuit.

However, he decided to stay and preach to them, and from a spiritual point of view his mission was a success. It was less so from a commerical standpoint, as the Greenlanders showed a propensity for preferring to trade with the Dutch, despite the fact that the Bergen Company, which had been formed to trade with Greenland, was given a theoretical monopoly in 1723. Between 1719 and 1728, 748 Dutch ships are reported to have called at Greenland, bringing back 1,250 whales and making a profit of 1.35 million guilders. Yet by 1729 the Bergen Company was in such financial straits that the state had to take it over and move its administration from Bergen to Copenhagen. There was still no improvement, and by 1731 King Christian VI was threatening to drop the whole scheme. An attempt to colonise Greenland by deporting convicts there in 1727 had also been a failure and had almost cost Egede his life.

In 1749 the Greenland Trading Company was given back to private enterprise in the period of mercantilism, but by 1774 it was in state hands again, this time under the name of Royal Greenland Trading Company. Trade did in fact improve at this time and the Danes had a stroke of luck in 1777 when 25 Dutch and German trading vessels were wrecked on the ice. Competition was less keen after this.

A further boost was given to trade with Greenland in the mid-nineteenth century by C. F. Tietgen, who during his stay in England had come across a new metal called aluminium, which could be made from cryolite. Cryolite was known to be in plentiful supply in Greenland, and Tietgen managed to have a ship equipped to bring home a cargo of it. Despite initial doubts as to the feasibility of the plan, it was a success.

Meanwhile the increased volume of trade between Greenland and the outer world brought about profound changes in her pattern of life. So far the Greenlanders had enjoyed a natural economy based on seal-hunting. The seal provided them with practically speaking all their needs — food, clothing, and the skins needed for their kajaks. Now, with the ships coming every summer from Denmark carrying cargoes of goods the Greenlanders had not known before, such as sugar and coffee, these luxury wares became coveted, accounting for almost half of Greenland's imports, and the Greenland population was prepared to barter far too much of its own produce for them, with the ironical result that hardship set in. The people had bartered so many skins that they lacked the warm clothes they needed for the winter. The dangers inherent in this were appreciated by the Danes and the Greenland trade monopoly was maintained very largely with a view to protecting the Greenlanders from themselves. It is easy to be sceptical about the maintenance of a monopoly for centuries and about keeping foreigners out of a colony the size of Greenland, but the motives of the Danes in this instance were genuinely humanitarian. They saw it as their duty, even as early as the eighteenth century, to preserve the Greenlandic civilisation, and it was for this reason that the trade monopoly was maintained there even when it was dropped in Iceland. This attitude persisted and earlier this century the Danes paid prices for Greenland fish which were above world prices, even increasing them gradually while world prices were falling.

It was decided at an early stage that despite the success of the paternalistic policy in Greenland, something should be done to bring the population to greater maturity and to give it at least some responsibility for running its own affairs. At a time of some social progress at home, H. J. Rink suggested in 1856 setting-up a management committee in each settlement consisting of both Danish and Greenland representatives. The aim of these councils should be to help in cases of social need, to exercise certain legal powers and also to obtain loans for building and for the general improvement of amenities. The experiment was introduced in south Greenland in 1857 and was so successful that it was later extended to the north.

Greenland, however, was entering a period of stagnation and even of decline. The increase in wealth and the changed economy resulted in an increasing population. Numerically this increase was small — from 7,500 in 1834 to 9,900 in 1855 — but in terms of percentage it was large. Moreover, it was accompanied by a decline in the number of seals caught, owing to the activities of European sealers off Newfoundland. Rink, who was director of the Greenland Trade organisation from 1871 to 1882, had to cope with more and more formidable problems on this count and also with a diminishing interest in Greenland on the part of the Danes themselves. It was not until after the turn of the century that Danish interest in Greenland revived. This revival found its expression through the activities of various members of a new organisation called the Danish Atlantic Islands, formed in 1901 to encourage concern for the various islands Denmark owned in the Atlantic, from the West Indies to Greenland. It consisted of people with varying interests, but those concerned with Greenland were overridingly humanitarian in their aims.

Efforts to encourage Greenlanders to strive for greater participation in their own affairs were made despite some opposition from the Greenland Trade organisation and its desire to keep to paternalism. Politicians adopted a sympathetic attitude and in 1908 a law on Greenlandic government was passed, introducing local councils and also a national council elected by the people and invested with considerable authority on internal matters. The Danish *Rigsdag*, of course, kept the final say through its Greenland Administration, originally a department in the Home Ministry and subsequently of the Ministry of State. The Greenlanders for their part were now better equipped to look after themselves, better educated, thanks to nineteenth-century educational policy and the founding of training colleges, and also because greater numbers had given up their traditional sealing and taken up a trade.

Seals were becoming more and more scarce, but this scarcity coincided with an increase in Greenlandic mean temperatures. In 1917 large quantities of cod appeared in Greenlandic waters and there was a gradual switch from sealing to fishing. The Danish government realised that the switch was vital and was prepared to give financial aid for the purchase of the new boats and equipment needed. Depots were built to treat and salt the fish, which were still sold though Greenland Trade and at prices decided by it — normally above world prices. Because of the revival of trade, the Greenlanders themselves could now import greater quantities of European food, and thereby completely changed their feeding habits. Further changes were brought about with temperatures increasing sufficiently to allow sheep to graze. Sheep-farming became a practical proposition — as it had been in the time of Erik the Red — and in 1914 a sheep station was opened in Qaqortoq/ Julianehåb to provide farmers with credit and to buy back their sheep for slaughter. Again Greenland Trade bought up the carcasses at inflated prices. Obviously the loss had to be made good by some means or other, and this was done by the export of Greenland cryolite.

A new law on Greenlandic administration, passed in 1925, aimed at fostering co-operation between the Greenlanders and the Danes, and giving, among other things, local rights to Danish civil servants who had been resident in Greenland for a minimum of two years. The two national councils, one for the north, one for the south, were now allowed certain judicial rights, though their decisions had to be accepted by the two sheriffs (*landsfogeder*), who thus had a veto, or by the Minister in Copenhagen. It was laid down that the councils should meet at least once a year. In the same year, but independently of the new Act, it was decided to start continuation courses for the best pupils from Greenlandic schools. There was still no higher education as such and those considered to be worthy of it were sent to colleges in Copenhagen.

In 1926 a new Education Act was passed giving Greenland broadly speaking the same school laws as existed in Denmark proper, though they proved difficult to enforce. Instruction was given in both Greenlandic and Danish, though it was not until about 1930 that Danish became firmly established and well taught.

There was no question of forcing a completely foreign language on the Greenlanders. They themselves wanted to learn Danish, which gave them their first direct opportunity of benefiting from European culture.

Danish jurisdiction over Greenland was almost universally accepted. Norway, however, to whom Greenland once belonged, still refused to acknowledge Denmark's right to the entire island. It should be remembered that Denmark had acquired Greenland together with Norway, with the establishment of the original Union in 1380, and that when Norway was taken from Denmark in 1814, many Norwegians felt that Greenland should not have been dealt with separately. Thus Norwegian interest remained and Norway maintained her right to fish off the coast of east Greenland. In 1931 a group of Norwegian hunters landed in east Greenland and occupied it in the name of King Haakon VII. They gained the support of the Norwegian government and it was only by going to the International Court of Justice at the Hague that Denmark reasserted her rights there. The verdict was gracefully accepted by Norway and since then Danish sovereignty has been acknowledged by all.

During the Second World War the question of sovereignty again arose in a different form. Because of the strategic importance of Greenland in a possible German attack on Canada or the United States, it was thought likely that either of these countries might occupy the territory, not least because the island was still nominally under the control of occupied Denmark. The Danish ambassador in Washington, Henrik Kauffmann, took it upon himself to draft a treaty with the United States allowing American bases in Greenland so long as there was thought to be a danger to America from enemy action. The two Greenland sheriffs agreed to the treaty and also decided not to recognise the government in Copenhagen, but to govern Greenland themselves as long as the Occupation lasted. A Greenland Commission was set up in the United States to take care of Greenland trade now that connections with Denmark were severed. The government in Copenhagen naturally protested about this and dismissed Kauffmann, but he was acknowledged as being the true representative of Denmark in the USA, and maintained this position throughout the war. In 1945 the agreement he had signed was then accepted by the liberation government.

In 1953, when Denmark adopted a new constitution, certain

clauses affected Greenland profoundly. Her colonial status was abolished and she was incorporated into Denmark proper, with representation by two members of the *Folketing*. Provision was also made for a Parliamentary Greenland Commission consisting of eight Danish and two Greenland representatives.

Prior to this, in 1950, the two west Greenland district councils had been merged into a single National Council elected by direct ballot by all Greenlanders over 23. This new Council was headed by a Governor, the *Landshøvding*. Local councils were also reorganised and given greater powers in local affairs and social legislation. Church and education, which had been one so far, were separated, and education has since been administered by a Board of Education consisting of the Governor, the Dean of Greenland and the Director of Education. The health service was extended to cope with modern conditions and provision was made for free medical treatment. State trading was maintained. In 1951 a Greenland Justice Act was passed bringing legal practice in Greenland into line with that in Denmark. The Greenlanders had hitherto enjoyed their own judicial organisation, much praised by Hans Egede in the eighteenth century, and there were those who regretted that a system which had stood the Greenlanders in good stead should be replaced by one based on entirely different principles.

By 1970 Greenland was moving towards home rule, and although the country joined the EEC in 1973 as a constitutional part of Denmark, it was against the wishes of the majority of the Greenland population. In 1975 a commission was set up to examine the problems associated with Greenland home rule, and in 1979 Greenland was finally granted internal self government under terms very similar to those already enjoyed by the Faroe Islands. There is now an elected assembly, the *Landsting*, of between 23 and 26 members, and a home rule government elected by the *Landsting* and responsible to it. Denmark is represented by a High Commissioner and retains responsibility for foreign affairs, defence, the police and the law courts.

Since the establishment of internal self government the country has undergone a period of intensive Greenlandisation, with a total reorganisation of the administration and the educational system. Danish, which had hitherto been the language of administration and schooling and enjoyed a status equal to that of Greenlandic, now occupies a secondary position, though it is still the first foreign language learned. The most immediately obvious signs of this to the outsider are the Greenlandic place-names which are now used instead of, or together with, the formerly established Danish names.

All this is taking place as the Greenlanders are making efforts to establish closer links with their Inuit counterparts on the North American continent. While this opens up new perspectives for Greenland, ties with Europe have been loosened to the extent that Greenland held a referendum to decide its future relationship to the EEC, with the result that it withdrew on 1 January 1985, since when it has enjoyed associate status. The reasons for withdrawal were partly economic — a desire to protect the fishing industry on which Greenland is so dependent — but partly also stemmed from a sense of the cultural differences between Greenland and its European partners. To that could be added the natural reluctance of a nation newly independent of one constitutional tie and concerned with establishing its own identity immediately to be incorporated into a major unit which was still more alien to it and which would have little understanding for the Greenlanders' aspirations, problems and points of view.

The change in Greenland's status and way of life since the end of the Second World War, with the abandonment of the old scattered hunting communities in favour of a consumer society's centralisation and industrialisation, with a resultant increase in individual wealth, has produced vast social problems. The people have in the space of some thirty years seen the end of an age-old system and its replacement with a new one, involving the rapid development of schooling, social services, health services and hospitals, with which they have had difficulty in coming to terms. The transformation has been the most radical in any country which has had close links with western Europe, and the final outcome is as yet far from determined. This is reflected in the words of Jonathan Motzfeldt, the then Prime Minister, in his introduction to a pamphlet published in 1983 concerning the reasons for wanting to withdraw from the EEC:

> Greenland must find its own way of doing things together with and aided by the Home Rule.
> Greenland must find its own point of equilibrium —internally as well as in relation to the outside world.
> It is up to Greenland itself to plan its future life, and to decide what it wants and how fast the country should be developed.

For all its dependence so far on subsidies from Denmark, that is exactly what Greenland has set about doing.

The arts in Greenland reflect a totally different tradition from those in the other Scandinavian countries. The literature was, of course, originally oral, and the first books were not printed until the eighteenth century. With the dawn of a national consciousness in the nineteenth century, publishing accelerated, and in particular many Inuit legends were collected and published.

It was not, however, until the twentieth century that Greenlandic literature began to move in the same direction as had been taken by European literature in general many decades earlier. Among the first products of the newer Greenlandic literature were the works of Henrik Lund — hymns, didactic poems, patriotic poems (he wrote the text now used as the national anthem). In many ways Henrik Lund's work can be compared with the poetry of the Danish Romantics, though it contains no Romantic philosophy as such.

The first novel in Greenlandic was Mathias Storch's *Sinnattugaq* ('A Dream'), published in 1914. A polemical treatment of contemporary problems, it derives its title from a dream envisioning the Greenland of the future. It was not, however, until 1976 that the first socially critical novel in a modern sense was published in the form of Hans Anthon Lynge's *Seqajuk* ('The Incompetent One'), treating the predicament of the rootless young in a modern Greenland in transition.

This problem is at the centre of much modern Greenland writing, which on the one hand is intensely patriotic, harping back to the ancient customs, and on the other seeking a new identity. The search for identity provides the title for one work typical of the late twentieth century, Kristian Olsen aaju's *Ballad about Identity*.

Greenlandic visual art is determined partly by Inuit legend, which relates it closely to the artistic products of the Inuit of Canada and Alaska, and partly by the kinds of material which have been available over the centuries — narwhal tusks, walrus teeth, the bones of sperm whale, driftwood and, now, soapstone. The ability to carve in and fashion these materials has developed in course of time to a fine art, and the products, reflecting the shape of the original material, project the superstitions and legends of an early age. With increasing contact with Europe in the nineteenth century, paintings of a simple nature made their appearance, and now, with the establishment of a School of Art in Nuuk, Greenlandic painting is moving into a phase in which the techniques are related to those practised in more artistically developed countries. The inspiration behind the school is its director, Hans Lynge, himself a painter and sculptor, a man able to work in a variety of media, but in all of them looking to the legend and tradition of his country and presenting them in a new guise.

BIBLIOGRAPHY

Aagaard, F. J. C. *Christensen* (Copenhagen, 1941)

Andersen, Hans Christian. *The Fairy Tale of my Life* (Copenhagen, 1955)

Andersen, H. Westergård. *Dansk politik i går og i dag* (Copenhagen, 1967)

Andersen, R. *Danmark i Trediverne* (Copenhagen, 1968)

Berntsen, Klaus. *Erindringer* (Copenhagen, 1923–5)

Berthelsen, Christian. *Grønlands litteratur* (Viborg, 1983)

Bille, Lars. *Danmark 1945–1980* (Copenhagen, 1980)

Borum, Poul. *Danish Literature* (Copenhagen, 1979)

Bredsdorff, Elias. *Bibliography of Danish Literature in English Translation* (Copenhagen, 1950)

Brøndsted, Johannes. *The Vikings* (Harmondsworth, 1960)

Danmarks statistiske Årbog

Dansk-Færøsk Samfund. *Færøerne* (Copenhagen, 1958)

Danstrup, John and Hal Koch (eds). *Danmarks Historie* (Copenhagen, 1962–6)

Engelstoft, Povl and Frantz Wilhelm Wendt. *Håndbog i Danmarks politiske Historie fra Freden i Kiel til Vore Dage* (Copenhagen, 1934)

Fabricius, L. P. *Danmarks Kirkehistorie*, vol. 1 (Copenhagen, 1934)

Foote, P. G. *On the Saga of the Faroe Islanders* (London, 1965)

Friis, Aage, Axel Lindvald and M. Mackeprang (eds). *Schultz Danmarkshistorie* (Copenhagen, 1941–3)

Friisberg, Claus. *Det moderne Danmark bliver til. Det danske samfund 1914–1984* (Varde, 1984)

Greenland Home Rule. *Why does Greenland want to leave the EEC?* (Nuuk, 1983)

Hammerich, Poul. *Danmarkskrønike 1945–1972* (Copenhagen, 1984)

Hansen, K. *Det danske Landbrugs Historie* (Copenhagen, 1934–5)

Heinesen, William. *Faroese Art* (Tórshavn, 1982)

Hurwitz, Stephen. *The Ombudsman* (Copenhagen, 1968)

Hvidt, Kristian. *Venstre og forsvarssagen 1870–1901* (Århus, 1960)

Jacob, Arthur and Gerhard Schepelern. *Klassisk musik* (Copenhagen, 1980)

Jensen, Orla. *Sociallovgivning* (Århus, 1962)

—— Carl Vigild, Arne Sørensen. *Studievejledning i den sociale lovgivning* (Århus, 1964)

Jones, W. Glyn. 'The end of a system', *The Norseman*, vol. 14 (1956), pp. 230–8.

—— 'Paulus Helie and the Danish Reformation', *The Month*, vol. CCX, no. 1176 (1965), pp. 160–70.

Jørgensen, Harald. *Studier over det offentlige fattigvæsen i Danmark i det 19. Aarhundrede* (Copenhagen, 1940)

Kaalund, Bodil. *The Art of Greenland* (Berkeley, Calif., 1979)

—— *Inuit Art. Greenland* (Copenhagen, 1983)

Kaarsted, Tage. *Dansk politik i 1960erne* (Copenhagen, 1969)

—— and Ole Samuelsen. *Kilder til Danmarks politiske historie 1920–1939* (Copenhagen, 1967)

Koch-Olsen, Ib. *Danmarks kulturhistorie* (Copenhagen, 1968)

Kristiansen, Erling *et al. Danmark og de Seks* (Copenhagen, 1968)

Kühlmann, Per. *Danskerne 4* (Copenhagen, 1983)

Larsen, T. *En Gennembrudstid* (Copenhagen, 1918–34)

Lorensen, Vilhelm. *Studier i dansk Herregaardsarkitektur* (Copenhagen, 1921)

Miller, Kenneth E. *Government and Politics in Denmark* (Boston, 1968)

Ministeriet for Grønland. *Grønland/Kalaallit Nunaat* (Copenhagen, 1985)

Mitchell, P. M. *History of Danish Literature* (Copenhagen, 1957)

Mørch, Søren, Anne Okkels Olsen and Knud Ryg Olsen. *Danmarks historie 1880–1960* (Copenhagen, 1984)

Nordisk Kontakt

Nørregård-Nielsen, Hans Edvard. *Dansk kunst* (Copenhagen, 1983)

Oakley, Stewart. *The Story of Denmark* (London, 1972)

Oehlenschläger, Adam. *Erindringer* (Copenhagen, 1850)

Ravnholt, Henning. *The Danish Co-operative Movement* (Copenhagen, 1950)

Royal Danish Ministry of Foreign Affairs. *Denmark* (Copenhagen, 1961)

—— *Danmark og Det europæiske økonomiske Fælleskab* (Copenhagen, 1962)

—— *Factsheets: Denmark* (Copenhagen)

Skovmand, Roar. *De folkelige bevægelser i Danmark* (Copenhagen, 1951)

Skrubbeltrang, Fridlev. *Der står en ny tids bonde* (Copenhagen, 1948)

────── *The Danish Folk High Schools* (Copenhagen, 1952)

Steensberg, Axel (ed.). *Dagligliv i Danmark* (Copenhagen, 1963)

Thomsen, B. Nüchel and Brinley Thomas. *Anglo-Danish Trade 1661–1963* (Århus, 1966)

Trap, J. P. *Danmark, 1–12* (Copenhagen, 1968)

Wamberg, Bodil (ed.) *Out of Denmark. Danish Women Writers Today* (Copenhagen, 1985)

Wendt, Frantz. *Danmarks historie 1939–1978* (Copenhagen, 1978)

Winding, Kjeld. *Danmarks historie* (Copenhagen, 1958)

INDEX

Note that in the alphabetical order the Danish letter å is treated as a, æ as ae and ø as o.